Media Law in Brazil

Media Law in Brazil

Clara Iglesias Keller
Dagoberto Luiz Moutinho de Miranda Chaves

This book was originally published as a monograph in the International Encyclopaedia of Laws/Media Law.

Founding Editor: Roger Blanpain
General Editor: Frank Hendrickx
Volume Editors: Peggy Valcke & Eva Lievens

Wolters Kluwer

Published by:
Kluwer Law International B.V.
PO Box 316
2400 AH Alphen aan den Rijn
The Netherlands
E-mail: lrs-sales@wolterskluwer.com
Website: www.wolterskluwer.com/en/solutions/kluwerlawinternational

Sold and distributed by:
Wolters Kluwer Legal & Regulatory U.S.
7201 McKinney Circle
Frederick, MD 21704
United States of America
E-mail: customer.service@wolterskluwer.com

ISBN 978-94-035-1566-3

e-Book: ISBN 978-94-035-1256-3
web-PDF: ISBN 978-94-035-1266-2

The Authors

Clara Iglesias Keller is a researcher, lecturer and legal counsel specialized in information technology, media and communications regulation. She holds a Doctorate and a Master's in Public Law from the Rio de Janeiro State University (Brazil) and an LLM in Information Technology and Media Law from the London School of Economics and Political Science (LSE, UK). She is currently Postdoctoral Researcher at the WZB Berlin Social Sciences Center and coordinator of the Digital Disinformation Hub in the Leibniz Institute for Media Research | Hans-Bredow-Institute. She is the author of the book *National Regulation of Internet-Based Services: Exception, Legitimacy and the Role of States*' (originally published in Portuguese as 'Regulação nacional de serviços na Internet: exceção, legitimidade e o papel do Estado', Lumen Juris, 2019).

Dagoberto Luiz Moutinho de Miranda Chaves is a lawyer, researcher and business advisor dedicated to entertainment, media, arts and technology industries since 2001. He has worked with the largest media conglomerates and audiovisual production companies in Brazil, as both in-house and outside counsel, participating in some of the most relevant deals for the national industry and the regulatory adequacy for foreign players' entry in Brazil. Dagoberto Chaves is the founding partner of Miranda Chaves Law Firm, assisting clients in the audiovisual, media, music and show business markets. He attended specialization and extension courses at George Washington University, State University of Rio de Janeiro and Getulio Vargas Foundation.

The Authors

Table of Contents

List of Abbreviations

ABERT	Brazilian Association for Radio, and Television Broadcasters (Associação Brasileira de Emissoras de Radio e Television)
ABI	Brazilian Press Association (Associação Brasileira de Impresa)
ABTA	Brazilian Association for Pay-TV Operators (Associação Brasileira de TV por Assinatura)
ADIN	Direct Unconstitutionality Action
ADPF	Allegation of Non-compliance with a Fundamental Principle (Arguição de descumprimento de preceito fundamental)
AGU	Federal Attorney General's Office (Advocacia Geral da União)
ANATEL	National Telecommunications Agency (Agência Nacional de Telecomunicações)
ANCINE	National Film Agency (Agência Nacional do Cinema)
ANEL	The National Association for Book Editors (Associação Nacional dos Editores de Livros)
ANVISA	National Health Surveillance Agency (Agência Nacional de Vigilância Sanitária)
BRL	Brazilian *Real* (official currency)
CABEQ	Brazilian Qualified Space Channels (Pay-TV Term)
CABEQ-I	Brazilian Qualified Space Channels Programmed by Independent Company
CADE	Administrative Tribunal for Economic Defense (Conselho Administrativo de Defesa Econômica)
CAEQ	Qualified Space Channels (Pay-TV Term)
CBT	Brazilian Telecommunications Act – Law 4.117/1967
CCS	Social Communications Council (Conselho da Comunicação Social)
CENP	Executive Council of Standard Norms
CFRP	Contribution for the Promotion of Public Broadcasting
CNJ	National Council of Justice
CONANDA	National Council for the Rights of Children and Adolescents

List of Abbreviations

CONAR	The National Council for Advertisement Self-Regulation (Conselho Nacional de Autorregulação Publicitária)
CONDECINE	Contribution to the Development of the National Film Industry (Contribuição para o Desenvolvimento da Indústria Cinematográfica Nacional)
CONTEL	National Telecommunication Council Formed in 1962
CSC	Senior Film Council (Conselho Superior do Cinema)
DTH	Direct-to-Home Television
ECA	Children and Juveniles Protection Act
EBC	Empresa Brasil de Comunicação
FTA	Free-to-Air Television
FTTH	Fibre to the Home
HDI	Human Development Index
HDTV	High-Definition TV
IACHR	Inter-American Commission on Human Rights
IBGE	Brazilian Institute of Geography and Statistics
IURD	Igreja Universal do Reino de Deus (Universal Church of the Kingdom of God)
LAI	Acronym for Law 12.527/2011, on Access to Information
MMDS	Multipoint Multichannel Signal Distribution Service
OECD	Organisation for Economic Co-operation and Development
OOH	Out-of-Home
OTT	Over-the-Top
PDT	The Democratic Labour Party (*Partido Democrático Trabalhista)*
RpTV	Repeater Stations
RTV	Retransmitter Stations
SBT	Sistema Brasileiro de Televisão (a Broadcasting Network)
SBTVD	Brazilian System of Digital Television
SeAC	Conditional Access Services (Serviços de Acesso Condicionado)
SECAP	Secretariat of Assessment, Planning, Power, and Lottery under the Ministry of Economic Affairs
SECOM	Special Secretariat for Social Communication (Secretaria Especial da Comunicação Social)
SDTV	Standard Definition TV
STF	Brazilian Supreme Federal Court (Supremo Tribunal Federal)
STJ	Superior Court of Justice (Superior Tribunal de Justiça)
TSE	Superior Electoral Court
TVA	Special Service of Pay-TV Signal Distribution in Ultrahigh Frequency
VOD	Video on Demand

General Introduction

§1. General Background of the Country

I. Relevant Geographical Aspects

1. The Federative Republic of Brazil is the largest country in Latin America and the fifth largest in the world, with a territorial area of approximately 8,510,295 km.[1,2] Its immense territorial mass, crossing four different time zones, is embedded in the southern part of the Americas, where it occupies about 50% of South America. The other half of the land is occupied by eleven countries, i.e., Argentina, Bolivia, Chile, Colombia, Ecuador, Guyana, Paraguay, Peru, Suriname, Uruguay and Venezuela. Brazil has land borders with all other South American countries except Chile and Ecuador.

2. Seven thousand three hundred and seventy kilometres of Brazil's total perimeter correspond to its coastline, bordered solely by the Atlantic Ocean. In addition to seawater, Brazil's hydrography is composed of twelve large hydrographic basins, which assure its access to about 12%[3] of all available fresh water on the planet.

3. For the most part, the country has a hot and humid climate due to its position in the intertropical zone. However, due to its dimensions and geographical variations, such as local land relief and exposure to different masses of air and ocean currents, Brazil has six types of climate. Such diversity imposes on local inhabitants a hydrological range from biblical floods to droughts. The areas affected by drought often suffer severe impacts, especially in Brazil's Northeast region, which has access to much less fresh water than the other parts of the country.

4. Brazil is divided into five regions (the North, Northeast, Midwest, Southeast, and South), a division meant to gather localities with similar characteristics in order to facilitate the development and application of public policies. These regions comprise twenty-seven Federation Units (twenty-six states and first Federal District), which in turn are composed of 5,568 municipalities (i.e., local governments).

1. IBGE Ordinance 177/2020.
2. For the sake of comparison, the US has approximately 9,800,000 km^2 and China 9,600,000 km^2.
3. Brazilian Ministry of Foreign Affairs. Available at https://www.gov.br/mre/en/subjects/sustainable-development-and-the-environment/environment-and-climate-change/water-resources (accessed 1 Dec. 2020).

5. According to an official estimate by the Brazilian Institute of Geography and Statistics (IBGE), in the second quarter of 2020,[4] Brazil had a total population of 211,755,692, of which 46,289,333 were in the State of São Paulo (Southeast region). Following more references to IBGE's official data,[5] 69.8% of Brazilian residents were economically active, and the unemployment rate was 13.3%. The country exhibits substantial social inequality levels.[6] In 2019, the State of São Paulo registered per capita monthly household income of BRL 1,946 (Brazilian *Reais*) as opposed to BRL 1,439, the average for Brazil as a whole, and an HDI (human development index) of 0.783 compared to an average HDI of 0.699 for Brazil. Brazil's highest HDIs are concentrated in the South and Southeast regions, while the lowest are found in the North and Northeast regions.[7]

II. Social and Cultural Values

6. Brazil's history is defined by the colonialist regime implemented around 1500 by what was then the Kingdom of Portugal, a regime that put the country through centuries of natural resource exploitation and violence against native peoples. Around 1550, this regime started a long-lasting practice enslaving African natives, which led to the captivity and torture of over 4 millions of people. It also rooted racial inequality deep into the country's foundations, so that over a century after the official abolishment of slavery (which happened in 1888), its consequences in Brazil's sociopolitical landscape are still notorious. Independence from Portugal was declared in 1822, and the country remained a monarchy until 1889, when the republican regime was implemented.

7. Throughout its history, Brazil has been a hotspot for waves of immigration from different continents. The first centuries after the invasion by the Portuguese were marked by the arrival of their own people as well as the enslaved African natives. During the seventeenth century, there was also some Dutch immigration, following a military invasion in the north-eastern areas. Other significant waves of immigration began in the nineteenth century, when there was a project to colonize the interior of the country with agriculture, after slavery was no longer legal. This attracted mostly Italian, Spanish and German immigrants.[8] Following the two world

4. IBGE. Research Directorate – DPE – Population and Social Indicators Coordination – COPIS. Available at https://ftp.ibge.gov.br/Estimativas_de_Populacao/Estimativas_2020/stimative_dou_2020.pdf (accessed 1 Dec. 2020).
5. IBGE – Gender Statistics – Working Population. Available at https://www.ibge.gov.br/apps/snig/v1/?loc=0&cat=128,-1,1,2,-2,-3&ind=4726 (accessed 1 Dec. 2020).
6. GINI was 0.50 in 2019.
7. IBGE – Cities. Available at https://cidades.ibge.gov.br/brasil/panorama (accessed 1 Dec. 2020).
8. Neide Lopes & Durval Campos, *Brasil: um país de imigração?*, Revista Internacional em Língua Portuguesa III, 24 (2011).

wars in the twentieth century, natives from these and other European countries continued to seek out Brazil as an alternative; now, they were accompanied by Japanese (an immigration wave that gained momentum from 1908).[9] Syrian and Lebanese immigration advanced between the decades of 1870 and 1940,[10] with the former accelerating in recent years due to conflicts in these Regions. Besides these examples, other waves of immigration have also reached the country, coming from different backgrounds and motivations (like, for instance, political and economic crises, such as the recent cases of Haiti and Venezuela).

8. Against this background, Brazil results from the amalgamation of diverse cultural and racial matrices and traditions. The country is also marked by religious syncretism (64.6% Catholic, 22.2% Protestant, 1.6% African religions in 2010 according to IBGE data[11]) and linguistic syncretism. The official and most commonly spoken language in Brazil is Brazilian Portuguese, a strand of Portugal's Portuguese that was highly influenced by the languages of the original peoples of the territory, African, French, Castilian, Italian, and Arab languages. The most significant difference between the Portuguese spoken in Brazil and that spoken in Europe is pronunciation. There are about sixteen dialects in Brazil, characterized by each region's quotidian communication. However, the dialects spoken in the capitals of Rio de Janeiro and São Paulo States exert more significant influence over the others, as they have greater exposure due to their economic relevance and media diffusion.[12]

9. Exploring Brazil through its dialects is an interesting exercise in understanding local cultures and certain regions' influence over others. This kind of influence is visible even from a superficial analysis of the origins of an apparent cultural uniformity. However, the causes and consequences of this influence reveal the essence of Brazil: a territory marked by social, racial, gender, and cultural inequality, with policies, resources, and decisions oriented to the most economically influential groups. This inherent inequality is also reflected in representation in the legislative and executive branches, as will be further discussed below.

10. Mass media has historically fallen short in representing the diversity of identity groups in the country,[13,14] which should be considered in light of access and the

9. Teliti Suzuki, *A imigração japonesa para o Brasil*, Revista Institucional de Estudos Brasileiros 39, 57–65 (1995).
10. Marcia Maria Cabreira, *Cultura e identidade em São Paulo: a imigração síria e libanesa*, 1 (3) EccoS Revista (2001).
11. IBGE Demographic Data – Brazilian Census. Available at: https://cidades.ibge.gov.br/brasil/pesquisa/23/22107 (accessed 1 Dec. 2020).
12. *For further references on Brazilian ethnic and linguistic composition, see* Darcy Ribeiro, *O povo brasileiro*. (Companhia de Bolso 2008).
13. *See* Wagner Machado da Silva, *A telenovela e os negros: A representatividade étnica na Rede Globo entre 2011 e 2017*, Intercom – Sociedade Brasileira de Estudos Interdisciplinares da Comunicação, 41° Congresso Brasileiro de Ciências da Comunicação (September 2018), https://portalintercom.org.br/anais/nacional2018/resumos/R13-0054-1.pdf (accessed 25 Mar. 2021).
14. *See* Fabio Sapaio de Almeida, Maria Cristina Giorgi & Maria Vitória Silva Paiva, The Non-Representation of Black People in Brazilian Soap Operas: The Gabriela's Case, Educare et Educare

relevance of broadcasting services and audiovisual content. In 2018, at least 96.4% of households had one television set (which already guarantees access to free-to-air television – FTA); this is a bigger proportion than that of households with a refrigerator, or even running water (which reaches 85.5% of households). Connectivity rates are expanding every year, and currently, 79.1% of households have Internet access, but only 44.1% have a computer or tablet. In terms of mobile connection, numbers from the same period of time showed at least one mobile cell phone in 93.2% of households.[15] Quality of Internet connection is also questionable, given that average speed connection is at 6.8 Mbp/s[16] and zero rating practices are widespread (despite incompatible with the principle of 'net neutrality' provided by Article 9 of Law 12.965/2014, known as 'Marco Civil da Internet').[17]

11. According to official data provided by the National Telecommunications Agency (ANATEL), Pay-TV in September 2019 had 16,010,000 Pay-TV paid terminals installed, corresponding to a density of 23.14% of households, and approximately 228,016,000 active mobile phone lines.[18]

12. The same report states that almost 50% of FTA channels' programming grid is occupied by entertainment shows, of which the soap opera genre[19] (with a typical Brazilian format) is popularly known as the national preference. 15.8% of the FTA Globo TV's programming grid (which enjoys the largest audience in the country) is occupied by soap operas produced by the channel itself in a 1.73 million[20] square meter studio complex located in Rio de Janeiro. It is important to note that this content is mostly transmitted during prime time (6 PM–12 AM), giving room only for news programmes (hard news). Sports content occupies 9% of Globo TV's grid, and together soap operas and national soccer championships attain the highest audience ratings on national television. In 2016, the six principal Brazilian FTA television channels broadcast 1,839 feature films, of which 22.2% were Brazilian.

UNIOESTE (July 2015), http://e-revista.unioeste.br/index.php/educereeteducare/article/download/12598/9012 10 20 573-583 (accessed 26 Mar. 2021).

15. IBGE 2018 National Continuous Household Sample Survey. Available at: https://biblioteca.ibge.gov.br/visualizacao/livros/liv101654_informativo.pdf (accessed 1 Dec. 2020).

16. Akamai [state of the Internet] Q1 2017 Report. Available at: https://www.akamai.com/us/en/multimedia/documents/state-of-the-internet/q1-2017-state-of-the-internet-connectivity-report.pdf (accessed 1 Dec. 2020).

17. Guy Thurston Hoskins, *Beyond 'Zero Sum': The Case for Context in Regulating Zero Rating in the Global South*, 8 Internet Policy Review 1 (2019).

18. *For up-to-date information about Brazil's telecommunications market, see the official information made available by Brazil's National Telecommunications Agency at* https://informacoes.anatel.gov.br/paineis/acessos/tv-por-assinatura.

19. Soap opera is a genre based on fictional characters and situations; in Brazil, they are shown every day, from Monday to Saturday, and last between 150 and 180 episodes, each 50 minutes long.

20. G1, *Globo inaugura estúdios nesta quinta-feira (8) e amplia seu complexo de produção no Rio*, G1.com (8 Aug. 2019), https://g1.globo.com/rj/rio-de-janeiro/noticia/2019/08/08/globo-inaugura-estudios-nesta-quinta-feira-8-e-amplia-seu-complexo-de-producao-no-rio.ghtml (accessed 10 Dec. 2020).

13. The influence of FTA television on the country's cultural identity can be referred to different political and economic factors, which will be explored throughout this monograph (and specially in Part III, where we will approach regulation of audiovisual media). At this introductory stage, it is worth noticing that, for many decades, FTA channels have played an important role in shaping social imaginaries, and influencing different aspects of day-to-day life. Some playful examples of this influence are well known. For instance, in January 2000, a Brazilian Internet portal adopted a West Highland White Terrier dog as a mascot in FTA television commercials. In the decade before the commercial was aired, pedigree records for this breed in Brazil totalled 645; but in the decade after the commercial was aired, there were 9,320 records.[21] Another example refers to a popular soap opera, aired in 1995. Until then, the female name 'Dara' had no cultural significance in Brazil, so much so that in the 1980s, only 163 girls with the name Dara were registered. However, the scenario changed in the following decade, after Globo TV exhibited a soap opera on prime time whose protagonist was named Dara: 7,648 new Daras were registered, i.e., a forty-seven-fold increase.[22] In the same sense, in the first week of exhibiting a soap opera set in Turkey, Globo TV caused a 66% increase in searches for accommodation in Istanbul.[23]

14. Besides influencing social and cultural references, audiovisual content in Brazil as edited by the mass media has also been perceived as an ignition for institutional change. In 1989, for instance, Brazil experienced a wave of kidnappings that not only victimized upper-class citizens but also instilled a state of permanent terror among publicly exposed figures. There was tremendous popular pressure for the kidnapping crime to be considered a 'heinous crime' (a legal classification that deprives suspects of certain crimes of possibilities such as bail or an amnesty). After tremendous pressure from the mass media and public opinion, the Heinous Crimes Law (Law 8.072/1990) was approved in just over one month from the bill's presentation.[24] When expressing his vote, federal deputy Plínio Sampaio summed up, in a single sentence, the pressure suffered by lawmakers:

> As a matter of conscience, I am a little concerned about giving my vote to legislation that I could not examine. I have every interest in voting on the proposal, but I do not want to do so under the threat that, tonight, on Globo TV,

21. Canal do Pet, *Raça west highland white terrier ficou conhecida graças ao IGuinho*, iG (29 Jan. 2020), https://canaldopet.ig.com.br/curiosidades/especiais/2020-01-29/raca-west-highland-white-terrier-ficou-conhecida-gracas-ao-iguinho.html (accessed 10 Dec. 2020).
22. IBGE database of names in Brazil is available at https://censo2010.ibge.gov.br/nomes/#/search (accessed 20 Dec. 2020).
23. G1, *Após novela, sobe busca por viagem à Turquia*, G1.com (12 Nov. 2012), http://g1.globo.com/turismo-e-viagem/noticia/2012/11/apos-novela-sobe-busca-por-viagem-turquia-veja-fotos-do-elenco-no-pais.html (accessed 10 Dec. 2020).
24. João José Leal, *Crimes hediondos: A Lei 8.072/90 como expressão do direito penal da severidade* 9 (Juruá 2007).

I will be accused of being in favour of the kidnapping, and it will certainly happen if I ask for the vote to be postponed.[25]

15. Interestingly, the Heinous Crimes Law was modified two more times, each time against public outcry related to or fomented by the mass media. The first amendment included homicide among the list of heinous crimes, after the actress, who was also the daughter of a famous author of soap operas, was violently murdered. The second amendment included the crime of counterfeiting medicines, after the mass media extensively reported cases of women getting pregnant after taking fake contraceptives (which became known as the 'flour pill') sold as genuine contraceptives.[26]

III. Political and Legal Systems

16. Brazil is a presidential republic in which the Federal Constitution[27] is the hierarchically superior legal diploma, which means that any other legal or infra-legal text needs to abide by its terms in order to be valid.

17. This rights charter was enacted in 1988 as a political letter intended to instal a democracy in Brazil after more than twenty years of military dictatorship – a regime based on total centralization of powers in the executive branch, which included strong governmental intervention in economic sectors. Authoritarianism pervaded all kinds of governmental policies, the epitome being the institutionalized censorship over any content publication, accompanied by violent repression of political opponents.

18. From 1964 to 1985, the authoritarian regime held six indirect elections, when the President was chosen by members of Parliament or by an 'electoral collegiate'.[28]The National Constituent Assembly was approved in 1985 after a series of political movements that hinted at the weakening of the military regime, including a popular campaign for direct elections (i.e., direct vote, of the people, for the election of lawmakers, mayors, governors, and the President of the Republic).

19. After three years of deliberation, the National Constitutional Assembly enacted the 1988 Federal Constitution, a legal diploma with the clear mission to establish a democracy in Brazil, guided by the ideals of participation, citizenship, political pluralism, and popular sovereignty (as proclaimed in the sole paragraph of

---

25. The Journal of the National Congress (29 Jun. 1990) is available at http://imagem.camara.gov.br/Imagem/d/pdf/DCD29JUN1990.pdf#page=121 (accessed 31 Dec. 2020).
26. Vanessa Haigh, *Falsificar remédio será crime hediondo*, Folha de São Paulo (1 Jul. 1998), https://www1.folha.uol.com.br/fsp/cotidian/ff01079819.htm (accessed 31 Dec. 2020).
27. The official translation into English of the Brazilian Federal Constitution is available at http://www.stf.jus.br/arquivo/cms/legislacaoConstituicao/anexo/brazil_federal_constitution.pdf (accessed 20 Dec. 2020).
28. TSE – Tribunal Superior Eleitoral, *Eleição indireta*. Available at: https://www.tse.jus.br/eleitor/glossario/termos/eleicao-indireta (accessed 1 Dec. 2020).

its Article 1). In the context of this democratization process, different and often clashing political interests were involved in the drafting of the Constitution, whose final result features a wide range of rights and guarantees (we will discuss these in General Introduction, §3, I below).

20. Among the Constitution's transition provisions, Article 2 mandated a plebiscite to determine the form of government (to be chosen between a republic or a constitutional monarchy) and the system of government (to be chosen between presidentialism and parliamentarianism). In 1993, the population chose a republican form of government and a presidential government system.

21. Institutionally, Brazil is structured as a federal republic consisting of a federal government (also referred to as 'Federal Union', or 'Union'), states, municipalities, the nations' capital and (eventually) territories. The latter refers to a specific category of administrative organization that is directly integrated into the Federal Union, but still has some level of local government administration. The 1988 Constitution eliminated the territories that existed in the country (by integrating them into pre-existing federation members, or turning them into states). Therefore the country currently has no territories, but the category is still present in the Constitution (and thus, so is the possibility of new territories being created in the future).

22. Even though municipalities are members of the Brazilian federation expressly named by the Constitution, official accounts refer to twenty-seven 'federations members' or 'federation units' – which refers to the total sum of twenty-six states, added the nations' capital (Brasília). As of March 2022, the National Institute for Geography and Statistics accounted for 5,568 municipalities.[29]

23. Each member of the federation is autonomous, and the unity of all members is administrated by the Federal Government (also known as the 'Federal Union'). According to Article 2 of the Constitution, the Federal Union has three branches that are independent, and harmonic among themselves, according to the principle of separation of powers: executive, legislative and judiciary. Besides their inherent attributions, the three branches exercise different mechanisms of control over each other, which are provided throughout the constitutional text, amounting to the adoption of a 'checks and balances' system.

24. Each member of the federation is governed by the head of its executive power: the President of the Republic of the Federal Union, governors at state level and majors at municipalities. All heads of the executive are directly elected by the people through majority voting, for a four-year term mandate with the possibility of a single re-election.

25. Legislative branches are also present in each federation, and members are all directly elected by the population, without limits to the number of possible

29. IBGE – Territory. Available at https://www.ibge.gov.br/geociencias/organizacao-do-territorio/estrutura-territorial/15761-areas-dos-municipios.html?=&t=o-que-e (accessed 1 Mar. 2022).

re-elections. At the federal level, legislative functions are carried out by the National Congress (or 'Parliament'). The National Congress' structure is defined by a bicameral system,[30] combining two legislative chambers that do not have any predominance over each other: the Senate (which represents federated states) and the House of Representatives (which represents the people).

26. The Federal Senate is composed of senators with an eight-year mandate term,[31] elected based on the absolute number of votes received from the state voters they represent (using the majority principle). The House of Representatives is composed of representatives with a four-year mandate, elected from the proportional vote[32] of those with electoral domicile in the state that such deputies represent. At states' and municipalities' levels, the legislative branch consists of one body, respectively, the State Assembly (in Portuguese known as 'Assembleia Legislativa') and the Council Chamber (in Portuguese known as 'Câmara dos Vereadores').

27. Legislative activity is carried out in periods called 'legislature', which have four-year terms.[33] As per the Brazilian Federal Constitution,[34] legislative activity aims to propose, debate, present and vote amendments to the Constitution, complementary laws, ordinary laws, delegated laws, executive orders and legislative decrees. This activity consists of a process that begins with the legislative initiative and ends with the promulgation and publication of laws, which then come into force after the vacancy period.

28. Legislative initiative is a prerogative that certain people, institutions, governmental bodies or groups hold the right to present a bill of law to the Legislative Power. In Brazil, it is possible that specific bills, given certain formalities and requirements, can be started by popular initiative. These requirements involve, for instance, a minimum number of signatures equivalent to 1% of voters, and are further regulated by Law 9.709/1998. After the presentation of a bill, it is submitted to the voting process in the legislative houses. Voting is usually preceded by studies and opinions carried out by specialized technical commissions of the legislatures themselves. After the vote, the bill is submitted to the sanction and veto of the head of the executive branch.

29. Not only voting rights are assured by the Constitution but also voting is actually mandatory for individuals older than eighteen years old, and optional for people older than seventy years old and for illiterate individuals. The first Brazilian Law that granted the right to vote was enacted in 1881, and it benefited only literate men. Women were granted a right to vote only in 1932, and gender imbalances in legislative representation are still present in the country.

---

30. Brazilian Federal Constitution, at Art. 44.
31. *Ibid.,* at Art. 46.
32. *Ibid.,* at Art. 45.
33. *Ibid.,* at Art. 44 para. 1.
34. *Ibid.,* at Art. 59.

30. In 2019, of 513 federal deputies (representatives of the Federation Units in the legislative process), only 77 were women,[35] making Brazil one of the countries with the lowest female representation[36] in elected positions (ranking 131st among the 189 countries analysed). An incomplete survey[37] conducted by the Federal Senate in 2014 inferred that one of the reasons for this low representativeness is the lack of political party support for female candidacies.

31. This understanding that women will suffer from a lack of support in political parties has deep roots in Brazilian patriarchy. According to the IBGE,[38] in 2018 women in Brazil generally received less than 80% of men's incomes, and less than 64.8% of men's incomes in the specific sector of scientific and intellectual occupations. In 2020, research conducted by the international accounting firm Grant Thornton indicated that women held only 34% of senior leadership positions in Brazilian companies.[39]

32. The judiciary branch is in charge of interpreting and enforcing the Law, and the Constitution gives every citizen the right to bring any violation of rights, or threat of violation of a right before courts (Article 5, XXXIV, a). As it happens with the other branches, the Judiciary is also granted administrative and financial autonomy, in order to guarantee the independence and impartiality of the courts.

33. In Brazil, the functional organization of the Judiciary is divided into bodies that operate in specific spheres, according to their respective jurisdiction.[40] At the top of this structure is the country's Constitutional Court – the Brazilian Supreme Federal Court (Supremo Tribunal Federal – STF). Its mission is to enforce the Constitution, which includes abstract and concrete disputes over constitutional matters. This means that STF exerts constitutional review directly (in matters disputing the constitutionality of laws and other legal forms, or in cases under its direct adjudicating competence) and indirectly, as the highest instance court for constitutional matters. Another part of the institutional design of the Brazilian Judiciary is the

---

35. Lara Haje, *Baixa representatividade de brasileiras na política se reflete na Câmara*, Brazilian Federal Deputies Chamber (29 Mar. 2019), https://www.camara.leg.br/noticias/554554-baixa-representatividade-de-brasileiras-na-politica-se-reflete-na-camara/ (accessed 20 Dec. 2020).
36. As described in Brazilian Federal Senate (DataSenado), *Women in Politics Survey*. Available at https://www12.senado.leg.br/institucional/procuradoria/proc-publicacoes/cartilha-mulheres-na-politica (accessed 10 Nov. 2020).
37. Brazilian Federal Senate, *Women on Politics* (2015). Available at: http://www2.senado.leg.br/bdsf/handle/id/510154 (accessed 20 Dec. 2020).
38. Agência IBGE, *Em 2018, mulher recebia 79,5% do rendimento do homem*, IBGE (4 Jul. 2019), https://agenciadenoticias.ibge.gov.br/agencia-sala-de-imprensa/2013-agencia-de-noticias/releases/23923-em-2018-mulher-recebia-79-5-do-rendimento-do-homem (accessed 10 Nov. 2020).
39. As described in Grant Thorton, *Women in Business 2020: Do plano de ação à prática*. Available at https://www.grantthornton.com.br/contentassets/158da8c0b7c04474a3cc43f4a5dc73af/women_in_business_2020.pdf?rdst_srcid=2041829 (accessed 10 Nov. 020).
40. As described in Superior Tribunal de Justiça – STJ, *Judiciário Brasileiro*. Available at: https://international.stj.jus.br/pt/Poder-Judiciario-Brasileiro#:~:text=%E2%80%8B%E2%80%8BO%20Poder%20Judici%C3%A1rio,entre%20cidad%C3%A3os%2C%20entidades%20e%20Estado.&text=A%20Constitui%C3%A7%C3%A3o%20Federal%20do%20Brasil,para%20a%20solu%C3%A7%C3%A3o%20de%20lit%C3%ADgios (accessed on 12 Dec. 2020).

National Council of Justice (CNJ), the body that controls the administrative and financial performance of the courts and the fulfilment of the judges' duties. The second-ranked highest court in the country is the Superior Appeals Court, in Portuguese known as Superior Tribunal de Justiça (Superior Court of Justice – STJ) which acts as an interpreter of the legislation in appeals coming from both the State Courts and the Federal Courts.

34. Below these institutions, the Federal Constitution organizes the Judicial Branch into two groups, with competencies in specific spheres: Common Justice and Specialized Justice. The Common Justice courts are in charge of solving conflicts and applying the law in all cases that do not fall within the competences of the Specialized Justice – which includes Electoral Justice, Military Justice and Labour Justice. Each Specialized Justice has their own specialized first instance and appeals courts.

35. The Common Justice has two jurisdictions: the Federal Justice, which operates within the scope of the Federal Union, and the State Justice, under the jurisdiction of each of the Brazilian states and the Federal District (the nation's capital). Municipalities do not have their own judicial organization. At the federal level, the judiciary is organized according to five regions that bundle a number of states. Each region has several first instance courts and one Regional Federal Court (which functions as an appeal court to that region). At state level, each state organizes their own first instance courts (including distribution among municipalities) and is provided with one State Appeals Court (known in the Portuguese as 'Tribunal de Justiça').

§2. The Media Landscape

I. Overview of Media Markets: General Landscape and Main Actors

36. As it happens in many countries, the current Brazilian Media Landscape is marked by shifts in consumption that affect different activities in this field. Many of these shifts can be linked to the expansion of digital platforms, streaming services and new forms of advertising, notably by bringing new (and often global) players to Brazilian markets. But despite their importance, the Brazilian media landscape is still populated by large national consolidated media conglomerates, who exert great cultural, social and political influence. In the next paragraphs, we will present some of the main actors in the current landscape.

37. Estimated advertising expenses in Brazil during 2020, according to a study conducted by Magna,[41] amounted to approximately USD 12 billion, of which 48%

41. MAGNA Global is one of the most used sources as a market reference for advertising investments around the world, used by agencies, advertisers and vehicles. The 2020 Report is available at https://s3.amazonaws.com/media.mediapost.com/uploads/MagnaYearEnd2020Forecast.pdf.

would have been directed to the digital segment, 43% to different types of television, and the other 9% distributed equally between print media, radio and out-of-home (OOH) advertising. Traditional media (i.e., TV and radio broadcasters, newspapers and magazines) represent a relevant market that is concentrated among only five groups, each one of them with high achievements in many market segments. Television reach is one of the elements of the equation that quantifies market relevance, and currently, the most relevant media groups in the country, by audience share,[42] are: (i) Globo Group, (ii) Record Group, (iii) Band Group, (iv) RBS Group, and (v) Folha de Sao Paulo Group. Due to the abundance of details in their composition, market dominance, and their influence on the Brazilian media landscape, we will focus in more detail on Groups (i) and (ii).

38. Nowadays, Globo Group controls the following print media: *O Globo* newspaper, *Valor Econômico* newspaper, *Extra* newspaper, and a series of printed magazines. Globo is also famed for operating diverse audiovisual and radio broadcasting services. Globo is also in charge of radio stations scattered all over Brazilian territory; a music record company; FTA television channel Globo TV (which is also expanded by an affiliated network, as described in Part III, Chapter 1); and the leading Pay-TV channels in Brazil (by audience numbers) among which the linear and pay-per-view channels that exhibit the most watched sporting events in the country, especially national and regional soccer matches, the most popular sport in Brazil.

39. Globo TV reaches 100 million Brazilians daily, corresponding to just under half of the country's population, and it exerts significant influence on national culture and politics.

40. It is possible to say that the emergence of Pay-TV in Brazil coincides with the launch of Globo Groups' subscription channels (formerly Globosat), which occurred in November 1991.[43] At the beginning of the operation, in addition to programming the channels, Globo also controlled their distribution means. Thus, it is natural that their own distributors were privileged with the content, so that no other company could run Globo content.

41. Globo content has long been synonymous with premium content, especially in the sports market, where the media group has consistently managed to place higher bids and hold exclusive rights in all available market segments. For this reason in 1991 the association NEO TV (which to date brings together several Pay-TV distributors) filed a petition with the Brazilian antitrust body (the Administrative Council for Economic Defense, or Conselho Administrativo de

42. As NGO Intervozes and Reporters Without Borders report, these companies held 71.1% of audience share in the period analysed, between January and March 2017. Research results are available at https://brazil.mom-rsf.org/en/findings/indicators/#!9fed61067e34232006ff7dcd0ed479d0 (accessed 10 Dec. 2020).
43. Memória Roberto Marinho, *Globosat*, Globo Group (3 Jul. 2019), https://robertomarinho.globo.com/empresas/inicio-globosat/ (accessed 10 Dec. 2020).

Defesa Econômica – CADE). In this lawsuit,[44] NEO TV accused Globo Group of anticompetitive practices by restricting competitors from accessing the linear channel SporTV and pay-per-view channels that broadcast the most relevant sporting events in the country.[45]

42. The second-largest media group in Brazil is the Record Group. Record TV occupies the second place[46] in terms of audience numbers and market share of FTA television. Record has under one umbrella a printed newspaper, a weekly newspaper for free distribution, radio stations and Pay-TV channels. In addition to that, the Igreja Universal do Reino de Deus (Universal Church of the Kingdom of God – IURD) is a religious institution with over 10 million followers and presence in 135 countries, as declared by Record in 2020.[47] Record's history with its current owner begins in 1989 with the acquisition of broadcasting stations by Mr Macedo, who is chief bishop of IURD and controller of the Record Group.

43. Besides the significant mobilization of people, IURD has potentially abundant political influence. In 2020, there were 120 lawmakers in Brazil declared[48] to be connected to evangelical religions, composing the so-called evangelical bench in legislative houses. The IURD is also linked[49] to a political party, the 'Republicanos', which housed most of the current President's, Jair Bolsonaro, supporting politicians during the 2020 regional elections. Mr Macedo is also an outspoken supporter of the current President Jair Bolsonaro.

44. Although it is a commercial television station, with varied content, religious proselytism is present in Record TV's programming grid in two visible ways: first, in the acquisition of programming grid space by IURD – meaning that IURD pays for Record TV so that it can occupy airtime transmitting their religious services.[50] And second, through the editorial guidelines of its programming. In addition to biblical soap operas aired during prime time,[51] all of Record TV's programming,

44. CADE administrative proceeding PA 08012.003048/2001-31.
45. Sports rights' antitrust cases involving Grupo Globo will be further approached in Part III, Ch. 9.
46. FTA television audience share data is available at https://www.kantaribopemedia.com/conteudo/dados-rankings/audiencia-tv-15-mercados/ (accessed 10 Dec. 2020).
47. R7, *Universal completa 43 anos com 10 milhões de fiéis pelo mundo,* R7.com (9 Jul. 2019), https://noticias.r7.com/brasil/universal-completa-43-anos-com-10-milhoes-de-fieis-pelo-mundo-09072020 (accessed 10 Dec. 2020).
48. Congresso em Foco, *Veja quais deputados e senadores fazem parte da bancada evangélica* (15 Sep. 2020). Available at https://congressoemfoco.uol.com.br/area/congresso-nacional/veja-quais-deputados-e-senadores-fazem-parte-da-bancada-evangelica/ (accessed 14 Feb. 2021).
49. For further details, *see:* Claudia Cerqueira, *The Church as a Political Party: The Relationship Between IURD and Republicanos* (2021). Available at https://www.scielo.br/j/rbcsoc/a/YWZWKnDk6LwvPpbSZ3PRnVQ/.
50. Esther Hamburger, *Religião toma conta do horário nobre*, Folha de São Paulo (26 Nov. 2003), https://www1.folha.uol.com.br/fsp/ilustrad/fq2611200315.htm (accessed 10 Dec. 2020).
51. Andréia Takano, *Relembre sucessos bíblicos da Record TV*, O Fuxico (26 Apr. 2020), https://www.ofuxico.com.br/noticias/relembre-sucessos-biblicos-da-record-tv/ (accessed 31 Dec. 2020).

journalism or entertainment follows the editorial agenda of the leading bishops of IURD.[52,53]

45. Other Brazilian commercial FTA television channels have space in their programming grid occupied by religious programming, including Globo TV, which produces and broadcasts a Catholic mass on Sundays. Band TV and RedeTV!(which are the other two of the five groups mentioned at the beginning of this section), for example, sell airtime for evangelical churches (mostly neo-Pentecostal churches like IURD) to broadcast their shows, masses and services. The NGO Intervozes reported that during 2016, 43.41% of RedeTV!'s programming grid was occupied by religious programmes.[54]

46. The commercialization of programming grid space (the so-called antenna-time) is done recurrently and openly, despite being expressly prohibited by the legislation. In this type of commercialization, the editor in charge of the programming grid sells space for an independent production company to broadcast their contents. It happens not only with religious institutions but also with any company willing to invest in this line of business – especially telesales content.

47. In the case of RedeTV! selling 43.41% of its grid to religious entities, it is not possible to fit this within the legal limit of advertising in FTA televisions programming grids. According to Article 124 of Law 4.117/1962, advertising should be under 25% of programming time. It is a very peculiar situation. If the content that fills the space sold by television broadcasters is not considered to be advertising, then it would be the case that a public service concessionaire is partially and temporarily assigning its concession contract to a third party.

48. As will be further touched on in Part III, according to Article 21, XII(a)[55] of the Federal Constitution, the broadcasting service is provided through public concessions, which must necessarily be preceded by public bids in accordance with Article 10 of Decree 52.795/1963. The bidding denotes the competition between players, so the public administration will grant the right to provide broadcasting services to those who have better conditions to provide it. Grantees are banned from licensing this public concession to a third party (even if temporarily). Under similar arguments, the prosecution office filed three public civil lawsuits[56] in 2019, against Record TV, Band and RedeTV!, enquiring into the programming time made

52. ANCINE, Observatório Brasileiro do Cinema do Audiovisual. Available at https://oca.ancine.gov.br/mercado-audio-visual-brasileiro. Accessed on: 15 Dec. 2020.
53. Olivia Bandeira, *Igrejas cristãs no topo da audiência*, Le Monde Diplomatique (16 Apr. 2018), https://diplomatique.org.br/igrejas-cristas-no-topo-da-audiencia/ (accessed 10 Dec. 2020).
54. Reporters Without Borders and Intervozes, *Fill the Airwaves and Subdue Them: Brazilian Churches as Media Owners*, Media Ownership Monitor Brazil (31 Oct. 2017), https://brazil.mom-rsf.org/en/findings/church-owning-media/ (accessed 10 Nov. 2020).
55. Brazilian Federal Constitution, at Art. 21: the Union shall have the power to: XII – operate, directly or through authorization, concession or permission: (a) the services of sound broadcasting and of sound and image broadcasting.
56. Brazilian Federal Prosecution Office, *ACP – tempo televisivo – igrejas*, http://www.mpf.mp.br/rj/sala-de-imprensa/docs/pr-rj/acp-tempo-televisivo-igrejas (accessed 10 Jun. 2020).

available to religious congregations in programming grids. These lawsuits, still pending in court, are the result of an investigation initiated in 2016.

49. While these are the main players in the broadcasting sectors, it is also important to highlight the main characteristics of the landscape regarding other media markets. Pay-TV services, for instance, are provided through a chain of actors that include production, programming, packaging and distribution. Even though the market was kicked off through the development of Globo's Pay-TV channels producer (formally known as Globosat), associated with the expansion of the infrastructure of cable distributor NET (of which Globo was a stakeholder until 2021), the market has evolved considerably since then. The turning point was the entrance of telecommunication companies in the market, which coincided with the approval of Law 12.485/2011, which unified the regulatory framework.

50. According to official data provided by the National Film Agency (Agência Nacional do Cinema – ANCINE),[57] in 2019 there were 276 Pay-TV channels distributed to subscribers in Brazil, of which only 46 were in HD. It is interesting to note that from 2018 to 2019, the total number of channels decreased by 13%. Still, in 2019, the number of subscribers to Pay-TV channels was 15.8 million, representing the most significant drop in subscriber analysis by year of 10% compared to the previous year. This drop meant the market size was slightly below the numbers of 2012 (16.2 million).[58] Following this downward trend, the number of Pay-TV subscribers in December 2020 totalled 14.9 million.[59,60]

51. The decline in the number of Pay-TV subscribers in Brazil is attributed to different factors. First, due to the boost in the subscribers base from 2010 on. In 2009, there were 7.5 million subscribers; in 2010, 9.8 million; in 2011, 12.7 million; in 2012, 16.2 million; in 2013, 18 million; in 2014, 19.6 million; and from 2015 on, the market started to show a decrease. The slide, which culminated in a more accentuated fall from 2017 on, is attributed to the entry of the socioeconomic classes with lower purchasing power (called classes C and D) into the Pay-TV consumer market. Such consumers are more susceptible to economic crises. In 2013, industry research indicated that 95% of new subscribers were from classes C and D.[61] For clarification, class C Brazilians in 2014 had an average monthly income

---

57. ANCINE, Observatório Brasileiro do Cinema do Audiovisual. Available at https://oca.ancine.gov.br/mercado-audio-visual-brasileiro (accessed 15 Dec. 2020).
58. *Ibid.* https://oca.ancine.gov.br/sites/default/files/repositorio/pdf/Informe_TVPaga_2013.pdf (accessed 15 Dec. 2020).
59. ANATEL, *Overview of Telecommunication in Brazil* (December 2020), https://sei.anatel.gov.br/sei/modulos/pesquisa/md_pesq_documento_consulta_externa.php?eEP-wqk1skrd8hSlk5Z3rN4EVg9uLJqrLYJw_9INcO6xQe_NCMYl6DFnwBVUZgGh_tcMajgdmgeIxfLBsexgpa-WjTV0U5SjhGZivpqHaU3OkTgkoMzUUKvaFLeLQeL8 (accessed 12 Jan. 2021).
60. Year-over-year study on the number of pay-TV subscribers in Brazil carried out by ANATEL is available at: http://www.abta.org.br/dados_do_setor.asp (accessed 12 Jan. 2021).
61. Exame, *95% de novos clientes de TV por assinatura são classe C ou D*, Exame Magazine (24 Apr. 2013), https://exame.com/tecnologia/95-de-novos-clientes-de-tv-por-assinatura-sao-classe-c-ou-d/ (accessed 12 Jan. 2021).

per person between BRL 320 and BRL 1,120.[62] At the same time, the cheapest package of Pay-TV channels was being offered for about BRL 55.[63]

52. In addition to that, from 2015 onwards, Brazil began to feel the effects of an economic crisis that culminated in successive falls in GDP.[64] Finally, the downtrend in the subscriber base is also attributed to the change in consumption habits, migration from linear to on-demand, and the emergence of cord cutters – i.e., people switching from cable or satellite television to Internet-based streaming services.

53. In 2019, according to unofficial data,[65] there were estimates that over-the-top (OTT) services were present in 39% of households against 26% of Pay-TV, although there is no official data for the segment, yet there are no official market surveys on video on demand (VOD) consumption since a regulatory framework for the segment is still under discussions. Without a regulatory framework demanding players to provide ANCINE with data, for instance, the agency does not yet have relevant aggregated data for disclosure.

54. Regarding the market share of Pay-TV distributors in 2020, Claro (a subsidiary of America Movil group), which operates in both direct-to-home television (DTH) and cable, concentrates 47.1% of subscribers, and Sky (AT&T subsidiary), which operates only in DTH, concentrates 30.4% of subscribers. At a smaller scale, Oi, which operates in both DTH and fibre to the home (FTTH), has 11.4% of total subscribers, and Vivo (Telefónica's subsidiary) has an 8.4% share. Smaller distributors, together, concentrate only 2.7% of the market.

55. According to official data released by the ANATEL in 2020,[66] the 14.9 million Pay-TV subscribers were mostly distributed between DTH (49.6%) and cable (42.9%), with a low but growing share of FTTH (7.5%), this last representing an increase of about 50% over the previous year in the segment. It is interesting to notice that, also according to ANATEL data, in 2020 Claro owned 27.1% of the 36.3 million wired broadband terminals and held a 25.7% share of mobile terminals.

---

62. Darlan Alvarenga, *Classe média brasileira é o 18º maior 'país' do mundo em consumo*, G1.com (18 Feb. 2014), http://g1.globo.com/economia/noticia/2014/02/classe-media-brasileira-e-o-18-maior-pais-do-mundo-em-consumo.html (accessed 12 Jan. 2021).
63. Bárbara Sacchitiello, *Brasil é o 30º em preço de TV Paga,* meioemensagem.com (29 Jul. 2014), https://www.meioemensagem.com.br/home/midia/2014/07/29/brasil-e-o-30-em-preco-de-tv-paga.html (accessed 20 Jan. 2021).
64. Instituto de Pesquisa Econômica Aplicada, Brazilian gross domestic product official calculation available at http://www.ipeadata.gov.br/exibeserie.aspx?serid=38414 (accessed 12 Jan. 2021).
65. Rafael Bucco, *TV paga no Brasil sofreu com os 'cord cutters' em 2018, diz AMDOCS* Tele Síntese (13 Feb. 2019), https://www.telesintese.com.br/tv-paga-no-brasil-sofreu-com-os-cord-cutters-em-2018-diz-amdocs/ (accessed 14 Jan. 2021).
66. ANATEL, *Overview of Telecommunication in Brazil* (December 2020), https://sei.anatel.gov.br/sei/modulos/pesquisa/md_pesq_documento_consulta_externa.php?eEP-wqk1skrd8hSlk5Z3rN4EVg9uLJqrLYJw_9INcO6xQe_NCMYl6DFnwBVUZgGh_tcMajgdmgeIxfLBsexgpa-WjTV0U5SjhGZivpqHaU3OkTgkoMzUUKvaFLeLQeL8 (accessed 12 Jan. 2021).

§3. SOURCES OF MEDIA LAW

56. Different normative instruments influence media law in Brazil. They originate from public and private instances and bind the media actors to different degrees. The media law framework encompasses a variety of activities, for which different sets of rules can be relevant. In general, the main sources to be considered are constitutional provisions, Parliament-enacted legislation, secondary legislation (i.e., regulatory norms enacted by direct and indirect public administration bodies), jurisprudence, and private codes of practices.

57. Throughout this monograph, we will detail these instruments' content, along with their relevance and limitations to the specific fields that make up media law. In this section, we provide a brief overview of their normative basis and hierarchy in the Brazilian legal system, focused on their origin and the degree to which they bind private and public agents in the media law field.

I. The 1988 Federal Constitution

58. As mentioned previously, the 1988 Brazilian Federal Constitution is considered the milestone of the country's re-democratization process because it was enacted after two decades of military dictatorship. It represents the adoption of the model of a liberal democracy, which is underpinned by political participation and separation of powers while also enshrining the protection of individual rights and liberties.[67] Because it was enacted in the context of re-democratization, several different stakeholders participated in the constituent assembly and deliberated over its terms, including public and private sectors, as well as civil society. As a result, the Constitution encompasses a variety of values and political interests. We can perceive this diversity of subject matters as both the result of 'a pluralist society, marked by the coexistence between different beliefs and values'[68] or as 'the reflection of a political context in which the fiscal crisis, high inflation, strong demand for social justice, and a fierce dispute for power resources from the organized sectors of Brazilian society lived together'.[69] If, on the one hand, this variety improved the set of individual protections with constitutional status, on the other hand, it hindered legal conflicts between hierarchically equal rights.

59. As it is for any legal field, the Brazilian Constitution is the ultimate binding legal instrument to influence media law, as its constitutionalism model presumes the subordination of legality to the terms of the Constitution, which is centred on democratic principles and individuals' fundamental rights. In this system, the validity of

67. Luís Roberto Barroso, *Vinte anos da Constituição Brasileira de 1988: o Estado a que chegamos*, 3, n.º 10 Revista de Direito do Estado (2008).
68. Antonio Moreira Maués, *Constituição e Pluralismo Vinte Anos Depois*, in Cláudio Pereira de Souza Neto, Daniel Sarmento e Gustavo Binenbojm (org.). *Vinte Anos da Constituição Federal de 1988*, 169 (Lumen Iures 2009).
69. *Ibid.*

rules does not depend only on compliance to procedural requirements for democratic rule-making but also on their content being coherent with the set of rights and guarantees provided for in the constitutional document.

60. This broad and ultimately binding Constitution provides a series of rights and guarantees that relate to the free exercise of expressions and media-related activities. The majority of the rights and liberties that express the constitutional vision for the Brazilian democracy can be referred to Article 5 of the Constitution. It provides for a diversity of guarantees to be promoted and protected in the Brazilian legal order, which are also varied among themselves, ranging from freedom of movement, communication guarantees to property rights, for instance.

61. Article 5 includes rights that have different levels of relevance for the application of media law. They vary from the very foundations of the field (such as the right to freedom of expression, free press, and access to information) to rights that apply collaterally (e.g., the right to financial reparation in the face of moral damage) or to a minimum degree (as with those related to freedom of movement and physical integrity). In the first group, one can find, for instance, 'the free expression of thought, while anonymity is forbidden' (Article 5, IV); 'the free expression of intellectual, artistic, scientific and communication activity, regardless of censorship or license' (Article 5, IX); and 'access to information is guaranteed to all and confidentiality of source is safeguarded, as long as it is necessary for the exercise of professional practice' (Article 5, XIV).

62. Aside from its dimension as a charter of rights, the 1988 Federal Constitution also has an organizational role, in that it sets out the basic premises upon which the Brazilian national state is organized. That is to say that the Constitution is also a document that allocates competencies among the federation members (i.e., the federal governments, states, municipalities, and the country's Federal District) and organizes the basic structures of the executive, legislative and judiciary branches.

63. Concerning the media sector, it places telecommunications and broadcasting regulation attributions under the Federal Government's competences (Articles 21 and 22), and it provides the legal regime for 'Social Communications' activities (Articles 220–224). The implementation and regulation of these provisions will be further addressed throughout this monograph.

II. Federal Legislation

64. By 'federal legislation', we mean the legal instruments approved by the National Congress, in both the House of Representatives and the Federal Senate. The pieces of legislation included under federal legislation encompass two types of laws that vary according to the required quorum for their approval (as per Articles 47 and 69 of the Constitution): ordinary laws (known in Portuguese as 'leis ordinárias', which require the majority of members of the Houses present on the day of the voting) and complementary laws ('leis complementares'). The latter requires approval by the absolute majority of each house – i.e., in order for it to be approved, a complementary law must have the votes of the absolute majority of the House's members, and not only the ones present at the voting. Overall, one can say that ordinary laws are the rule, and complementary laws are exceptions, given that the Constitution demands their adoption in specific cases (e.g., federation-related matters as specified by Article 18 §3 and labour regulations, as per Article 7, I of the Constitution).[70]

65. Given that the Constitution provides that communications are a matter under the Federal Government's competence, federal legislation (in the form of ordinary laws) plays an essential role in regulating this field. Some of the most relevant sources of media law in Brazil were enacted in this form. For instance, Law 9.472/1997 established the Telecommunications Act, and Pay-TV services are regulated by Law 12.485/2011. The content and relevance of these legal instruments will be further developed throughout this monograph.

III. Secondary Norms: Regulations

66. Secondary norms are normative regulations that allow for proper enforcement of the law. They consist mostly of norms originating from direct and indirect public administration bodies and provide details as to how a Parliament-enacted law should be enforced, thus making it applicable in practice. These norms vary according to the administrative authority that is responsible for enacting them.

67. First, it is within the President's competence to enact 'Decrees' which he signs along with those Ministries of State whose functions relate to the object of regulation. After Parliament passes legislation, decrees are the next hierarchically superior legal instrument and are bound by the terms of the bill they regulate. That means that the text of a Decree cannot, under any circumstances, innovate or add on to what is provided by the original statute. For instance, Law 12.965/2014 (known as the Internet Civil Rights Framework, or, in Portuguese, 'Marco Civil da Internet') is regulated by Decree 8.771/2016 (which brings specific provisions regarding, for instance, net neutrality and data storage). In a similar vein, the Telecommunications Act (Law 9.472/1997) is further regulated by different decrees, such as Decree 10.610/2021 (which provides for a plan to improve general access to telecommunications services). The existence of a regulatory Decree is not a condition for a statute's validity or enforceability.

68. After decrees, normative instruments enacted by specialized administrative bodies can also play an important role in regulating laws. There are several different public administration bodies whose competencies encompass the enactment of sectoral regulation, besides legislation monitoring and enforcement (as will be

70. For a further analysis of the different legal instruments in the Brazilian system *see* Cristiana Belon Fernandes, Renato Maluf & Gabriella Tuna Garamvolgyi e Silva Mamede, *Constitutional Law in Brazil*, 51 (Wolters Kluwer Law and Business 2012).

described in Part V of this monograph). To name a few, the Ministries of State and their Secretaries and Departments can play an important role, as well as diverse autarchy bodies and, of course, regulatory agencies. These bodies can enact different sorts of normative instruments. Some of the regulations have mostly organizational management content (e.g., 'Administrative Ordinances'); others are distinguished by their regulatory function (which is the case of 'Normative Instructions', and 'Resolutions') – and some express deliberative decisions taken by collegial bodies, including boards of directors (these are often called 'Deliberations'). It should be noticed that each body enacts normative instructions relevant to the industry under its jurisdiction, and Part V will describe the supervisory bodies that influence media law.

IV. Jurisprudence

69. The term *jurisprudence* refers to judicial precedents, whether considered as single cases or as a collection of decisions resulting from the 'enforcement of the same precepts on similar cases'.[71] Even though the Brazilian legal system is based on a civil law tradition, jurisprudence continuously gains importance as a law source. This importance is reflected in the Brazilian Civil Procedure Code, whose Article 927 provides that judges and courts are bound by previous higher court decisions (especially when they adjudicate repetitive lawsuits or appeals) and by the form known as 'binding precedent' (known in Brazilian Portuguese as 'Súmula Vinculante').

70. Binding Precedents were inserted into the Brazilian legal order by Constitutional Amendment 45/2004. According to Article 103-A of the Constitution, STF may enact Binding Precedents in order to settle constitutional interpretations, after it has enacted repeated decisions on specific matters. The Binding Precedents shall be approved by two-thirds of the Court's members, and as from its publication in the official press, the Precedents are binding on the other organs of the judiciary and on the direct and indirect public administration, at the federal, state and municipal levels. Until the time of writing this monograph, STF had enacted fifty-eight Binding Precedents.[72]

71. It is safe to say that jurisprudence plays an important role as one source of media law, especially in terms of defining the scope of media and communications-related rights – such as freedom of expression, access to information, and rights to image, and honour. For this field, the most relevant jurisprudence sources rest in higher court decisions, particularly STF (the country's Constitutional Court) and STJ (the highest-ranked appeals court for the enforcement of the federal laws).

71. Humberto Dalla & Renata Berlinski, *Civil Procedure in Brazil* 16–25 (Wolters Kluwer Law and Business 2020).
72. STF, *Súmulas Vinculantes*. Available at: https://portal.stf.jus.br/textos/verTexto.asp?servico=jurisprudenciaSumulaVinculante. Accessed on 19 Apr. 2022.

V. Private Codes of Practice and Other Soft Law Instruments

72. Outside of the state's regulatory competencies, media law is also influenced by the values and standards embedded in the practices of the media sector. The degree to which this influence is effective will depend on how institutionalized these practices are, e.g., if they were agreed upon and formalized by a professional category or sectoral association. This is the case, for instance, for the Brazilian Press Association (Associação Brasileira de Impresa – ABI), which, besides formalizing its bylaws (and other constitutive documents), has also enacted a Journalists' Code of Ethics.[73] The Code sets out a series of obligations for journalists to abide by in their activities, and the sanctions to be applied within ABI and the Labour Union in the case of non-compliance.

73. Media companies are also frequently organized in sectoral associations that play an important role in presenting their agendas before governmental authorities and promoting debates among their member and civil society. There are a few examples that illustrate the adoption of such sectoral institutions at a federal level. Broadcasting companies, for instance, are gathered under the Brazilian Association for Radio and Television Broadcasters (Associação Brasileira de Emissoras de Radio e Television – ABERT). The Brazilian Association for Pay-TV Operators (Associação Brasileira de TV por Assinatura – ABTA) represents private broadcasting services, and the E-Commerce Chamber represents most digital platforms businesses in Brazil ('Câmara Brasileira de Comércio Eletrônico').

74. Even though such entities play an important role in the sector's dynamics, in terms of sources of media law, the self-regulating institution for the advertisement sector can be considered the most influential private source of media regulation. As further detailed in Part III, Chapter 6, the National Council for Advertisement Self-Regulation (Conselho Nacional de Autorregulação Publicitária – CONAR) is a non-governmental organization that 'aims to promote freedom of advertising expression and defend the constitutional prerogatives of commercial advertising'.[74] Its activities include sectoral organization and representation, as well as receiving and adjudicating complaints about publicity pieces from consumers, authorities, associates, or by members of its board. These complaints are judged by the Ethics Council, according to the due process guarantees established in the bylaws. After analysing a complaint, the Council can impose a warning penalty, recommend changes to its content, or recommend its suspension. Given this scope, CONAR exercises its influence on the media landscape through its code of practice, decisions, binding precedents, and technical opinions.

---

73. Associação Brasileira de Imprensa, *Código de Ética,* http://www.abi.org.br/institucional/legislacao/codigo-de-etica-dos-jornalistas-brasileiros/.
74. CONAR – Missão. Available at: http://www.conar.org.br/ (accessed 10 Oct. 2020).

Part I. Freedom of Speech in Brazil

75. The right to freedom of expression has been part of the Brazilian legal order since the promulgation of the 1824 Constitution, which provided every person's right to 'communicate their thoughts through words and to publish them in the press, without censorship, as long as they remain liable for any abuses of such right'.[75] As is the case in various democratic charters, freedom of expression remained a fundamental right in the later Brazilian constitutions – including that of 1967, promulgated during the military dictatorship that started in 1964.

76. The authoritarian regime later replaced the Constitution published in 1967 with Constitutional Amendment No. 1/1969, which reads that freedom of expression and thought did not apply to 'propaganda of war, subversion of the order or prejudices of religion, race or class and to publications and expressions contrary to morals and good customs'.[76] Exceptions such as these references to morals and good customs were nothing more than an instrument to promote a positive view of the totalitarian regime, something which enabled stigmatization of the media, formalized censorship and enabled the compromise of free speech at an institutional level.

77. The dictatorship censored various cultural expressions, including public spectacles, songs, audiovisual content, and press publications. The legal basis for censorship of public presentations was Decree n. 20.493/1949, enacted before the military regime. It created the 'Service for Censorship of Public Recreations' – a police authority under the Ministry of Justice's supervision, with the power to partially or entirely censor these events. After 1964, press publications were censored based on Law 5.563/1968 and Decree-Law n. 1.077/1970. While the former created a 'Superior Council for Censorship', the latter imposed heavy restrictions on press activities. For instance, it provided a no-tolerance policy towards publications considered 'contrary to morals and good costumes' and allowed for *ex ante* censorship, search, and apprehension of books and periodicals.[77]

75. Luis Roberto Barroso, *Constituição, Liberdade de Expressão e Classificação Indicativa. Invalidade da imposicao de horarios para exibicao de programas televisivos,* 11 Revista de Direito do Estado 342 (2008).
76. *Ibid.*
77. See Lucas Borges de Carvalho, *Os meios de comunicação, a censura e a regulação de conteúdo no Brasil: aspectos juridicos e distinções conceituais,* 4 (1) Revista de Direito, Estado e Telecomunicacoes 51–82 (2012).

78. These policies lasted until the country began the process of re-democratization. As it did for other political and social life sectors, the 1988 Constitution broke the totalitarian paradigm in the field of media law. It established a legal regime for the media to protect citizens' free speech rights, contemplating various individual and collective guarantees related to the different dimensions of free speech. The core of this protection rests in items IV and IX of Article 50, which read as follows:

> Art. 50. All people are equal before the Law, without distinction of any kind. The rights to life, freedom, equality, security, and property are guaranteed to all Brazilians and foreigners residing in the country, in the following terms:
>
> [...]
> IV – the expression of thought is free, while anonymity is forbidden;
> [...]
> IX – the expression of intellectual, artistic, scientific, and communication activity is free, regardless of censorship or license.

79. The protection of free speech spread through other provisions of the Constitution, which secures rights and guarantees that are contained in, or related to freedom of expression, in different degrees. In the Brazilian legal framework, freedom of expression can be interpreted as a broad right that encompasses a series of guarantees that are distinct from each other but brought together by a philosophy centred on developing the human subject and the sustainment of the democratic process. Some of these guarantees are commonly referred to as 'freedom of thought', 'freedom of opinion', 'freedom of the press', 'freedom of information', 'right to information', 'broadcasting freedoms' and 'freedom of conscience', among others. In this sense, constitutionalist author José Affonso da Silva adopted the expression 'freedoms of communication', to refer to the 'set of rights, forms, processes and vehicles that allow for the coordination of creation, expression, and diffusion of thought and information'.[78]

80. Although the 1988 Constitution assured a rupture with institutionalized censorship and paved the way to a new paradigm regarding freedom of speech, this right has not necessarily gone unthreatened in the last three decades. While the dictatorship's institutional mechanisms are no longer in place (i.e., the communications landscape is no longer conditioned to massive and structural state suppression of speech), other social and political factors deserve our attention, as they also can affect the fruition of a free and plural free speech institutional landscape. Some of the most relevant factors are the high rates of violence perpetrated against journalists;[79] the use of judicial claims of libel and defamation to intimidate journalists and

78. José Affonso da Silva, *Curso de Direito Constitucional Positivo* 242 (São Paulo: Malheiros 2003).
79. As of September 2020, Reporters without Boarders reports that Brazil continues to be an especially dangerous country for the media, as many journalists continue to be threatened or killed in connection with their work. Source: Reporters without borders, County report: Brazil. Available at: https://rsf.org/en/brazil (accessed 17 Sep. 2020).

press vehicles;[80] and some characteristics of Brazil's media services regulatory landscape, which, whether by omission or by existing institutional mechanisms, is still permeated by economic concentration and maintained privileges of traditionally powerful political groups. One example of the latter is the practice known as *coronelismo eletrônico* (or 'electronic colonelism'), which allows elected politicians to own local and national broadcasting licences.[81]

81. These factors represent a different kind of threat than the institutionalized and non-institutionalized violent practices of the past dictatorships. The new constitutional paradigm allowed for a more democratic public sphere of debate and a free speech tradition that moved away from the totalitarian regime. Nevertheless, there can be no real comprehension of Brazil's free speech environment without understanding the cultural, political, and legal barriers that still stand in the way of a free, plural, and safe public debate. These barriers will be further addressed throughout this monograph, along with their significant impacts on the institutional landscape.

82. In the following three paragraphs, we will describe the constitutional scope of free speech protection in Brazil. Paragraph 1 will illustrate the constitutional protection of both its subjective and collective dimensions, and paragraph 2 sets out the legal restrictions on free speech. Lastly, paragraph 3 will provide an overview of jurisprudence, notably regarding the most influential Constitutional Court precedents.

§1. Free Speech as an Individual and Collective Right

83. The protection of freedom of expression can be justified from two different perspectives: (i) as an individual's subjective right to express themselves without external interference, and (ii) as a collective right to access free and plural information in order to allow each person to participate in public debate. These two perspectives can also be referred to as the *subjective* and *objective* dimensions of free speech – wherein the subjective dimension refers to the individual perspective and the objective dimension to the collective one.

84. These dimensions have complementary normative contents. As a subjective right, free speech demands the protection of an individual's moral right to disseminate their ideas and thoughts without obstruction. In this perspective, freedom of expression is an individual right of the citizen, which derives from human dignity and constitutes a moral guarantee that each person has to manifest their identity

80. Carlos Eduardo Lins da Silva, *Censura judicial à imprensa no Brasil: autorregulação e maturidade democrática*, Revista de Direito Administrativo 253 (2010).
81. The practice of 'electronic colonelism' will be further addressed, together with its impacts on Part IV. For further details, *see:* Venício A. de Lima Machado & Cristiano Aguiar Lopes, *Coronelismo eletrônico de novo tipo (1999–2004): as autorizacoes de emissoras como moeda de barganha política* 3 (Observatório da Imprensa, Instituto para Desenvolvimento do Jornalismo: Sao Paulo 2007).

before the community and exercise their autonomy.[82] In this sense, free speech implies a *negative* duty for states. In order to protect and promote it, they must abide by an obligation of abstention and refrain from interference.[83]

85. In turn, the objective dimension implies that freedom of expression is also a collective right, according to which the public, in general, is entitled to free and plural information. Ultimately, its goal is to protect the public sphere of debate necessary for the democratic state's legitimate operation. Under the guidance of its objective dimension, freedom of expression assumes the role of a prerequisite for functioning democracies, associated with both an instrumental function of conducting public debate and substantive content related to rights of access to information, diversity, and plurality. In this realm, states must protect and promote freedom of expression through *positive* policies. Aside from refraining from interference (as the protection of the subjective dimension demands), states must act to promote conditions such as equal access, plurality, and regional presentation. Despite the theoretical dichotomous treatment given to these two elements, they are inseparable and enable true preservation of these rights – sometimes through an absentee state stance, and sometimes through active measures.[84]

86. The Brazilian Constitution provides for negative and positive state duties to protect free speech by promoting its both subjective and collective dimensions.[85] One can assert that only an interpretation that extracts negative and positive state duties about freedom of expression is proper to the systems of rights and guarantees provided by the 1988 Constitution. According to Daniel Sarmento, this is due to the Constitution having established a democratic legal order centred on fundamental rights, whose full accomplishment can only be achieved through public power activism. The author further argues that the consecration of freedom of expression would be no exception to this rule, based on the assumption that violations are not produced only by the state's action, but often as a result of its inertia.[86]

87. A thorough analysis of the Constitution confirms this reasoning, as the text brings express provisions regarding the ties of abstention and action for the state. Regarding the subjective dimension, a few of the rights provided by Article 5 clearly express concerns with guaranteeing individual free expression and freedom of thought (items IV, IX), as well as an absolute ban on censorship provided in §2. Similarly, the same Article 5 provides for the right to a free press and freedom of any cultural and artistic manifestation. Negative duties of non-intervention are also reflected in Article 220, notably in §1, according to which 'no law shall contain any

82. Daniel Sarmento, *A Liberdade de Expressão e o Problema do Hate Speech in Livres e Iguais: Estudos de Direito Constitucional*, 242 (Lumen Jures 2010).
83. Jónatas M. Machado, *Liberdade de Expressão. Dimensões Constitucionais da Esfera Pública no Sistema Social*, 379 (Coimbra Editora 2002).
84. Owen Fiss, *Democracia y Disenso. Una Teoria de La Libertad de Expressión,* 46 (Ad-Hoc 2010).
85. Gustavo Binenbojm, *Meios de Comunicação de Massa, Pluralismo e Democracia Deliberativa – As liberdades de expressão e de imprensa nos Estados Unidos e no Brasil*, 6 Revista da EMERJ 23 (2003).
86. *Ibid.*

obstacle to the full freedom of journalistic information in any media'. These are defensive guarantees, in the sense that they need to be protected by public authorities from public and private obstacles external to their exercise.

88. The Constitution also provides positive duties to protect freedom of expression, with the intent to preserve access to the public sphere of debate and conditions for the exercise of free expression. Yet at an abstract level, item XIV of Article 5 provides that 'access to information is guaranteed to all'. Furthermore, throughout the text, one can find series of provisions aimed at specific actors of the media and communications sector embedded with free speech as a collective right-related concern. As per their nature, these provisions demand positive policies to be implemented by state authorities.

89. For instance, aiming at promoting pluralism in the media sector, Article 220, §5 prohibits media outlets from being owned by direct or indirect monopoly or oligopoly. Although monopoly bans are essentially antitrust policies, they are also a mechanism that can be applied to media and communication sectors as a means to achieve *external pluralism* – which occurs when citizens can 'find a full range of political views expressed among the existing media outlets in an overall media market'.[87] Mechanisms aiming at *internal pluralism* (i.e., individual media outlets hosting various opinions across the ideological spectrum[88]) can also be listed as examples of how the Constitution recognizes the collective dimension of freedom of expression. In this sense, Article 5, item V provides that 'the right of reply is guaranteed, proportional to the appeal, in addition to the indemnity for material, moral or image damage'. The nature of the right of reply will be discussed in more detail in Part II, Chapter 4. For now, it is enough to highlight that, in Brazil, the right to reply is grounded not only on the need for personal compensation of offended people but also on the importance of offering different points of view on the matters in the public debate.

90. There are still other provisions in the Constitution that presume a positive duty of states regarding freedom of expression. Article 221 provides a series of obligations for radio and TV broadcasting services in this sense, such as: setting preferences for educational, artistic, cultural, and informational purposes; promoting national and regional culture, especially by favouring independent production that aims to disseminate it; and observing regional and cultural differences in terms of their artistic and journalistic production.

91. In most cases, the Constitution does not provide for the detailed implementation of these obligations, which means that their fulfilment depends on infra-constitutional regulation. Thus, the explicit obligation, along with applicable sanctions and enforcement competencies, is to be defined by Parliament, whose task in these cases is to interpret the applicable constitutional provisions and carry out

---

87. Michele Polo, *Regulation for Pluralism in the Media Markets*, 3 (Universidade de Bocconi and IGIER 2005).
88. *Ibid.*

the positive policy that they express. In this spirit, Law 12.485/2011 establishes policies that institute national, regional, and independent content quotas for Pay-TV services (as follows in Part III, Chapter 4), and Decree-Law 236/1967 sets the rules for local limits on broadcasting licences. According to the sectors to which they apply, these legislations will be further described in the next chapters.

92. Since the Brazilian Charter provides for negative and positive state provisions regarding free speech, a constitutionally responsive regulatory landscape needs to address both these requirements, ensuring that this fundamental right is fulfilled in the whole of its dimensions. In this spirit, it is not enough that institutionalized censorship is no longer in place; the government has a constitutional duty also to provide access to information and a democratic public sphere.

93. While a few laws have regulated these constitutional obligations, there is disagreement on whether they have indeed fulfilled the democratic media landscape aspirations expressed in the Constitution. To a certain degree, the prioritization of negative duties can be associated with a long-lasting political culture that is still traumatized by the harms of institutional censorship. However, critiques of media and communications regulation in Brazil are mostly focused on the post-1988 maintenance of systemic privileges of dominant media conglomerates[89] – such as a concentrated broadcasting licensing system and different political mechanisms that continue to favour the access of privileged economic and political groups to media and communications infrastructure.

§2. Restrictions on Freedom of Expression

94. As with most democratic constitutional orders, freedom of expression is not an absolute right in Brazil since the Constitution itself provides for several exceptions to the rule of no intervention. These exceptions encompass restrictions on freedom of expression when in conflict with other fundamental rights and state intervention in communications services. Concerning the latter, the Constitution establishes, for instance, guidelines for broadcasting programming, such as the aforementioned 'preference for educational, artistical, cultural and informative finalities' or 'the promotion of national culture and incentive to regional and independent audio-visual content' (both in Article 220). This sort of positive state interference should not be mistaken for censorship. It is justified under the collective dimension of this right and thus equated with its very promotion, as we describe in paragraph 3.

95. It is part of the courts' original functions to deliberate on the scope of fundamental rights, which includes the right to freedom of expression when in conflict with other constitutional guarantees – such as child protection or even a person's

89. Enrique Saraiva, *O novo papel regulatório do Estado e suas conseqüências na mídia*, in Saravia, Enrique; Martins, Paulo Emílio de Matos e Pieranti & Octavio Penna (org.), *Democracia e regulação dos meios de comunicação de massa* 6465 (Rio de Janeiro: Editora FGV 2008).

right to their own image, honour, and privacy. As the Constitution prohibits prior restraints (formerly known as previous censorship) and with it any sort of *ex ante* interference, free speech-related abuses are to be assessed and penalized by judges' *ex post* (which is done through the wide adoption of balancing techniques and proportionality tests). This means that, in theory, only after a particular content has been made public, can a judge hold somebody civil or criminally liable for violating other rights.

96. According to the Brazilian Criminal Code, some abuses of the right to freedom of expression are considered crimes (Law 2.848/1940). Under, Title I, Chapter V (entitled 'Crimes against one's honour'), there are three provisions that criminalize defamatory conduct. The first two are imputing that a person committed a crime, as per Article 138 (punishable by six months to two years of detention and a fine); and imputing someone with conduct that is offensive to their reputation, as per Article 139 (punishable by three months to one year of detention and a fine). These crimes are in the realm of what is known as *libel* and *slander*. The third conduct, provided by Article 140, can be translated as *injury*. It happens when a person offends another's 'dignity or decency' and is punishable by one to six months of detention or by a fine. All these sanctions can be made harsher in the face of determined circumstances; for instance, injury can be punished by one to three years of detention plus a fine when it is directed at one's race, ethnicity, religion, origin, elderly or disabled condition (Article 140, §3). These crimes are further discussed in Part II, Chapter 3.

97. While these 'crimes against one's honour' are all punishable by detention, according to Law 9.099/1995, they can also be considered crimes of minor offensive potential, as the equivalent penalty is up to two years of detention (which might not happen according to aggravating circumstances, such as the aforementioned racial injuries). As such, detention sanctions are often replaced with other penalties, such as fines, loss of assets, community services, and temporary rights restrictions.

98. In parallel to criminal liability, courts also adjudicate civil reparation claims, whether or not these are related to the criminal conducts described above. These claims might be based on abuses of the right to freedom of expression that already took place (e.g., regarding an allegation that has already been published) or on potential violations (e.g., when somebody identifies a potential threat that has not yet taken place). Regarding the latter, most common pleas request that the defendants abstain from performing the conduct that would abuse their right to free speech.[90] As per reparative litigation, pleas can also encompass some sort of duty

90. In this sense, *see*, for instance, in August 2011 a first instance judge forbade an evangelical church of displaying billboards with biblical citations that were, in that context, interpreted as homophobic messages. The billboards were to be installed in the eve of the annual Gay Pride Parade of the City of São Paulo, an iconic event for the promotion of civil rights. The appeal's court upheld this decision, stating that: 'is not a simple expression of religiosity, something that could perfectly happen in the interior of a temple, in the presence of the church goers, and thus respecting the freedom of religious faith and cult. However, the church intended to make lobby for its religious convictions and

of abstention, even though requests for financial indemnification (a constitutional right as per Article 5, items V and X) and for the exercise of the right to reply are more common.

99. Given that the Constitution expressly bans *ex ante* censorship, pre-emptive speech-abuse-related claims are more vulnerable to rulings of unconstitutionality and disproportionate restrictions on freedom of expression. The constitutional legislator's choice for speech-related infringements only to be punished *ex post* privileged freedom of expression by not preventing an idea or information from reaching the public. It is the basis for a public sphere free of pre-emptive control and less likely to generate chilling effects. Nevertheless, this goal might be compromised depending on how courts exercise their adjudication competencies. Literature frequently expresses concerns towards the judicial stipulation of high amounts of monetary compensation in the face of civil defamation or moral damage claims.[91]

100. The main risks to be considered in these cases are that not only an individual or a media vehicle can be penalized with a disproportionate financial burden but also that this systemic practice is highly likely to generate chilling effects. *See*, for instance, the case of a local newspaper from the city of Santa Cruz do Rio Pardo (a rural area in the state of São Paulo). In 2009, the newspaper was sentenced to reparations of BRL 593,000 for moral damages against a judge for reporting that the local city hall had covered his home rental fees and telephone line costs.[92] At the time, the owner of the newspaper declared that this would mean 'a financial capital punishment', as his company would not be able to survive such a financial burden. In a similar case, a small newspaper from Rio Grande do Sul announced, also in 2009, that it was going out of business after twenty-four years due to not being able to afford a series of judicial indemnifications.[93] They were all stipulated in judicial claims presented by family members of an influential regional political

---

this practice confronts the sexual orientation of others and should not prevail. The self-determination of a person gives her the right to opt and eventually to practice her own sexuality the way she wants. The State and no religion cannot publicly confront such a liberty. In the democratic rule of law, the human dignity must prevail. For this reason the inadequate behaviour of the appealing church must be abolished, since it is not admissible any incentive to prejudice. Furthermore, the religious support of the condemned practice affects those who do not comply with the religious dogmas. Besides, a free society requires that all of his members exercise their individual freedom without limitations and the billboards don't follow such requirements and should be taken away since they do not take into consideration the human dignity which also includes the sexuality'. 4th Private Law Chamber of the São Paulo Appeal's Court. Decision n. 0045315-08.2011.8.26.05. The translated excerpts were extracted from the analysis of the case law provided by Ronaldo Porto Macedo Junior, *Freedom of Expression: What Lessons Can We Learn from U.S. Experience?*, 13 Revista Direito GV 1, 274–302, 275 (2017).

91. Fábio Carvalho Leite, *Por uma posição preferencial do direito de resposta nos conflitos entre liberdade de imprensa e direito à honra*, civilistica.com, 7, 1 (2018).
92. TJSP, 9147829-03.1998.8.26.0000. Available at: https://esaj.tjsp.jus.br/cposg/show.do?processo.codigo=RMZ011KTL12L1&uuidCaptcha= (accessed: 23 Mar. 2022).
93. TJRS, 06110290820118217000. Available at: https://consulta.tjrs.jus.br/consulta-processual/processo/resumo?numeroProcesso=70022063242&codComarca=700 (accessed: 23 Mar. 2022).

leader, as the newspaper had published denunciations made against him in a parliamentary enquiry.[94] These two cases are an illustration of a much wider set of judicial decisions that encompass cases against both communications vehicles (bigger and smaller) and journalists, and involve political and non-political actors. What they have in common is that they lead to decisions where high reparation values ended up derailing press activities and potentially preventing future information from reaching the public. In fact, this practice is commonly referred to in Brazilian media and literature as *judicial censorship.*[95]

101. According to Fábio de Carvalho Leite, this system equates freedom of expression with the possibility of bearing monetary compensation derived from civil liability over speech abuse. These indemnifications are determined by judges considering the specificities of each case, and as noted, they can often reach high amounts. Considering that Brazil is among the world's most unequal societies, the author highlights the worrisome reality that a significant part of the population cannot afford this risk and is therefore potentially prevented from the full exercise of free expression. In contrast, individuals and media conglomerates provided with the financial power to bear those same risks become holders of an 'absolute right' to free speech.[96]

§3. Jurisprudence

102. The assessment of Brazilian jurisprudence in this field can be challenging. Since judges and courts at different hierarchical levels can adjudicate civil and criminal claims of defamation, the judicial review on freedom of expression is somewhat fragmented. It is not possible to identify one single sense or tradition among the first instance and appeals court's decisions that could amount to a single 'Brazilian theory on free speech' – as much as balancing techniques and proportionality tests are popular. For this reason, a comprehensive precedents-based approach to the first instance and appeal court jurisprudence is unlikely to be representative of this universe.

103. Since liability over speech abuse can only be assigned to courts, they end up playing a relevant role in defining the scope of freedom of expression. As mentioned previously, the Constitution protects a variety of rights alongside freedom of expression, i.e., with the same hierarchical position in the Brazilian legal order.

94. Both these examples were retrieved from: Carlos Eduardo Lins da Silva, *Censura judicial à imprensa no Brasil: autorregulação e maturidade democrática*, Revista de Direito Administrativo 253 (2010).
95. *Ibid.*
96. Fábio Carvalho Leite, *Por uma posição preferencial do direito de resposta nos conflitos entre liberdade de imprensa e direito à honra*, civilistica.com, 7, 1 (2018).

When concrete cases present conflicts between these rights, courts solve them according to the 'balancing doctrine and a vague conceptualization of human dignity'.[97]

104. The most significant advantage of this model is that any restrictions on free speech will only be carried out by the judiciary – the branch with legitimacy and expertise to assess threats to fundamental rights. Furthermore, judicial decisions are presumed to be the righteous interpretation of the law, self-executable and provided with legal certainty. On the other hand, its main disadvantages relate to the fact that in a judicial system where any judge or court is competent to arbitrate constitutionality conflicts, the scope of freedom of expression ends up lacking 'a more deep and defined reflection that could reveal some theoretical coherence that could lie behind these cases'.[98] This leads to a scenario where one finds various interpretations of the same rights conflict, which can lead to different and yet (allegedly) equally constitutional solutions. Theoretical and empirical studies have already hinted at the fact that, in this system, 'the different standards adopted in these decisions are a mere expression of the ideological biases that guided the judge's preferences'[99] instead of solutions extracted from the applicable legal framework.

105. This fragmentation of free speech interpretations is amplified by libel and defamation litigation becoming a widespread practice in Brazil, to the point of weighing on the country's free press landscape. As Carlos Eduardo Lins da Silva illustrates it, the non-governmental organization Freedom House classifies Brazil as a 'partially free press' country. This is due to a series of factors that include the civil and criminal defamation lawsuits that are used by politicians, government authorities and businesspeople to intimidate journalists and press vehicles.[100] In the 2017 Freedom of the Press Dark Horizon Report, the organization identifies this sort of threat as a tendency in other Latin American countries where journalists face 'violence, lawsuits and police interference'.[101] The report cites one case that can be considered a symbol for these practices and their destructive potential. This case was from 2016, when nearly fifty lawsuits were filed against five reporters who had worked on news articles revealing the suspiciously high earnings of members of the judiciary in the State of Paraná. According to the Report, 'the lawsuits were coordinated, using similar language, but were spread out geographically, forcing the journalists to spend considerable resources traveling between the courts'.[102] Aside

97. Ronaldo Porto Macedo Junior, *Freedom of Expression: What Lessons Can We Learn from U.S. Experience?*, 13 Revista Direito GV 1, 274–302, 275 (2017).
98. *Ibid.*
99. *Ibid.*, 274–302, 281. *See also* Guilherme da França Couto Fernandes de Almeida & Fábio Carvalho Leite e Ivar Allan Rodriguez Hannikainen, *Liberdade de expressão e direito à honra: medindo atitudes e prevendo decisões*, 21 (1) Espaço Juridico Journal of Law (2020).
100. Carlos Eduardo Lins da Silva, *Censura judicial à imprensa no Brasil: autorregulação e maturidade democrática,* Revista de Direito Administrativo 253 (2010).
101. Freedom of the Press Dark Horizon (2017). Available at: https://freedomhouse.org/report/freedom-press/2017/press-freedoms-dark-horizon. Accessed: 19 Oct. 2020.
102. *Ibid.*

from generating chilling effects and compromising equal enjoyment of free speech rights, such practices undoubtedly contribute to a fragmented and dispersed jurisprudence.

106. Other than the broad constitutional framework and the adjudication-centred system for restrictions on free speech, this characteristic of the Brazilian jurisprudence can also be associated with a lack of clear and informative precedents coming from the STF. According to Ivar A. Hartmann,[103] the Constitutional Court's decisions offer no guidance to lower courts about the boundaries between freedom of speech and moral damage, focusing mostly on procedural issues.[104] He argues that there is a 'precedent crisis', given that when STF's decisions do not inform lower courts, the whole jurisprudence will lack predictability and legal certainty. Thus, one can argue that this uncertainty over the interpretation of free speech protections and restrictions in Brazilian Courts is also reflected, to a different degree, in the STF's jurisprudence.

107. Regardless of a possible lack of a consistent method and substantive interpretational boundaries, there are a few exemplary precedents that reflect the STF's treatment of freedom of expression. Overall, this approach can be associated with a libertarian perspective, where free speech is a right mostly defined by its subjective dimension (i.e., a right whose protection demands non-interference). This perception was, in great part, evoked by *The Press Law Constitutionality* judgment (ADPF 130), when in 2009 the Court annulled a law enacted during the military regime to regulate press activities. Among other important grounds for the judicial interpretation of free speech, this decision stated the unconstitutionality of any sort of legislative intervention over the 'nuclear content' of press freedom.[105] This perspective inspired other iconic precedents, such as the one known as *Journalist's Diploma* case (which overthrew the requirement of bachelor's diploma for one to pursue the journalist profession), the *Non-authorized Biographies* case (about the requirement of one's authorization previous to the production of literary or audiovisual works on their biographies) and the *Right to be Forgotten* case (by means of which the STF fixed the understanding on the incompatibility of a right with such a purpose with the Brazilian legal system). Despite this libertarian tendency, there is also an important precedent on the restriction of free speech. In *Siegfried Ellwanger v. STJ* (HC 82424), the STF drew a clear line between free speech and the dissemination of racist and antisemitic content.

108. In the next pages, we will offer an overview of three out of these four precedents: *the Press Law Constitutionality* case, the *Non-authorized Biographies* case,

---

103. Ivar A. Hartmann, *Crise dos precedentes no Supremo: o caso dos precedentes sobre liberdade de expressão,* 6 Journal of Institutional Studies 1, 109–128 (2020).
104. *Ibid.*
105. STF, ADPF 130, tried on 30 Apr. 2009. Available at: http://redir.stf.jus.br/paginadorpub/paginador.jsp?docTP=AC&docID=265928. Accessed: 26 Oct. 2020.

Siegfried Ellwanger v. STJ, and the right to be forgotten thesis. The *Journalist's Diploma* case will be further detailed in Part II, Chapter 1, herein below (which approaches the journalist profession).

I. *The Press Law Constitutionality* Case, ADPF 130

109. Law 5.250/1967 ('Press Law') was enacted during the military dictatorship that governed the country between 1964 and 1983, aiming at 'regulating the exercise of freedom of thought and information' in the country. In practical terms, the Press Law regulated communication activities, establishing duties and limits, as well as sanctions to be applied in case of non-compliance. For instance, the law forbade 'clandestine' publications, or any content that 'attempted to work against morals and good customs'. It also regulated the conditions under which a right to reply could be granted and exercised. Under its terms, press publications, their printing infrastructure, broadcasters and any sort of mass communication vehicle needed to be registered by a public notary, which included filing broad information on the individuals who claimed responsibility for those entities. It became illegal to 'abuse one's right to freedom of thought and information' and the law also deemed a number of conducts to be crimes, such as 'to disseminate propaganda promoting war or intended to subvert the political and social order', or 'to offend public morals and good customs'. Provisions such as these were based on vague legal concepts, which allowed for the criminalization of speech that was considered to be contrary to the authoritarian regime's interests and beliefs.

110. Even though the country's re-democratization process started in 1983, Law 5.250/1967 had its constitutionality challenged before the STF only in 2008, through a judicial procedure that could be translated to English as 'allegation of non-compliance with a fundamental precept' (in Portuguese, *arguição de descumprimento de preceito fundamental* – ADPF).[106] The Democratic Labour Party (*Partido Democrático Trabalhista* – PDT) claimed that the Press Law was incompatible with the 1983 Federal Constitution, which provided a robust framework for protecting free speech, access to information, and freedom of the press. The case was decided on 30 April 2009, and the STF ruled for the abrogation of the entire Press Law, meaning that all of its provisions were no longer valid in the Brazilian territory. The wording of the decision stated that:

- Full freedom of the press presumes no previous censorship of any kind and no legislative power over what the STF understood to be the 'nuclear content' of press freedom. In this sense, Parliament could only legislate over subject matters that are 'collateral or related' to press activities, and under no circumstances would that include the content of what a press vehicle can or cannot publish.

106. ADPFs are the procedural mechanisms used to control the constitutionality laws that were enacted previously to the 1988 Constitution.

According to the decision, these collateral or related matters are the ones provided by the Constitution, such as the right to reply, journalistic source protection, criminal liability for defamation, and limitations on foreign ownership of communication companies.
- The 1988 Constitution does not allow for any previous restrictions on press freedom, but only for the investigation of civil and criminal liability, accompanied by sanctions when appropriate. In this sense, freedom of the press would be the first value to be considered, and abuses of this right would still be addressed and penalized on *ex post* terms. It also highlighted that proportionality must be respected when measuring financial compensation for abuse.
- It is impossible to reconcile the Press Law with the democratic Constitution, given that: (i) the Press Law contained an interlacing of commands, where for each general rule that affirms freedom, a range of exceptions were established, which practically invalidated the freedom commands in the first place; and (ii) in practical matters, Law 5.250/1967 depicted a real intent to go beyond 'a project of government' into a 'project of power'. Thus, its ultimate goal was to fully realize a long-lasting authoritarian power project, dependent on stifling all critical thinking in the country – an ambition deemed by the Court as absolutely incompatible with the 1988 Constitution.

111. ADPF 130 is perhaps the biggest symbol of STF's interpretation of the scope of freedom of expression. As these selected excerpts show, the trial not only consecrated a libertarian approach but was also embedded with a judicial statement, conveying that no authoritarian violations of speech would be tolerated under the democratic constitutional order. Nevertheless, some of its critics argue that the decision did not put enough effort into differentiating authoritarian violations from the regulation of illegal content and its boundaries, or from the provision of measures that would assure the very exercise of free speech.[107]

II. *Non-authorized Biographies*, ADI 4815

112. In 2012, the National Association for Book Editors (Associação Nacional dos Editores de Livros – ANEL) filed a lawsuit before the STF pleading partial unconstitutionality of Articles 20 and 21 of the Brazilian Civil Code (10.406/2002), which regulate the use of a person's image.[108] Specifically, the lawsuit pursued the declaration of unconstitutionality of the obligation which accrues from these provisions, according to which it was necessary to get a person's authorization prior to publishing their biography. According to the claimant, these provisions violate freedoms of expression, of thought, intellectual, artistic, scientific and communication activities (Constitution, Article 5, IV and IX) and the right to information (Article

107. As we will detail further below, this was the case, for instance, of the right to reply provision. It was invalidated with the whole of the Press Law and remained unregulated for years, until a new law was enacted.
108. STF, ADI. 4815, tried on 10 Jun. 2015. Available at: http://redir.stf.jus.br/paginadorpub/paginador.jsp?docTP=TP&docID=10162709 (accessed 19 Oct. 2020).

5, XIV) by not providing any exception that contemplates biographical works. ANEL further argued that, as per their wording, these provisions ground a mechanism of 'private censorship', which would be the prohibition, by judicial means and motivated by private reasons, of unauthorized biographies.

113. In 2015, STF ruled in favour of the claimant and granted Articles 20 and 21 of the Civil Code a 'constitutionally conforming interpretation',[109] declaring that authorizations of image use are not required for literary or audiovisual biographic works. According to the decision:[110]

– the prohibition of censorship provided by the Federal Constitution presumes that such conducts are not to be tolerated, whether they are motivated or performed by the state or by private actors;
– the Constitution also provides a right to access information, which encompasses the freedom to inform, receive information, and seek information. These also relate to a free process of formation of public opinion;
– the requirement for previous authorizations for the purposes of biographic works and to seize published works are acts equivalent to 'private censorship', and thus forbidden by the constitutional order.

III. Restrictions on Freedom of Expression, HC 82424 (STJ)

114. Siegfried Ellwanger was an editor who published a book containing discriminatory content against the Jewish people.[111] In 1996, he was convicted of the crime of racism by the Court of Appeals of the State of Rio Grande do Sul, after being cleared on a first instance trial. The STJ later confirmed this conviction, and in 2003 the case was examined by the STF through a writ of habeas corpus. The decisions that convicted the defendant were based on the Federal Constitution, which provides that 'the practice of racism constitutes a crime neither subject to bail nor to the statute of limitations' and on Article 20 of Law 7.716/1989, according to which it is a crime to 'practice, induce or incite discrimination or prejudice of race, colour, ethnicity, religion or national origin', punishable by one to three years of detention and a fine.

115. As a case that discusses whether a publisher shall be criminally liable for publishing books with discriminatory content, the *Ellwanger* case is of fundamental

109. While adjudicating the constitutionality of legal diplomas which bear more than one interpretation, the STF can apply the interpretation mechanisms called 'constitutionally conforming interpretation', which allows the Court to determine which interpretation is constitutional and should therefore prevail (instead of deeming the law unconstitutional). *See* Virgílio Afonso da Silva, *Interpretação conforme a Constituição: entre a trivialidade e a centralização judicial*, 2 (1) Revista Direito GV (2006).
110. STF, ADI. 4815, tried on 10 Jun. 2015. Available at: http://redir.stf.jus.br/paginadorpub/paginador.jsp?docTP=TP&docID=10162709 (accessed 19 Oct. 2020).
111. STF, HC 82424, tried on 17 Sep. 2003. Available at: http://redir.stf.jus.br/paginadorpub/paginador.jsp?docTP=AC&docID=79052 (accessed 19 Oct. 2020).

importance to the disputes on the limits to freedom of expression, notably in the face of hate speech and racist content. Nevertheless, while analysing the wording of STF's decision, one can notice that the core of the constitutional discussion on this case was focused on the concept of 'race' and 'racism'. Most of the STF's justifications were directed at the defendant's argument that the Jewish people are not a race, and thus the conduct for which he had been convicted would not 'have the racial connotation necessary for barring the statute of limitations'.[112] This assertion refers to the fact that the crime of racism is not subject to prescription under the Brazilian Constitution, and therefore a person can be prosecuted and convicted even after the expiry of traditional statutory prescription terms. This is relevant to the case because Mr Ellwanger's defence argued that, given that his conduct could not be classified as racism, prescription terms would apply, and it would be no longer possible to indict and convict him. In this regard, the Court stated that 'the division of human beings into races results from a process of purely socio-political content. Racism accrues from this assumption, and in turn generates discrimination and segregationist prejudice'.[113] Accordingly, it also stated that discrimination against the Jewish people results 'from the core of National-Socialist thought that Jews and Arians form distinct races' and that it is hence 'irreconcilable with the ethical and moral standards defined in the Constitution'. In this sense, 'the crime of racism is verified by the simple use of these stigmas, which constitutes an assault against the principles upon which human society is built and organized, such as the respectability and dignity of the human being and his peaceful coexistence in the social environment'.[114]

116. The decision also settled a discussion on the limits to freedom of expressions, notably in the face of racism and hate speech. Regarding this matter, the Court decided that the exercise of free speech is not under constitutional protection when used to harm someone's dignity. In this sense, the decision stated that:

- racism is a crime not subject to bail under the Brazilian legal order, and to edit and publish content which retrieves and enhances credibility of racial conceptions defined by Nacional Socialist regimes constitutes a crime of racism, either by arguing a supposed inferiority of the Jewish people or by denying the holocaust;
- freedom of expression is not an absolute constitutional guarantee, and it does not protect immoral content which is classified as criminal conduct; public liberties are not unconditioned and shall be exercised in harmony with the other rights and guarantees that are also provided by the Constitution;

112. Ronaldo Porto Macedo Junior, *Freedom of Expression: What Lessons Can We Learn from U.S. Experience?*, 13 Revista Direito GV 1, 274–302 (2017).
113. STF, HC 82424, tried on 17 Sep. 2003. Available at: http://redir.stf.jus.br/paginadorpub/paginador.jsp?docTP=AC&docID=79052 (accessed 19 Oct. 2020).
114. Translation extracted from Ronaldo Porto Macedo Junior, *Freedom of Expression: What Lessons Can We Learn from U.S. Experience?*, 13 Revista Direito GV 1, 297 (2017).

– the Court considered that, in this concrete case, 'the guarantee of freedom of expression was retracted in the name of the principles of dignity of the human person and judicial equality'.[115]

117. The *Ellwanger* case became one of the most studied precedents in the STF recent history – also for reasons other than reflecting a critical fundamental rights conflict and setting important limits to freedom of expression. In fact, some will argue that *Ellwanger* also marks a transformation in the 'narratives used by the Court´s Justices in order to justify the power and role of the Court – whose task, focus and source of legitimacy would then be the protection of human dignity in all its dimensions'.[116]

IV. Right to Be Forgotten, RE 1010606 (STF General Repercussion Theme 706)

118. According to STF, the right to be forgotten – understood as the right to prevent, due to the passage of time, the disclosure of truthful and lawfully obtained facts or data published in analogical or digital media – is incompatible with the Brazilian Federal Constitution.[117]

119. The first steps of the lawsuit that culminated in the trial of RE 1010606 were taken in 2004, in Rio de Janeiro. The siblings of Mrs Aida Curi, murdered in a brutal way in 1958, sought indemnification on account of an alleged unauthorized exhibition of their sister's image in a journalistic programme aired on Globo TV. The plaintiffs argued that, almost fifty years after the crime happened, there would be no reasonable justification for, or public interest that could ground, the re-enactment of their sister's murder, along with the display of photographs of the crime scene. The case had numerous outcomes and appeals before being judged by the STF almost two decades after the initial petition.

120. The decision that determined the incompatibility of the right to be forgotten with the Brazilian legal system was based on the following understandings:

– The passage of time must not prevent the circulation of information that has been lawfully obtained and processed because the passage of time cannot have the power to make a publication or data contained therein illicit. In other words, if the information was produced when the data was lawfully available, the unavailability of the data will not cause the future circulation of the information to be unlawful.

115. *Ibid.*

116. Diego Werneck Arguelhes, *Ellwanger e as transformações do Supremo Tribunal Federal: um novo começo?* (Direito e Praxis 2022).

117. STF, RE 1010606, tried on 11 Feb. 2021. Available at: https://portal.stf.jus.br/processos/downloadPeca.asp?id=15346473757&ext=.pdf (accessed 20 Feb. 2022).

- Restrictions on freedom of expression cannot occur because of alleged historical decontextualization due to the passage of time.
- Public interest presupposes lawfulness; therefore, if data has not been obtained lawfully, there will be no public interest in its circulation.
- The right to be forgotten would impact the entire community, as it would be deprived of knowing the facts in all their amplitude.
- Admitting the right to be forgotten would mean privileging the right to image and private life, to the detriment of freedom of expression and the right to information regarding relevant facts of social history.

121. The Rapporteur Justice also understood that the matter object of the lawsuit has constitutional density and goes beyond the involved parties' interests. For that reason, he recognized its general repercussion, being registered as Topic of General Repercussion n. 786 ('Tema de Repercussão Geral'), and the following thesis became effective: 'The idea of a right to be forgotten is incompatible with the Constitution, understood as the power to prevent, due to the passage of time, the disclosure of truthful and lawfully obtained facts or data published in analogical or digital media. Possible excesses or abuses in the exercise of freedom of expression and information must be analyzed on a case-by-case basis, based on constitutional parameters – especially those related to the protection of honor, image, privacy, and personality rights in general – and the express and specific legal provisions in the criminal and civil spheres.'

Part II. Regulation of the Press

Chapter 1. The Journalists' Profession

122. In Brazil, the journalist profession can be exercised regardless of obtaining a university journalist's degree in a university course. This understanding accrues from a Supreme Court decision dated June 2009. When judging the lawsuit RE 511.961, the STF considered that the rule that imposed the mandatory graduation course in journalism for the profession's exercise (Decree-Law 972/1969) was not compatible with the 1988 Federal Constitution.

123. The STF's trial had, on one side, the Union of Radio and Television Companies of the State of São Paulo and the Federal Public Ministry, and, on the opposite side, the National Federation of Journalists and the Federal Union, together with other representative institutions. In essence, contrary to the requirement for a diploma, the first group claimed that the need for graduation in journalism was not met by the Federal Constitution of 1988 while it would violate its Article 5, IX, and XIII. Such provisions are situated in the chapter dedicated to fundamental rights, and prescribe, respectively, the right to the free expression of intellectual, artistic, scientific, and communication activities, regardless of censorship or licence, and the free exercise of any profession (*see* Part I herein above). The claimants also argued that Article 220 of the Federal Constitution prohibits any legal means that may cause embarrassment to the exercise of the rights of freedom of expression of thought, creation, expression, and information, and that such requirement is not compatible with Article 13 of the American Convention on Human Rights (San Jose Pact), ratified by Brazil in 1992. Going further, Union of Radio and Television Companies of the State of São Paulo and the Federal Public Ministry also stated that the lack of technical qualifications to practise the journalism profession, unlike medical doctors, engineers, and aircraft pilots, could not cause society to be exposed to any risk that could justify this limitation on freedom of expression through statutory regulation.

124. Due to the re-framing resulting from this trial, blogger journalists, citizen journalists, and professional journalists are granted the same treatment as professionals with a degree in journalism. However, a journalist shall be duly registered with the Labour Secretariat in order to exercise their profession. This requirement comes from the same Decree-Law 972/1969 that was attacked by the decision that considered graduation in journalism unnecessary. As observed, the decree remains in force, although the provision related to graduation in journalism is no longer applicable.

125. In its decision, STF considered that journalism is not a public service per se, and the lack of technical qualification for the exercise of a journalist's profession would not expose society to any risk since graduation in this field would not be the ideal way to prevent the profession's exercise to expose third parties to risks. It is important to remark that a Proposal for Amendment of the Constitution (PEC 33/2009) is currently under the scrutiny of the legislative houses. Such Proposal for Amendment 33 aims to bring back the requirement for graduation in journalism to practise the profession.

Chapter 2. Journalists' Rights

126. Due to its intimate link to rights of freedom of thought, information, and communication in general, professional journalists are granted a few guarantees meant to support the exercise of their profession and fulfilment of such rights. Before approaching them, there are two overarching observations to be noted.

127. The first one refers to the relevance of labour legislation. Journalists, as professionals hired by third parties, hold labour rights like all other workers. The vast majority of these rights are granted by the 'Brazilian Labour Framework', formalized under Decree 5.452/1943 (and known in Portuguese as 'Consolidação das Leis do Trabalho'). Labour Courts (both about general work relations and the journalist professions specifically) also apply, as is the case, for instance, of Precedent 55 of the Superior Labour Court (Tribunal Superior do Trabalho – TST), which states that 'the employer is obliged to mention in the employment agreement the press agency in which the journalist is going to work'.[118]

128. Second, as creators of content, journalists hold copyright protection over their work. As it happens in most labour relations that encompass content creation, copyright over works produced under the term of the labour contract is usually assigned to the employer. However, there is an unavailable portion as determined by Brazilian law, the so-called moral rights, which cannot be transferred or abdicated. Among moral rights, there are, for instance, the right to be credited as the author and the right to oppose oneself to modifications of the original work (as per Article 24 of Law 9.619/1998). For this reason, any provision in which the journalist himself gives up or transfers, for example, the moral right to have his name linked to the work is null and void, and whoever fails to give credit to the author of the work is subject to the relevant legal statutes.[119]

§1. Role of Journalists as Watch-Dogs of Society

129. No less important than the non-specific rights of journalists are intrinsic rights to participate in journalistic activities, which have a vital social function. Freedom of expression, the right to criticism and sources protection are some of the guarantees necessary to assure journalists with minimum conditions to act as watchdogs of society in safety. Unfortunately, this goal is often not accomplished in Brazil, where the press field is still marked by moral attacks and violence against journalists.

---

118. For more information about the Brazilian labour regulation, please refer to Ronald Amorim e Souza, *Labour Law and Industrial Relations in Brazil* (International Encyclopaedia of Laws, Wolters Kluwer).
119. For more information about the Brazilian labour regulation, please refer: Maristela Basso, *Intellectual Property in Brazil* (International Encyclopaedia of Laws, Wolters Kluwer).

130. In March 2020, after a series of attacks propelled by President Jair Bolsonaro against journalists from various media outlets, and in response to a recommendation issued by the Inter-American Commission on Human Rights (IACHR) in 2014, the Brazilian Ministry of Family and Human Rights edited a thirty-page booklet on the protection of journalists' rights entitled 'Cartilha Aristeu Guida da Silva: Protection of the Human Rights of Journalists and Other Communicators'.[120] Aristeu Guida da Silva was a journalist murdered in 1995 after reporting on specific groups of professional killers. This crime inspired the filing of a complaint against the Brazilian state at the IACHR, for failing to comply with international parameters for freedom of expression and journalistic protection. The complaint of human rights violations reached the IACHR through the Inter-American Press Society in 1999, which alleged that the crimes resulted from the journalist's professional practice, thus violating Articles 1.1,[121] 4, and 13 of the American Convention on Human Rights. For this reason, Mr Silva's name became the reference for this initiative that aimed at increasing journalists protection.

131. There are numerous notorious cases of violence against journalists throughout Brazil's history. Specially recently, we can highlight countless other cases of human rights violations closely linked to the exercise of the profession of journalist. According to the National Federation of Journalists' annual report,[122] in 2019, there was a 54% increase in the number of attacks on journalists and media outlets in Brazil over the previous year, totalling 208 attacks. According to this report, 144 of these events had a connection with politicians. According to a screening carried out by the digital magazine *Midia Ninja*, 121 offences were committed against the press and their vehicles, enacted by the President himself, Mr Jair Bolsonaro.[123] Among the attacks carried out in 2019, there were 2 cases of murder, 15 incidents of physical aggression, 20 occurrences of verbal aggression, 28 incidents of threats, 5 events of restriction on freedom of expression by judicial means, 10 cases of censorship, and 114 cases of discredit to the press, 10 cases of suspension of the right

120. Ministry of Woman, Family and Human Rights, *Cartilha Aristeu Guida da Silva: Proteção dos direitos humanos de jornalistas e de outros comunicadores e comunicadoras* (2020), available at https://www.gov.br/mdh/pt-br/assuntos/noticias/2020-2/marco/mmfdh-apresenta-cartilha-governamental-sobre-a-protecao-de-jornalistas-e-outros-comunicadores-e-comunicadoras/cartilha-aristeu-guida-da-silva-mmfdh.pdf (accessed 10 Jan. 2021).
121. The States Parties to this Convention undertake to respect the rights and freedoms recognized herein and to ensure to all persons subject to their jurisdiction the free and full exercise of those rights and freedoms, without any discrimination for reasons of race, colour, sex, language, religion, political or other opinion, national or social origin, economic status, birth, or any other social condition.
122. Annual reports of violence against journalists in Brazil organized by Federação Nacional dos Jornalistas (Brazilian National Journalists Association) are available at https://fenaj.org.br/relatorios-de-violencia-contra-jornalistas-e-liberdade-de-imprensa-no-brasil/ (accessed 12 Jan. 2021).
123. Renata Mielli, *Cartilha nenhuma vai mudar a realidade – Bolsonaro é o maior inimigo da imprensa e da liberdade de expressão*, Midia Ninja (4 Mar. 2020), https://midianinja.org/renatamielli/cartilha-nenhuma-vai-mudar-a-realidade-bolsonaro-e-o-maior-inimigo-da-imprensa-e-da-liberdade-de-expressao/ (accessed 12 Jan. 2021).

to practise the profession, 2 cases of racism, and 2 cases against the union organization. Television, newspapers, and digital media journalists are the biggest targets, accounting for 28.23%, 26.61%, and 18.55% of attacks, respectively.[124]

132. Against this context, the booklet Cartilha Aristeu Guida da Silva stresses the role of government in not only protecting but also setting the example for respect and diligence regarding how press activities are addressed. This includes a provision according to which:

> State agents should not adopt public speeches that expose journalists and other communicators to risk of violence or increase their vulnerability. It is essential that state authorities constantly, explicitly and publicly recognize the legitimacy and value of journalism and communication, even in situations where the information disclosed may be a criticism or inconvenient to the interests of the government.

133. As important as this initiative is, violence against journalists is a long-established defect of Brazilian democracy that has been exhaustively documented through the years. Recently, the Brazilian Chapter of the NGO Reporters Without Borders published the report 'Protection Paradigm: Making Protection Mechanisms Work for Latin American Journalists', where it accounts for violence against journalists in Brazil, Mexico, Colombia and Honduras. Among their recommendations, Reporters Without Borders include, among others: that the National Parliament enacts a legal framework aimed at building a protection programme for journalists at national level; national coordination that includes states and regions where media workers are mostly endangered; and the adoption of journalists protection protocols that account for diversity of professionals and therefore increases protection for more vulnerable groups (according to gender, race, ethnic origin and sexual diversity).[125]

§2. Right to Criticism and Prohibition of Censorship

134. The free press is an essential instrument for the exercise of democracy. As highlighted throughout this monograph, the Brazilian Federal Constitution establishes several provisions aimed at guaranteeing rights to express oneself, to inform and to access information.

135. Notably, all sorts of previous censorship are forbidden in the Brazilian legal order. As already described in §1 of this Part I, this prohibition was enacted in the

124. National Federation of the Journalists (Federação Nacional dos Jornalistas – FENAJ). 2019 report of violence against journalists and freedom of the press in Brazil (January 2020). Available at: https://agenciabrasil.ebc.com.br/geral/noticia/2020-01/brasil-registra-mais-de-200-ataques-contra-jornalistas-em-2019 (accessed 12 Jan. 2021).

125. Reporters Without Borders, *Protection Paradigm: Making Protection Mechanisms Work for Latin American Journalists*. Available at: https://rsf.org/sites/default/files/protection_paradigm.pdf (accessed 21 Apr. 2022).

context of democratization of the legal order after decades of a military dictatorship, which institutionalized censorship of all sorts of expression as a public administration practice. Despite the scope of freedom of expression being object of a mixed jurisprudence, the precedents enacted by the Brazilian Supreme Court (STF) do follow the constitutional rule. As mentioned in §3 of this Part I, STF has reiterated the prohibition of censorship in some of its most iconic decisions on the scope of freedom of expression. This includes the Press Law Constitutionality trial (ADPF 130), when the Court sealed the unconstitutionality of state interference in freedom of expression. With this stance, the STF recognized the freedom of the press as a key element of democracy. Going further, the rapporteur at the STF in his vote justified the importance of freedom of the press as 'an immaterial heritage that corresponds to the most eloquent attestation of the political and cultural evolution of an entire people', and stated that the relationship between the press and the public interest cannot be 'a priori susceptible to censorship, even by legislators or judges'.[126]

136. Regarding journalistic guarantees specifically, STF has confirmed the relevance of non-intervention on expression in a 2015 trial, this time focused on the role of courts themselves. In lawsuit Rcl 21.504 AgR/SP,[127] it decided that even in the context of preventive injunctions, judges and courts shall not inhibit the constitutional freedom of expression and communication, which would result in public censorship. This trial relates to concerns regarding 'judicial censorship' – the practice of successively filing civil and criminal lawsuits against journalists for content published under their press activities (*see* Part I, §2). These concerns are also addressed by the CNJ – the organ responsible for controlling and supervising administrative and financial duties of judiciary organs, as well as judge's compliance with their functional duties. In 2018, CNJ released a report with data related to press freedom in Brazil from 1997 until the middle of the second half of 2017.[128] According to this report, 704 lawsuits (59.5%) were motivated by allegations of defamation, 19.5% concerned electoral legislation violations, 10.9% were around privacy violation, and 10.2% concerned infringement of intellectual property rights. Rio de Janeiro, concentrating 18.4% of the share, leads the ranking, followed by São Paulo with 14.3%. The most sued press company is Globo (18.1% of the lawsuits).

137. Related to the prohibition of censorship, and also essential for the free and safe exercise of the journalistic profession, is the 'right to criticism'. The right to criticism rests within the content of the right to freedom of expression itself, but its foundations also rest in political pluralism – one of the basis for the Brazilian democracy, as stated by Article 1, V of the Constitution. In this sense, the right to criticism was expressly named in a 2011 STF precedent as one of the dimensions of

---

126. STF, ADPF 130, tried on 30 Apr. 2009. Available at: http://redir.stf.jus.br/paginadorpub/paginador.jsp?docTP=AC&docID=265920 (accessed: 26 Oct. 2020).
127. STF, Rcl 21.504 AgR/SP, tried on 17 Nov. 2015. Available at: https://redir.stf.jus.br/paginadorpub/paginador.jsp?docTP=TP&docID=9975288 (accessed 20 Feb. 2022).
128. 2018 Report on Freedom of the Press by Conselho Nacional de Justiça (National Council of Justice), https://www.cnj.jus.br/wp-content/uploads/2011/02/fe4133ad3d044846ba3b8ff5594bb7a7.pdf (accessed 12 Jan. 2020).

press freedom. According to the final decision enacted in lawsuit AI 690841 AgR/SP, the dimensions of press freedom, as regarded by the Brazilian Constitution, include: (a) the right to inform, (b) the right to seek information, (c) the right to express an opinion, and (d) the right to criticize. The decision further established that the Constitution supports the right to carry out journalistic criticism directed at public people, no matter how hard and vehement it may be. This understanding was ratified in other STF decisions, including the 2018 tried ADIN 4451. The lawsuit was centred on the constitutionality of Article 45, II and III, and its paragraphs 4 and 5 of Law 9.504/1997 (which regulated electoral timeframes). The provisions under scrutiny imposed restrictions on political propaganda and on content aimed at criticizing election candidates. These provisions were declared unconstitutional by STF, which understood that they would represent previous state interference in the right to criticism during the electoral process. The wording of the decision, once again, grounds the right to criticism in freedom of expression and political pluralism, also expressly stating that 'any legal provisions that attempt to annihilate or control critical thinking are unconstitutional'.[129]

§3. Protection of Journalistic Sources

138. The secrecy of sources has constitutional protection in Brazil under Article 5, XIV of the Federal Constitution, according to which 'everyone is guaranteed access to information and the source's confidentiality is safeguarded, when necessary for professional practice'.

139. This provision is associated with freedom of information, as the right to seek information and to be informed, without any restrictions, except among other fundamental and limiting rights set also by the Federal Constitution. Source protection is a relevant guarantee for reporting and press activities, according to which journalists cannot be obliged to reveal their sources. This does not apply to personal opinions – which is a right also constitutionally guaranteed, but not the purpose of this specific provision. In fact, the same article of the Constitution contains a provision prohibiting anonymity (Article 5, IV), which must not be mistaken for source secrecy. Source protection is essentially linked to the journalist profession, but can also apply to other professions that rest on secrecy. As any other right provided by the Brazilian legal order, source secrecy is not an unlimited right, and in theory, can be restricted when in collision with other fundamental rights. However, the STF jurisprudence is prone to maintaining source secrecy, as breaking it could enhance state censorship and repression of political opponents.[130]

129. STF, ADI 4451, tried on 26 Jun. 2018. Available at: https://redir.stf.jus.br/paginadorpub/paginador.jsp?docTP=TP&docID=749287337. Accessed on: 21 Apr. 2022.
130. In this sense, STF, Rcl 21,504/SP, tried on 13 Oct. 2015. Available at: https://portal.stf.jus.br/processos/detalhe.asp?incidente=4814991. Accessed on 21 Apr. 2022.

Chapter 3. Journalists' Liability

140. The abusive exercise of journalism can cause severe individual and collective damages. However, any state measure that seeks prior control to prevent such injuries could lead to censorship. For this reason, the Brazilian Legal System supports the 'a posteriori' civil and criminal liability model, as seen in Chapter 1 of this Part I.

§1. General Information on the Liability System

141. Civil liability in Brazil arises from the damage someone causes to another person. It is the due for those who committed a determined offence that injured a third party's rights, and when verified by a judge, it binds the agent who committed the damage to return the victim of its acts to its situation prior to the damage (whether this reparation is pecuniary or moral in nature).

142. Three elements are required for civil liability: the damage, the illegal act, and a causal link between the conduct and the damage. In the case of damage caused by a press vehicle, both the company (i.e., the press vehicle) and the journalist who signed the piece that caused the damage can be considered liable. While the latter will only respond for reparation if its 'fault' is proven, the press vehicle can be held liable regardless of fault.

§2. The Liability System

143. There is no legal system applicable specifically to journalists and publishers, meaning that, overall, liability will be assessed according to the rules that apply to everyone. Through general legislation and precedent court decisions, however, it is possible to analyse some of the elements that determine who will respond in case of liability, and when it will happen.

144. The Brazilian legal system, through Article 932, III of the Civil Code establishes the possibility of attributing liability to the employer, entrepreneur, and hiring company for unlawful conduct carried out by persons in their service. In our analysis, the unlawful conduct would refer to abuses of the right to freedom of expression and free press.

145. It should be noted that Precedent 221 of the STJ asserts that 'The author of the writing, as well as the owner of the dissemination vehicle, are civilly responsible for the compensation of the damage.' This precedent serves as a guide for several court decisions that directly impose accountability on the journalist. It is essential to point out that the courts understand that it is sometimes impracticable to identify the journalist's conduct when editors and other internal business microstructures can influence the message's content, or how it is framed, to adapt it to different editorial lines or even political interests. Because of this, in countless cases when dealing with television media, given the creative and editorial structure of the medium, it is understood that the company is held responsible,[131,132] without prejudice, of course, of the company having the right to sue the person responsible for the content, to seek for indemnification to cover the expenditures on the indemnifications previously paid to a third party.

146. High courts jurisprudence has also already settled the fact that media companies might be liable for damages regardless of guilt or fault, when their transmitted content causes damage to others. This understanding is grounded on the assumption that the television activity, given its scope and its production dynamics, entails risks that are essential to these dynamics, and such risks are to be borne by the company.[133] The assessment of liability for damages is done by courts, through the applicable judicial procedures. We can find constitutional exceptions to the right to freedom of expression in the constitutional text, which already hints at the sort of conduct that could inspire reparation for speech abuses. The Constitution's text establishes that freedom of thought, creation, expression and information will not be subject to any restrictions, 'subject to the provisions' in Article 5, IV, V, X, XIII and XIV, which provides, respectively: (a) prohibition of anonymity; (b) right of a proportional response to the offence; (c) inviolability of intimacy, private life, honour, and image, ensuring the right to compensation for material or moral damage resulting from any violation; (d) free exercise of professional activities; and (e) confidentiality of the source.

§3. Defamation and Libel

147. Freedom of the press, an activity of paramount importance for democracies, is faced with ethical limits and the obligation not to transmit content that taints others' honour and image. In Brazil, the cases of excesses committed by the press are not uncommon.

148. A few cases in recent history became notorious for illustrating the darn consequences of irresponsible reporting from the press. One of them happened in 1994, when a group of mothers accused the owners of a school and the school transport driver of paedophilia. Without any evidence, and before the competent courts could judge the accused, the press exhaustively reported on the case with focus on the complaints and exposing the people denounced. The news was broadcast in prime time by dissemination vehicles that enjoyed great viewing figures, which culminated in high levels of popular pressure, causing the accused people to be arrested

131. Luis Gustavo Grandinetti Castanho de Carvalho, *Responsabilidade Civil dos Meios de Comunicação,* Revista da EMERJ, 5, 17 (2002).
132. STJ, REsp 207.637/PR, tried on 20 Apr. 2006. Available at: https://processo.stj.jus.br/processo/revista/documento/mediado/?componente=MON&sequencial=2367837&tipo_documento=documento&num_registro=199900220781&data=20060530&formato=PDF. Accessed: 20 May 2022.
133. *See*, for instance, STJ, REsp 331182/SE, tried on 3 Sep. 2002. Available at: https://stj.jusbrasil.com.br/jurisprudencia/7492048/recurso-especial-resp-331182-se-2001-0092115-6/inteiro-teor-13121023. Accessed: 21 Apr. 2022.

without any evidence against them. Shortly after, the police investigation was discontinued, as the chief of police realized that there was no evidence against the accused. Press vehicles and Government of the State of São Paulo were sentenced to indemnify those who were unjustly and undeservedly accused, and this case became a symbol of the importance of responsible reporting.[134]

149. In Brazil, companies are civilly liable, which makes them liable for damages; however, there is a systemic limitation that prevents companies from being criminally liable.[135]

150. This is also the case for libel and defamation, meaning that those who commit crimes against an individual's honour should respond individually, under criminal law. Defamation is a criminal conduct as defined in Article 138 of the Brazilian Criminal Code, as falsely attributing to someone a fact or action defined as a crime. The rule also stipulates that those who know that the accusation is false, and then proceed to propagate or disclose it, are subject to the same penalty. Defamation against dead people is also punishable.

151. The author can be acquitted if he proves that what he divulged is true unless the imputing crime is subject to private criminal procedure and the victim has not yet been convicted; if the crime is against the President of the Republic or the head of foreign government; or if the victim is found not guilty by an unappealable court decision, even if it is a public criminal action. The penalty is a fine and imprisonment that can vary between six months and two years.

152. In libel, unlike defamation, a criminal act is not imputed to a third party, but an offence to someone's reputation is propagated. The only possible exception of truth is if the victim is a civil servant, and the offence is related to his functions' exercise. The penalty is a fine imprisonment that can range from six months to two years. This is different from defamation, where fines and imprisonment penalties are cumulative.

153. In both crimes, penalties are aggravated when it relates to offences against the President of the republic or head of foreign government, people over the age of 60, people with disabilities, or if the crime is committed in exchange for payment or reward. However, the offender can retract prior to the court conviction. In this case, he or she will be exempt from the penalty – but the retraction should be done by using the same means of communication that was used to commit the original crime.

---

134. STJ, REsp 1215294/SP, tried on 17 Dec. 2013. Available at: https://scon.stj.jus.br/SCON/jurisprudencia/doc.jsp?livre="ESCOLA+BASE"&b=ACOR&p=false&l=10&i=1&operador=e&tipo_visualizacao=RESUMO. Accessed: 26 Oct. 2020.

135. Except for specific exceptions that hold companies liable for crimes against the environment and for financial crimes (Brazilian Federal Constitution, at Arts 73 and 225).

154. These criminal law provisions are intended to protect the individual's public image (objective honour) and do not prevent the victim from taking civil action to repair the injury.

§4. Image and Privacy

155. In Brazil, image protection is based on the Federal Constitution. The constitutional text describes a whole protective arrangement, including the attribution of remedies for possible violations.

156. Understood as a fundamental right, the right to image is non-transferable, inalienable, non-renounceable, imprescriptible. Therefore, under Brazilian law, any agreement that deals, for example, with the definitive transfer of image rights is ineffective. Likewise, any assignment, assignment promise, permanent alienation, or waiver of such rights will be null and void. This requires caution with contractual clauses that seek to obtain an unrestricted authorization for the use of images without specific limitations. These are the applicable constitutional provisions:

> Art. 5, X: the privacy, private life, honour and image of persons are inviolable, and the right to compensation for property or moral damages resulting from their violation is ensured. (…)
> Art. 5, XXVIII: under the terms of the law, the following are ensured:
>
> a) protection of individual participation in collective works and of reproduction of the human image and voice, sports activities included.

157. Further regulations were set by the Brazilian Civil Code and, concerning artistic participation, by the Brazilian Copyright and Neighbouring Rights Law (Law 9.619/1998, the 'Copyright Law'). Concerning sports activities, the applicable framework was set by Law 9.615/1998 (the so-called Pelé Law).

158. In its Article 21, the Civil Code states that:

> Unless authorized, or if necessary for the administration of justice or the maintenance of public order, the dissemination of writings, the transmission of the word, or the publication, display or use of the image of a person may be prohibited, at their request and without prejudice to the indemnity that may apply, if they injure the honour, good reputation or respectability, or if they are intended for commercial purposes.

159. Particular emphasis shall be given to the necessity to obtain authorization, the possibility of prohibition, and the duty to indemnify unauthorized commercial use of images. In this sense, there are abundant precedents in jurisprudence that enabled the approval of STJ Precedent 403, which steers judicial decisions on the subject. Precedent 403 states that 'Reparation for the unauthorized publication of a person's image for economic or business purposes is due regardless of proof of the damage.' Therefore, an assumption of damage surges from the economical use of a third party's image without prior authorization. However, such protections are not absolute, and can still bear exceptions and balance against other fundamental rights. This is the case, for instance, of non-authorized biographies. As already shown in this monograph, in 2015, Brazil's Constitutional Court ruled against the requirement of authorization from subjects of literary or audiovisual biographies. The decision sealed an interpretation of Article 21 of the Civil, according to which such a requirement would be over restrictive of freedom of expression, thus equating to a form of private censorship (for further details, *see* Part I, §3, II).

160. Artistic participations, even though not considered copyrighted work, are protected in the form of neighbouring rights, as provided for in the Copyright Law and in Law 6,533/1978, the so-called Artist's Law:

> (Copyright Law) Art. 89: The provisions on authors' rights shall apply, mutatis mutandis, to the rights of performers, producers of phonograms and broadcasting organizations.
> Sole paragraph. The protection under this Law of the rights referred to in this Article shall leave intact and in no way affect the guarantees afforded to the authors of literary, artistic or scientific works.

161. The Copyright Law also provides for a variety of guarantees for interpreters (also under the guise of neighbouring rights), as seen in its Articles 90, 91, and 92. These provisions encompass the rights to authorize or prohibit the recording, broadcasting, any use, and public communication of their interpretations, in addition to the right to the integrity of artistic interpretations. In addition, Law 6.533/1978 establishes in its Article 13 that 'the assignment or promise of assignment of copyrights and neighbouring rights arising from the provision of professional services will not be allowed'. The same Article 13, in its sole paragraph, determines that the copyright and neighbouring right is due by reason of the exhibition of the work.

162. Finally, the Pelé Law, as per its Articles 87 and 87-A, concerning athletes' image rights, assures them the right to commercially use their name, symbols, and surnames separately from the special labour contract signed with the sports entity. The assignment of image exploitation rights granted by athletes must have a time limitation, considering that, as seen previously, the Brazilian legal system prohibits the assignment, transfer, and definitive sale of these rights. The full text of these provisions reads as follows:

> Art. 87. The denomination and symbols of a sports administration entity or sport practice, as well as the sporting name or surname of the professional athlete, are their exclusive property, with legal protection, valid for the entire national territory, for an indefinite period, without the need for registration or registration with the competent body.

Sole paragraph. The legal guarantee granted to the entities and athletes referred to in this Article allows them to commercially use their name, symbols, names and surnames.
Art. 87-A. The right to use the athlete's image can be assigned or exploited by him through a private arrangement and the adjustment of rights, duties, and conditions separated from the sports contract.

I. Image and Privacy Rights Versus Public Interest

163. Image and privacy rights are often in collision with the right to freedom of expression, specially with regard to journalistic activities. For a full comprehension of how courts position themselves in such conflicts, and thus shape the right to freedom of expression, we must consider not only the applicable constitutional and legal provisions but also a series of circumstances and practices that contribute to how much image and privacy rights can be compromised in favour of the public interest. These practices and circumstances include the system-based reparations *a posteriori*, the resulting varied jurisprudence (from which it is challenging to extract one single tendency, either pro privacy, or pro public interest) and tendencies of 'judicial censorship' – all aspects already covered throughout this chapter.

164. Regarding privacy and image rights of convicted criminals, it is possible to argue a jurisprudential tendency to favour the public interest, as illustrated by the cases selected below.

165. In the Court Appeal 1108361-27.2019.8.26.0100 judged by the São Paulo Court of Justice on 6 July 2021, Mr Leandro Pires da Costa, sentenced to prison for murder years before, sought damages against Medialand (an audiovisual production company) and Netflix. He claimed the accused parties produced and exhibited a documentary series, whose purpose is to bring criticism and analysis of notorious crimes, containing his image, depicted as a criminal, without prior authorization. The plaintiff sought reparation, as well as a ban on the exhibition of the series. In the ruling, the Rapporteur Justice denied their requests, arguing that:

- After committing the crime, of national repercussion, the author came out of anonymity and became a public person. The trial was followed by the press and everything about him was published, including his pictures. The crime's investigation and trial, in turn, took place without the imposition of secrecy;
- STJ precedent 403[136] does not apply to the disclosure of notorious facts and people, with such a purpose, even if it is recognized that there is an economic/profitable activity behind this type of cinematographic production.

136. 'The indemnity for the unauthorized publication of a person's image for economic or business purposes is independent of proof of the damage.'

166. Previously, the same Netflix documentary series was the subject of other lawsuits, filed by different convicted criminals, Mr Mizael Bispo dos Santos[137] and Mr Sandro Dota.[138] The first argued that the series used images of him, without authorization, and that the interviewees made derogatory judgments about himself. The Rapporteur Justice ruled these requests unfounded. Mr Sandro Dota argued that the journalistic nature of the series was only to 'cover up' its commercial nature. For this matter, the Rapporteur Justice sustained that there was no 'exaggeration or offense to the plaintiff's honour, since the series portrayed the facts that were in the investigative process'.

167. In April 2020, the STJ judged REsp 1.736.803,[139] by means of which Paula Nogueira Peixoto, convicted for the murder of a famous Brazilian actress in 1992, sought, through the application of a thesis that defended the existence of the right to be forgotten in Brazil, to prohibit news reports related to the crime committed, under the pretext of news published twenty years after the crime was committed. The ruling stated that 'in view of the evident social interest in cultivating the historical and collective memory of a notorious crime, it is inappropriate to accept the thesis of the right to be forgotten in order to prohibit any future publication of journalistic articles related to the criminal fact, under penalty of constituting prior censorship, prohibited by the Brazilian legal system'.

168. Regarding the right to privacy, a relevant precedent concerns the content of a telephone wiretap on a conversation between the then Minister of Communications and the President of the National Bank for Economic and Social Development (BNDES), disclosed by a weekly magazine. The Minister expressed his preference for one of those interested in the ongoing privatization process of telephone companies. In a judgment dated May 2020 (RE 685.493), the STF ruled by a majority that 'In view of the conflict between the freedom of expression of a political agent, in defence of public affairs, and the honour of a third party, the collective interest must prevail.'[140]

---

137. Court Appeal TJSP 1105964- 92.2019.8.26.0100 judged on 26 Nov. 2020.
138. Court Appeal TJSP 1110417-33.2019.8.26.0100 judged on 18 Jun. 2021.
139. STJ, REsp 1.736.803, tried on 28 Apr. 2020, available at https://processo.stj.jus.br/processo/revista/documento/mediado/?componente=ATC&sequencial=102328872&num_registro=201700267279&data=20200504&tipo=5&formato=PDF (accessed 20 Feb. 2022).
140. STF, RE 685.493, tried on 22 May 2020, available at http://redir.stf.jus.br/paginadorpub/paginador.jsp?docTP=TP&docID=753486649 (accessed 12 Jan. 2021).

Chapter 4. Right to Reply

169. The right to reply is a popular statute in media law, consisting of a right to publish an alternative version of information previously disclosed by media vehicles. The right to reply was enshrined in Article 5, V of the Brazilian Federal Constitution, which secures 'the right to reply, proportional to the harm, in addition to indemnity for material or moral'.

170. In Brazilian law, the right to reply is traditionally understood as a subjective right, which assists every human person or institution to deny, defend or rectify harmful information about themselves using the same media vehicle as the media vehicle where the harmful piece was published in the first place. In these terms, the right to reply plays an important role in protecting and compensating those who consider themselves harmed by a particular news outlet, and its constitutional justifications include the 'protection against offensive and harmful imputations to human dignity and honour, which, when they occur through the media, gain amplified notoriety'. The potentially broad reach of a communication vehicle is what would justify the need for a guarantee of defence 'against the media', according to which offended individuals can offer their perspective with an equivalent degree of disclosure.[141]

171. Notwithstanding its importance as subjective right of defence and compensation, the right to reply is a multidimensional guarantee – as it is with many statutes that regulate the exercise of free speech. As it allows for the diffusion of an alternative version of the facts presented by a media vehicle, it also plays an important role as a collective right of access to plural information, in the sense that it guarantees plurality of perspectives concerning the same facts or issues in the public debate.

172. In that sense, L.G. Grandinetti Castanho de Carvalho highlights the importance of abandoning restrictive approaches to the right of reply – restricted to its role to repair damage, or as a statute related to self-defence – and embracing its collective perspective. According to the latter, not only the personally offended subject but also society holds a right of reply, as per its right of access to true, impartial, and authentic information.[142] Against this background, the right of reply is considered a part of the right to information and thus can also be considered a collective right.

173. This understanding has already been ratified by the jurisprudence of the Brazilian Constitutional Court, in the judgment of Precautionary Action 2695.[143] In a monocratic decision by Justice Celso de Mello, the STF ruled that the right to reply has a 'dual constitutional vocation', aiming at the preservation of personality

141. All quotes in this paragraph are extracted from Vital Moreira, *O direito de resposta na comunicação social* 101–102 (Coimbra: Coimbra Editora 1994)
142. L.G. Grandinetti Castanho de Carvalho, *Liberdade de Informação e o Direito Difuso à Informação Verdadeira.* 121–122 (Renovar: Rio de Janeiro 2003).
143. Tried on 25 Nov. 2010 and published on 1 Dec. 2010 edition of *Diário de Justiça Eletrônico.*

rights and of the exercise of the right to accurate and precise information. In recognizing this second function, Justice Celso de Mello stated that:

> It is necessary to reiterate that any person (as much as the community itself) has the right to obtain and have access to truthful, honest and reliable information, in such a way that the violation of this right, if and when consummated, can fully justify the exercise of the right of reply. Thus, far from imposing an improper restriction on freedom of expression, the right of reply, as per its multifunctionality, qualifies as an instrument to overcome the state of dialectical tension between rights and freedoms in situations of conflict.

174. This rendering exemplifies the interpretation of the constitutional text depicted in Part I of this monograph, according to which the 1988 Charter recognizes the collective dimensions of freedom of expression – and hence, the importance of a free and plural public sphere. In this sense, the rightful interpretation of the right of reply in the Brazilian legal order is inextricable from the free speech order implemented by the country's democratic Constitution.

175. At first, the right to reply provision was regulated by the now revoked Law 5.250/1967 ('Press Law'), which provided, in addition to the guarantee itself, a definition, form and limits for its exercise. Following the STF decision in ADPF 130,[144] these provisions were invalidated, along with the rest of the law. It is worth mentioning the unsuccessful understanding of Justice Gilmar Ferreira Mendes in this trial, according to which the plea should be partially upheld, and Law 5.250/1967 should not have been completely revoked. At the centre of the Justice's argument was the necessity to maintain the rules that governed the right to reply and assure its certain and uniform provision by the legal system. As per his wording, 'the right of reply is guaranteed at the constitutional level, but in the infra-constitutional provides organizational and procedural rules that enable its effective exercise'.[145]

176. After the ADPF 130 trial invalidated the right to reply to legal provisions, its exercise remained unregulated, resting solely on the constitutional provision. In practical terms, this meant that its scope, form and limits were uncertain, and thus varied according to negotiations between media vehicles and offended parties, or according to the judicial determinations on single cases brought to the judiciary.

177. Six years after the judicial decision that revoked the Press Law, the National Parliament approved Law 13.188/2015, which regulates the right to reply regarding content that is matters disclosed, published or transmitted by the media. The law provides, once again, for detailed guarantees and conditions implied in the exercise of this constitutional right. In the following paragraphs, we highlight the main aspects regarding scope, form of exercise and limitation of the right to reply currently in place.

---

144. *See* Part I of this monograph.
145. STF, ADPF 130, tried on 30 Apr. 2009. Available at: http://redir.stf.jus.br/paginadorpub/paginador.jsp?docTP=AC&docID=265928. Accessed on: 26 Oct. 2020.

178. According to Article 2, the right of reply consists of an answer to, or rectification of, information published or transmitted on the media, free of charge and in means proportional to the original information's scope and reach. For these purposes, 'media' is understood as any article news piece, regardless of the means or platform of distribution, publication or transmission that it uses. This right is applicable when harm is inflicted concerning a natural or legal person's honour, intimacy, reputation, concept, name, brand or image, regardless of such harm being intentional or not. The same section provides that any spontaneous retraction or rectification, even if given the same prominence, publicity, periodicity and size of the appeal, does not prevent the victim from exercising the right of reply, nor does it impair legal action for reparation of moral damage. Article 2, §2 excludes from this rule 'comments from Internet users on websites', which means that there is legally no guarantee of a right to reply to harms caused by the types of comments.

179. The right of reply must be exercised within sixty days from the date of the original publication, by the natural or legal person affected by the original content, or by their legal representative, spouse, descendant, ascendant or sibling, in case the victim is absent from the country or has passed away before the due date of the right to reply. In order to exercise it, the holder of the right to reply must send a written extrajudicial notification to the media platform that published the harmful information, or to the person identified as its author, requesting the publication of their reply.

180. Upon receiving such a request and deciding to publish the reply, the author or publication must assure that the content of the rectification or alternative version is presented in the same feature, publicity and periodicity of the original publication. In addition to these, if the harmful content was published on print media or the Internet, the reply must also be presented in the same physical dimension as the original publication; in case it was transmitted in radio or television, the reply must also have the same duration and geographical reach.

181. If a media vehicle publishes a reply that is not in accordance with these requirements, it will be considered non-existent for legal purposes. If a media platform receives a notification requesting the exercise of a right to reply and does not promote its publication within seven days, the holder of the right to reply will be entitled to file a lawsuit (Article 5), which shall follow a special procedure.

182. This special procedure is clearly embedded with the legislator's intent to guarantee a speedy publication of corrections or alternative perspectives to information displayed by the media – as it is well illustrated by its shorter time frames and the fact that the lawsuit keeps being processed during forensic vacation (Article 9, §1). Law 13.188/2015 provides for this detailed special procedure, as described herein below.

183. A right to a reply-based lawsuit must be processed within the maximum deadline of thirty days (Article 9). As of its filing, the plea must be briefed with the original content that is being contested, proof of the reply notification that went unanswered, as well as with the text of the response or rectification that the right to reply holder desires to be published. Article 8 also provides that the response intended must be clearly related to the information contained in the original piece, in order to be processed according to this law.

184. Upon receiving a right to reply complaint, the judge must notify the media vehicle or author of the original publication within twenty-four hours, and they will have the same amount of time to explain their refusal in airing the reply or three days to challenge the victim's lawsuit. Whether or not they respond, in twenty-four hours, the judge must evaluate the available information about the victim's request and, if there is evidence that their request is legitimate, the judge shall determine and establish the date and conditions for the publication or transmission of the reply (Article 7). This is later referred in Article 8 as an 'anticipatory measure'. Such a mechanism is yet another indication that the law favours the publication of the reply above its merit, since regardless of the contestation deadline being open, the judge must still rule on the publication of the reply, based on a possibly incomplete legitimacy assessment (since it would only be complete if by the time the decision was made deadlines had already run and the judge had assessed all information provided by all the parties involved). In case the defendant refuses to abide by the judicial order, the judge can impose a daily fine on them, or determine any appropriate measures in order to enable compliance with their decision. The anticipatory measure may be reconsidered or modified by the judge, in a reasoned decision, at any time.

185. In case the final ruling is in favour of the defendant, i.e., if the plaintiff loses, they must bear the costs of the judicial process and the costs referring to the publication of the reply (Article 11). If the decision for the right to reply is sustained and the defendant loses, the plaintiff can also file another action to request reparation for moral, material or image damages. This different lawsuit will be processed in ordinary time frames, in accordance with the procedural code. By no means the filing of this action impedes the processing of a right to reply lawsuit.

Chapter 5. Access to Public Information

186. Media vehicles access public information through the means available for the general public. For this reason, the framework herein described applies to any media platform, or to any interested citizen, as opposed to it being a particular regime for print media. In Brazil, this access is guaranteed by the 1988 Federal Constitution, and in most part, regulated by Law 12.527/2011 (Access to Information Act – LAI) and by Law 13.105/2015 (Civil Procedure Code – CPC).

187. The Federal Constitution expressly provides for a right of access to public information, according to which every citizen 'has the right to receive information of their particular interest, or of collective or general interest, from public bodies, which will be provided within the terms of the law, under penalty of liability, except for the cases where secrecy is essential to the security of society and the State' (Article 5, XXXIII). This is reinforced by the constitutional regime reserved for the public administration, which, among other principles, must abide by a duty of publicity (Article 37).

188. The Constitution also lays down specific provisions regarding public finances and environmental policy. The first one is established in Article 163-A, according to which the federal, regional and local governments 'shall make their accounting, budgetary and fiscal information and data available, according to the periodicity, format and system established by the central accounting body of the Federal Government, in order to guarantee the traceability, comparability and publicity of the collected data, which must be disclosed electronically, allowing for wide public access' (Article 163-A). As per the second one, Article 225, IV requires the publicity of environmental impact studies produced previously to the implementation of construction work or activity potentially causing significant degradation of the environment.

189. In the following paragraphs, we will describe the provisions that regulate this set of constitutional guarantees, with special attention to the most relevant mechanisms that allow journalists and media vehicles to access public information.

§1. Public Documents and Meetings

190. Law 12.527/2011 is Brazil's LAI, according to which the people (including journalists and media vehicles) can access public interest information through two central means: by consulting information actively disclosed by public bodies and other entities (mostly through websites whose adoption is mandated by the law) or by filing requests to access specific pieces of information held by a public body or other entity (and in this case, LAI provides that the bodies bound by its terms must all implement an access to information service).

191. Before LAI was enacted, the exercise of access to information of public interest in Brazil was approached by different laws, notably fiscal liability regulation, environmental protection statutes and custody of public archives. This meant access to information was submitted to different standards and legal interpretations, as these rules were dispersed in multiple and distinct orderings.[146] While the Brazilian institutional framework was still fragmented, neighbouring countries – such as Colombia, Chile, Perú and México – had already advanced in building unified legal frameworks,[147] which are associated with systems that are more efficient in providing equal access, promoting transparency and guaranteeing secrecy and data protection when needed. Against this background, LAI was enacted in 2011, after years of legislative debate, and it not only established a single consistent framework for access to public information in Brazil but also revoked pre-existent norms that conflicted with its terms.[148]

192. LAI sets out a system that is based on the assumptions that: public interest information publicity is the rule, and secrecy is reserved for exceptional cases to be provided and regulated by legislation; public interest information is actively disseminated, irrespective of whether or not requested; legislation encourages the use of means of communication made possible by information technologies; a culture of transparency in public management must be fostered; and the access to institutional information framework must contribute to the development of social control over public administration acts.[149]

193. Based on the given factors listed above, LAI distinguishes itself from previous national regulations for transitioning from a ‘passive transparency’ model (where the public administration discloses information on demand), to an ‘active transparency’ one, in which information is disclosed and diffused by public entities on their own initiative, spontaneously, irrespective of whether or not requested.[150]

194. Its terms are binding for a number of public and private institutions, namely: all public organs within the Federal Government, states, the Federal District and municipalities; public bodies that are part of the direct administration of the executive, legislative and judiciary branches (including independent control courts and public prosecution offices); autarchies, public foundations, public companies, mixed-capital companies and other entities controlled directly or indirectly by the federal, state or local government; and private non-profit entities that receive public resources for carrying out actions of public interest, whether directly from

---

146. Eneida Bastos Paes, *A construção da Lei de Acesso à Informação Pública no Brasil: desafios na implementação de seus princípios*, 62 (4) Revista do Serviço Público, ia 407–423 (2011).
147. Andrea Monteiro A. Esmanhoto, *La Transparencia y el Acceso a la Información en Brasil*, Revista Internacional de Derecho de la Comunicación y de las Nuevas Tecnologías, 1, 3 (2010).
148. Eneida Bastos Paes, *A construção da Lei de Acesso à Informação Pública no Brasil: desafios na implementação de seus princípios*, 62 (4) Revista do Serviço Público, ia 407–423 (2011).
149. Marcelo Gruman, *Lei de Acesso à Informação: notas e um breve exemplo*, Revista Debates, v.6, n.3, 97–108 (2012).
150. *Ibid.*

budget or through social grants, management contract, partnership agreement, covenants, agreements, adjustments or other similar instruments (*see* LAI, Articles 1 and 2). Regarding private non-profit entities, the obligations of publicity prescribed by LAI refer only to the portion of public funds received and their destination.

195. LAI states that it is the responsibility of public bodies to ensure that information is managed transparently, not only by providing access to it but also by assuring its wide dissemination through different means; public bodies are also responsible for protecting public interest information by assuring its availability, authenticity and integrity, and the same time they also protect confidential and personal information, according to the access restrictions made in accordance with its Article 6.

196. LAI, Article 7 specifies what the access to information obligation regulated by the law implies, i.e., what conducts, procedures and safeguards must be assured by public bodies. These include, among others: guidance on the procedures for accessing specific information, as well as on the location or system where the desired information can be obtained; information contained in records or documents, produced or accumulated by public bodies, whether or not they were originally collected from public archives; information produced or held in custody by an individual or private party resulting from a relation with a public entity (even if that relation has already ceased); primary, complete, authentic and updated information; information on activities carried out by an entity, including those related to their policy measures, organization and services; information pertinent to the management of public assets, use of public resources, bidding, administrative contracts; information that relates to the implementation, monitoring and output of programmes, projects and actions performed by the entity, as well as proposed goals and indicators; and information related to the results of inspections, audits, services and accounts carried out by internal and external controlling bodies.

197. Concerning what cannot be accessed, the rights guaranteed under LAI do not include information regarding scientific and technological research and development projects whose secrecy is essential to national and societal security (Article 7, §1). Information can also be considered partially confidential, in which case access to the non-confidential part of a public document is ensured by means of an extract or a copy, with concealment of the part under confidentiality.

198. Regarding active transparency, Article 8 states that the entities bound by LAI must promote access to information irrespective of whether or not it is requested, through disclosure of an ‘easily accessible means’, providing that maintenance of an official website in the world wide web is mandatory. The provision goes on to list what kinds of information shall be actively disclosed, which includes:

(1) competencies and organizational structure, addresses and telephone numbers of the respective units and opening hours to the public;
(2) records of reception and transfer of financial resources; expense records;

(3) information regarding bidding procedures, including the respective notices and results, as well as all contracts signed by the entity;
(4) general data for monitoring programmes, actions, projects and works of agencies and entities; and answers to frequently asked questions;
(5) other than this information, the mandatory websites must:
   - include a content search tool that allows access to information in an objective, transparent, clear and easy to understand language;
   - adopt several electronic formats, including open and non-proprietary ones, such as spreadsheets and text, in order to facilitate the analysis of the information;
   - enable automated access by external systems in open, structured and machine-readable formats;
   - disclose the formats used for structuring the information;
   - guarantee the authenticity and integrity of the information available for access;
   - keep available information updated for access;
   - indicate the location and instructions that allow the interested party to communicate, electronically or by telephone, with the organ or entity that owns the site; and
   - adopt the necessary measures to guarantee accessibility of content for people with disabilities.

199. As for passive transparency, LAI also mandates the entities bound by its terms to establish and maintain a citizen information service responsible for assisting and guiding the public regarding access to information, informing about the processing of documents and receiving, processing and filing documents, and requirements of access to information (Article 9).

200. Such requests can be presented by any citizen and must include their identification and specification of the required information (Article 10). The information required must be 'feasible' (i.e., findable, possible), and the entity responsible for it cannot impose any requirements on the request related to its motivation; i.e., the information must be provided regardless of the reasons that justify the request. These requests shall be received and processed through the website, but the entity must also ensure another means of filing them, allowing citizens without access to the Internet to also profit from such services.

201. The public agency or entity must authorize or grant immediate access to the available information, and if this is not feasible, it must within twenty days either inform the applicant of another date, place and method for a new consultation or provide credible reasons for partial or complete refusal of the request; or even inform that it does not possess such information and indicate another entity to be consulted (Article 11). In case of partial or complete refusal, the applicant must be informed about the possibility of appeal, conditions and deadline for filing – which according to Article 15 is ten days after notification of refusal. The authority hierarchically superior to the one that issued the contested decision must decide on the appeal within five days. Ultimately, another appeal can also be directed to the

National Controller Body (in Portuguese referenced as *Controladoria Geral da União* – CGU). LAI also states that public authorities that deny access to information without sufficient grounds are too subject to disciplinary measures.

202. The citizen information service must be free of any charge, unless there is a request for reproduction of documents, in which case the cost of these services and materials can be charged. There is, however, an exemption for people whose economic situation does not allow them to do so without prejudice to their own or their family's sustenance.

203. LAI establishes a secrecy classification to be implemented by the entities bound by its terms, regarding information that is secret.

204. For these purposes, information that is essential for national and societal security and that shall be classified is any information whose disclosure could:

- jeopardize national defence and sovereignty or the integrity of the national territory;
- harm or jeopardize interstate negotiations or the country's international relations;
- jeopardize the life, safety or health of the population;
- offer a high risk to the country's financial, economic or monetary stability;
- harm or risk strategic plans or operations of the Armed Forces;
- harm or risk scientific and technological research projects, as well as systems, property, infrastructure or areas of national strategic interest;
- jeopardize the security of institutions or senior national or foreign authorities and their families;
- compromise intelligence actions, as well as ongoing investigations (Article 23).

205. Article 22 also highlights that these provisions do not exclude other legal hypotheses provided by legislation (including secrecy, secrecy of justice or industrial secrecy resulting from the direct exploitation of economic activity by the state or by an individual or private entity in association with the public administration).

206. According to Article 24, this type of information must be classified by the public entities provided by the law as either ultra-secret (which means it should be protected for twenty-five years); secret (implying protection for fifteen years); or reserved (in which case it must be kept confidential for five years). Classification of information can be appealed against by any citizen interested in accessing it, according to Article 17.

207. LAI also imposes restrictions on the right to access in the area of personal information related to one's intimacy, privacy, honour and image (Article 31, §1). Section 31 prescribes special conditions for the handling and treatment of personal data. It states that access to such information is restricted to the information holder and authorized public authorities for the term of hundred years, regardless of classification. It recognizes exceptions to this rule, in cases where their disclosure is expressly authorized by the data holder or by law (Article 31, §1, I, II). Nevertheless, this authorization will not be required if the information is necessary for prevention and medical diagnosis, when the person is physically or legally incapable, and for use solely and exclusively for medical treatment; statistics and scientific research of evident public or general interest provided by law (anonymization being required); compliance with court order; defence of human rights; and in the face of protection of the public interest.

§2. Court Hearings and Documents

208. According to the Federal Constitution, all judicial procedures are public, and legislation can only restrict access to them when done in order to protect one's personal life, or when 'social interest' so demands (Article 5, LX). In addition, Article 93, IX provides that 'the law can only restrict access to judicial procedures when the defence of privacy or social interest so requires' and that 'all trials shall be public, as well as all judicial decisions, under penalty of nullity, and the law may limit the presence, in certain cases, to the parties themselves and to their lawyers, or only to them'.

209. These constitutional provisions are anchored in the principle of democratic control over the actions of the judiciary branch, and they are regulated by the Civil Procedure Code. According to Article 189, all process actions that are not in conformity in terms of public access will be considered null. As per this rule, confidential judicial processes are to be treated as exceptions, provided by legislation when the protection of an individual's privacy or when the public interest so requires.

210. These cases can be treated by different legal instruments that shall be considered by the circumstances for confidentiality already laid out by Article 189. They include: cases where the public or social interest demands secrecy; lawsuits related to marriage, affiliation, separation of spouses, divorce, and child custody and support; lawsuits which comprise data protected by the constitutional right to intimacy; lawsuits regarding matters that were submitted to arbitrage, as long as the interest parties can prove that the arbitration was originally established under confidentiality. Judges have discretion to extend these exceptions to other cases not specifically contemplated in the legal text, provided that its decision is justified since it is restricting a constitutional guarantee.[151]

151. Humberto Dalla & Renata Berlinski, *Civil Procedure in Brazil* 16–25 (Wolters Kluwer Law and Business 2020).

Part III. Regulation of Audiovisual Media

211. The Brazilian audiovisual media framework includes a variety of activities that are classified as both telecommunication and broadcasting services, whose provision is based on different types of infrastructure and regulated by different sets of public policies. In order to paint a comprehensive picture of what is in fact a complex and diverse regulatory landscape, in this part of our monograph, we will discuss this framework through two groups of services: broadcasting (which encompass three types of broadcasting systems – public, private and state); and Pay-TV services. Even though OTT (or Internet-based) audiovisual services are currently in expansion in Brazil, there is not yet a comprehensive regulatory framework that applies to these services. For this reason, we opted to refer to them along the text, whenever relevant vis-à-vis the regulation of other media.

212. For the sake of clarity, references to the 'audiovisual market', 'audiovisual sector' or 'audiovisual regulation' will always refer to the greater market and policy context that includes all these types of services. In turn, references to 'broadcasting services' (or market, regime, system or regulation) refer exclusively to the audiovisual services that are provided through the use of the electromagnetic spectrum (FTA). As we will further clarify, this distinction is a relevant one in the Brazilian context due to the Constitution's provision of differentiated legal regimes for telecommunications and for what is understood as broadcasting.

213. Ahead of a more detailed description of the policies that are currently applicable to the Brazilian audiovisual sector, we propose a brief review of its history, which allows for a greater understanding of the current landscape.

214. Unsurprisingly, this history starts with the introduction and expansion of broadcasting technologies in the first half of the XX century. As depicted in the chapters that follow this introduction, the current Brazilian broadcasting system is a hybrid one, where these activities can be performed under three different legal regimes – i.e., public, private and state broadcasting – and regulated by different sets of public policies. Even though this framework depends heavily upon the provisions of the 1988 Constitution, some of its defining characteristics have been in place since the 1930s, when the government enacted the first broadcasting regulations (at that time mostly focused on radio services).

215. These first policies were established on authoritarian principles, mostly reflected in centralized and discretionary control by the public administration over the content of broadcasts and the process for renewing licences. As highlighted by Lucas Borges Carvalho, strong state intervention in the broadcasting policy framework lived in 'relative harmony' with the commercial exploitation of these services by private agents.[152] In fact, the broadcasting system established by then was mostly inspired by the North American model, based on the economic exploration of electromagnetic spectrum by private companies – as opposed to European traditions such as the German and the British ones, where broadcasting was essentially a public service.[153] This influence of the North American system in Brazil can be observed in the adoption of granting public licences to private companies to make use of the spectrum. The system that was implemented is also marked by the possibility of granted companies placing adverts and thereby collecting profits from exploiting broadcasting services. In turn, this allows for cost-free fruition of these services by the general public, which, in other experiences, is a goal achieved by the collection of a fee to cover the cost of the public service or its universalization.[154]

216. In spite of these choices allowing the participation and fulfilment of private companies' interests, the legislation also provided for a series of state-based mechanisms of control concentrated in the federal executive branch of government. In this way, content censorship was also adopted by authoritarian governments in the 1930s and 1940s, and Decree 20.047/1931 stated that broadcasting services should abide by the 'national interest and educational purposes'. In 1938, the government implemented mandated slots for governmental content diffusion ('Hora do Brasil', or 'Voz do Brasil'), a facility that nowadays still binds radio services to honour these slots and content. This mix of a private initiative-based system and the implementation of heavy-handed mechanisms of control by the state prevailed during the following decades and later through the military dictatorship period.

217. Commercial audiovisual broadcasting (Free TV, FTA services) started in 1950,[155] and the Brazilian Telecommunications Act (CBT) was approved in 1962 (Law 4.117/1962). It stipulated the Federal Government's competence to manage, exploit and delegate exploitation of broadcasting and other telecommunication services such as landlines and telegraph (which by then were not yet submitted to different classifications). The Act also created a regulatory body centred on the Presidency (National Telecommunication Council – CONTEL), which was responsible for producing technical norms, monitoring and enforcing regulation with

152. Lucas Borges de Carvalho, *The Broadcasting Policy in Brazil and Its Legal Framework: From Authoritarianism to Ultraliberalism*, 264 Revista de Direito Administrativo, 245–277 (2013).
153. *Ibid. See also*: Suzy dos Santos & Sérgio Capparelli, *Coronelismo, radiodifusão e voto: a nova face de um velho conceito*, in Valério Brittos & César Bolaño, *Rede Globo: 40 anos de poder e hegemonia* (Paulus 2005).
154. Lucas Borges de Carvalho, *The Broadcasting Policy in Brazil and Its Legal Framework: From Authoritarianism to Ultraliberalism*, 264 Revista de Direito Administrativo, 245–277 (2013).
155. Jonas Valente, *Regulação Democrática dos meios de comunicação*, 37 (Coleção O Que Saber 2013).

respect to all of these services. CONTEL was hierarchically linked to the Ministry of Communications and ultimately to the Presidency.[156]

218. The 1967 Constitution (enacted during the military dictatorship) maintained the commercial exploitation of broadcasting under state control, and the most significant legislation to be implemented during this period was Decree 236/1967. Some of its most important and controversial provisions were: limitation of broadcasting licences per person, per company and per location; creating rules for 'educational broadcasting' (specific broadcasting licences which should prioritize educational content between 7AM and 5PM, e.g., classes, conferences, lectures and debates); and it stipulated a series of conducts that figured as 'abuse of broadcasting freedom'. These conducts included: incitement to disobedience of laws or judicial decisions; disclosure of state secrets or matters that undermine national defence; insult to the national honour; promoting war or processes of subversion of the political and social order; promoting colour, race or religion-based discriminatory content; instil rebelliousness or indiscipline in the Armed Forces or public security; offend public family morals, or good manners; slander, insult or defamation of the Legislative, Executive or Judiciary Powers or their members; depicting false information with danger to the public, economic and social order; and collaborating in the practice of rebellion, disorders or prohibited demonstrations.[157]

219. As highlighted by Miriam Wimmer, during the authoritarianism of the military period, which hindered the freedom of broadcasting companies with regard to content, the years of dictatorship enabled the expansion and consolidation of broadcasting services in Brazil.[158] These governments managed to maintain the private sector's logic of operation of the broadcasting system while also recognizing its value for the integration and formation of national identity. Among the contributions that were determinant to the system that is still in place nowadays, she cites the state investments for the construction of national communication infrastructure, loans from public banks, tax exemption on imports of equipment and the absence of effective controls on economic concentration (which assured big media conglomerates the freedom to expand their market through the formation of national networks, a defining arrangement of the Brazilian broadcasting system, as we will further explore).

220. Even though the legal instruments mentioned above were enacted in historical and technological contexts drastically different from the current ones, many of their provisions are still operative – especially with regard to broadcasting services, whose regulation was the least affected during the re-democratization process and state reforms that followed.

---

156. Miriam Wimmer, *Direitos, Democracia e Acesso aos Meios de Comunicação de Massa*, 188 (2012).
157. *Ibid.*, 190–192.
158. *Ibid.*, 191.

221. The promulgation of the 1988 Constitution marks the beginning of a new system not only for freedom of expression but also for audiovisual regulation. The Constitution paved the way for a series of changes in the legislation (and later even in the text of the Federal Constitution) that led to the regulatory framework currently in place. It implemented a new paradigm for freedom of expression,[159] which no longer allowed for the maintenance of institutional censorship. Together with public spectacles, print publications and all sorts of expression, audiovisual content was no longer subject to previous analysis and approval by state authorities in order to reach the public. This guarantee is reflected in constitutional provisions Article 5, IX, as well as Articles 220–224 (that provide guidelines for Social Communications).

222. According to Article 220, '[t]he expression of thought, creation and information, in any form, process or vehicle, will not suffer any restrictions'. Paragraphs 1 and 2 of the same article further establish that '[n]o law will contain any provision that may constitute an obstacle to the full freedom of journalistic information in any media, observing the provisions of Article 5, IV, V, X, XIII and XIV' and that 'censorship of any political, ideological and artistic nature is prohibited'. Paragraph 3 establishes that federal legislation will be responsible for regulating public entertainment and spectacles (i.e., informing the public about their nature, parental ratings, place and time slot authorizations) and for establishing the legal means that guarantee the person and 'the family' the possibility of defending themselves against radio and television programmes that contradict the provisions of Article 221 (as well as from advertising products, practices and services that may be harmful to health and the environment).

223. Article 220 further established principles for advertising, according to which the advertising of tobacco, alcoholic beverages, pesticides, medicines and therapies will be subject to legal restrictions, which include, whenever necessary, a warning about the harm caused by their use (paragraph 4), as further detailed in Part III, Chapter 6. Moreover, paragraph 5 lays down that social communication mediums cannot, directly or indirectly, be the object of a monopoly or oligopoly, and paragraph 6 states that publication of printed communication vehicles does not depend on state authorization or any sort of licence (in a clear reinforcement to the prohibition of previous censorship of any kind).

224. Article 221 establishes content guidelines specifically targeted at broadcasting services, according to which '[t]he production and programming of radio and television stations will comply with the following principles: i – preference for educational, artistic, cultural and informational purposes; ii – promotion of national and regional culture and encouragement of the independent production that aims to disseminate it; iii – regionalization of cultural, artistic and journalistic production, according to percentages established by law; and iv – respect for the ethical and social values of the person and the family'.

---

159. *See* Part I.

225. Article 222 sets out restrictions on ownership of journalistic and broadcasting companies, as further detailed in Part IV of this monograph.

226. As of its enactment, the Constitution also mitigated decision-making centralization and administrative discretion by including the Parliament in the processes of granting and renewing broadcasting licences.[160] In this sense, Article 223 provides that the executive branch shall grant and renew broadcasting concessions, permission and authorizations, even as they abide by the principle of the complementarity of the private, public and state broadcasting systems. The mitigation of its power over broadcasting licences is reflected in the rule of paragraph 1, according to which Parliament will be responsible for analysing and deliberating on these administrative acts. Deliberations for the non-renewal of such licences shall be taken by at least two-fifths of the House members (paragraph 2), and licences can only be cancelled before their term ends in case there is a final judicial decision in this sense (paragraph 3).

227. Article 224 of the Constitution lays out that Parliament shall establish, as its auxiliary organ, the Social Communication Council – a consultative body without any law enforcement powers whose role will be further explored in Part V of this monograph.

228. A brief analysis of these constitutional provisions unveils that the system elected by the constitutional legislator still mirrors the tension between state intervention and private initiative. Nevertheless, while pre-1988, this tension tended towards state control (in terms of censorship, the decision-making centralization in the executive branch and the wide discretionary power to grant licences) that changed after re-democratization,[161] when the principle of free enterprise came to prevail over the state's regulatory action. As stated by Lucas Borges de Carvalho, this change had a positive side, as a policy that did not allow any form of censorship or concentration of powers. Nevertheless, he argues that this new model was 'selectively adopted', given that a few measures that reflected the old public policy mentality remained untouched – e.g., the distribution of licences still concentrated on politicians and traditional media conglomerates. At the same time, much of the private initiative-led broadcasting system remained unregulated,[162] granting economic agents full freedom and no restrictions in providing a service of public interest that is based on a scarce public good (i.e., the electromagnetic spectrum).

229. Another distinctive characteristic of the audiovisual framework designed in the Constitution was inserted by Constitutional Amendment n. 08/95, which separated broadcasting from telecommunication services. The same amendment also

160. Lucas Borges de Carvalho, *The Broadcasting Policy in Brazil and Its Legal Framework: From Authoritarianism to Ultraliberalism*, 264 Revista de Direito Administrativo, 245–277 (2013).
161. *Ibid.*
162. *Ibid.*

provided for the creation of a regulatory body to manage the exploitation of telecommunication services, which were privatized and had their exploitation delegated and auctioned to the private sector.[163]

230. In fact, the separation between broadcasting and telecommunication services was promoted amidst a series of economic reforms that took place in the 1990s, led by President Fernando Henrique Cardoso (these reforms were initiated when he was Minister of the Economy and carried on during two terms of his presidency, 1995–1998 and 1999–2002). Under the guise of modernization and privatization, these reforms redesigned the Brazilian State's approach to the economy and the structure of the public administration, having affected key economic sectors (beyond telecommunications like transportation and energy).[164] Even though it has been reported that high-ranked authorities leading the processes of privatization in the Ministry Communications wanted to include the whole of social communication in the process, that did not happen. The final wording of Amendment 08/95 left aside broadcasting services,[165] which remained subject to the previous legal regime, sealing these services' status quo and allowing for the maintenance of a separate and pre-established regime for broadcasters using electromagnetic spectrum.

231. As a result, there are two constitutional categories that include audiovisual services: telecommunications and broadcasting. In fact, as we will approach in the next sections, each of these categories also encompasses non-audiovisual services.

232. The first one consists of broadcasting in the strict sense, i.e., services that are provided through the infrastructure of electromagnetic spectrum. This includes what the Constitution refers to as 'sound broadcasting' (i.e., radio services) and 'sound and image broadcasting' (i.e., television services that can also be referred to as 'FTA' TV). Telecommunication services, on the other hand, are the ones that offer 'transmission, emission or reception, by wire, radio-electricity, optical means or any other electromagnetic process, of symbols, characters, signs, writings, images, sounds or information of any nature' (as per Res Anatel n 73/1998, Article 2). They encompass a variety of services that are not audiovisual (e.g., mobile and landline operators) and also all sorts of Pay-TV operators (which provide audiovisual services through the exploitation of telecommunication infrastructures, e.g., cable, FTTH, DTH, special Service of Pay-TV signal distribution in ultrahigh frequency (TVA), Multipoint Multichannel Signal Distribution Service (MMDS)).

233. Besides the infrastructure on which they are based, the greatest conceptual distinction between audiovisual services that are considered to be broadcasting (FTA) and to be telecommunications is that the former are freely provided without any direct cost to the population. At the other end of the spectrum, Pay-TV services

163. Miriam Wimmer, *Direitos, Democracia e Acesso aos Meios de Comunicação de Massa*, 197 (Amazon 2012).
164. *Ibid.*
165. *Ibid.*

are only provided under a private regime, and are hence submitted to different regulatory rules (which can also vary according to the infrastructure on which the service is based, as it will be further addressed in the chapters that follow this introduction).

234. As noted above, the Constitution establishes a broadcasting system formed by private, public and state systems, which must abide by the principle of complementarity (Article 223) – however, this wording does not include clear guidelines on what distinguishes these systems. Each of these classifications encompass different types of broadcasters, and further analysis of this system reveals that it exhibits considerable contradictions and imprecisions.[166] For the purposes of this Introduction, it suffices to define each of these systems as follows.

235. In the *private* system are the broadcasters who are either private entities licensed by the state to commercially exploit the service or broadcasters that are licensed to exploit the service without commercial purposes, such as associations and foundations with public interest purposes. The latter are also referred to as 'educational TV' or 'educational broadcasting'.[167] Besides these, the private broadcasting system also includes 'Community TVs' ('TVs Comunitárias'), which are privately operating broadcasters bound by rules that promote its public character, allowing any member of the respective community to participate in any way in the broadcaster.[168]

236. The *state* system encompasses the institutional broadcasters of governmental authorities, like, for instance, the Justice TV (judiciary branch), Senate TV and TV Câmara (the Houses of the Parliament). These entities provide state services, with the goal of offering citizens informative, cultural and educational content related to the governmental entity's activities.[169] The entities are also responsible for financing their broadcasting channels system, appointing its holders and exercising control over programming.[170]

237. As per the *public system*, it consists of the Brazilian model for what is internationally referred to as a 'public service broadcaster', i.e., broadcasting companies controlled by the state and founded on 'democratic and participative management models, with a control body with the presence of society and its representations, and with stable and robust financing mechanisms that ensure autonomy and not create

166. Cláudia R. F. Lemos, Maíra de Brito Carlos & Antonio Teixeira Barros, *TV Câmara. TV Pública? As TVs legislativas na transição para a plataforma digital*, 5 (2) Observatorio (OBS*) (2011).
167. Jonas Valente, *Regulação Democrática dos meios de comunicação*, 38 (Coleção O Que Saber 2013).
168. *Ibid.*
169. Ericsom Meister Scorsim, *O controle dos serviços públicos de radiodifusão (Rádio e Televisão) no Brasil,* Revista da Faculdade de Direito da UFPR, 34, 161 (2000). There is, however, some degree of disagreement regarding the legal nature of Community TVs, and some authors may refer to them as being part of the public system of broadcasting.
170. Jonas Valente, *Regulação Democrática dos meios de comunicação*, 38 (Coleção O Que Saber 2013).

market dependency'.[171] The most relevant representative of this category is Empresa Brasil de Comunicação (EBC), created in 2007 to fulfil the long-standing gap of a public service broadcaster (whose main characteristics will be highlighted in Chapter 2 below).

238. The only legislation that expressly regulates the tripartite broadcasting system established by Article 223 of the Constitution is Law 11.652/2008, which by creating the public service broadcaster EBC also defined what is the broadcasting public system. As it brings no reference to what constitutes the private and the state systems, and neither does any other legislation, these conceptual frameworks depend on an interpretation exercise considering a greater set of legal and regulatory diplomas.

239. In its turn, telecommunications services also encompass a vast group of activities. While the federal branch's competence to regulate and manage these services is embroidered in the Constitution (Articles 21, IX and 22, IV), further policies towards these services are established in specific legislation (e.g., the General Act for Telecommunications – 'LGT', Law 9.472/97) and regulatory norms enacted by ANATEL, the regulatory authority. Considering audiovisual telecommunications services, different services are designated by different technological infrastructures, but they can be referred to as Pay-TV or Conditional Access Services (as is the terminology adopted by Law 12.485/2011, which provides a unified regulatory framework for these audiovisual services).

240. The insertion of Internet-based services into this Pay-TV regulatory framework is still disputed in public policy fora (like regulatory agencies and Parliament) by the telecommunications, technology and broadcasting representatives. As shown in the introduction to this monograph, the sector has consistently grown in the national market for the last years, but this growth has not been accompanied by a unified and organized legal framework. Thus, Internet-based audiovisual services remain regulated by sparse legislation.

241. As it appears, the Brazilian audiovisual market is defined by diversity and decentralization, whereas many different services – that are submitted to different classifications that abide by different legal regimes and are supervised by different authorities – compete with each other at different levels.

242. In this context, it is worth highlighting that in its recent report 'Telecommunications and Broadcasting Review of Brazil 2020', the Organisation for Economic Co-operation and Development (OECD) included a set of key recommendations for this audiovisual regulatory framework, some of which are targeted precisely at the long-standing constitutional foundations of this model. It recommends the creation of a converged, independent regulator, as a means to simplify the regulatory regime and address the convergent reality. That would encompass, for instance, reuniting the assignments of broadcasting and communication services in

171. *Ibid.*

one single administrative authority, as well as the adaptation of framework to a simple class-licensing regime for communication and broadcasting services.

243. In the next chapters, we will approach the regulatory framework for each of these services according to the classification that is available in the legislation while also pointing out its limitations and inconsistencies.

Chapter 1. Private Broadcasting: FTA television

244. The private broadcasting system encompasses services of different natures, which have in common the fact that they are provided by private entities and offered to the public without any cost. For this reason, they are also commonly referred to as 'FTA TV' (in Portuguese, referred to as 'TV Aberta').

245. Even though the Brazilian communications landscape follows the global tendency of expansion of digital communications, with growing connectivity numbers,[172] the services known as private broadcasting (especially the commercial grants) remain the audiovisual medium with the highest reach in terms of geographical coverage and population usage.[173] Also, as already addressed in the Introduction to this part of the monograph, the history of broadcasting technologies and their regulation by the state has played a relevant role in the configuration of its media law landscape.

246. In this chapter, we will approach what is a complex and yet incomplete regulatory landscape, with focus on the most relevant legal aspects and controversies around private broadcasting regulation, as well as defining characteristics of this market which accrue from this framework.

§1. Different Categories of Private Broadcasters

247. Private broadcasters are submitted to different and usually overlapping classifications. In the next paragraphs, we will approach them according to the type of grant, the technology, type of service and broadcasting station. As the latter type of broadcasting allows for the contractual arrangement that founded television networks (also known as the 'affiliate system'), we will also describe the main characteristics and implications of this commercial organization.

I. Types of Grant: Commercial, Educational and Community

248. Even though Article 223 of the Constitution expressly refers to three systems of broadcasting – public, private and state broadcasting – there is no clear regulation concerning which type of broadcasting grants supports each of these systems. For the purposes of this chapter, we will approach what is known as commercial TV, educational TV and community TV as parts of the private broadcasting system. While there is little controversy about commercial and educational TVs being classified as such, community TV can also be referenced as part of the public broadcasting system (even though these channels are not operated by EBC).

---

172. World Bank, *Individuals Using the Internet*, available at: https://data.worldbank.org/indicator/IT.NET.USER.ZS?end=2017&locations=AR-BO-BR-CL-CO-EC-MX&start=2017 (accessed 16 Jan. 2021).
173. OECD Telecommunication and Broadcasting Review of Brazil 2020.

249. Commercial TVs are the private agents licensed by the state to exploit the service with commercial purposes and their profits are mostly originated from negotiation of advertising space. There is no legal impediment for a non-profit organization to act through this concession.[174] The main legal instruments that regulate commercial broadcasting are the 1962 Brazilian Telecommunications Code (CBT), Decree-Law 236/1967, and Decree 2.108/1996.

250. Educational TVs are broadcasting services provided without profit-making purposes by public and private universities, foundations, associations, or by members of the Brazilian federation (i.e., local, state and federal governments). Among these, public entities shall be given preference over private ones when it comes to obtaining these grants. Educational TVs are expected to air educational and cultural programmes that complement educational systems at any level or modality, thus including basic education and higher education, adult education and vocational training, in addition to covering content related to educational, cultural, pedagogical and professional activities. Recreational, informative or sports-related programmes may fit this definition if they are distinguished by an instructive educational or cultural approach. Since their services are not commercial, educational TV cannot air any form of direct or indirect advertisement (which includes announcing sponsorship of their programmes). The main regulatory instruments that detail these other aspects are Decree-Law 236/1967, Decree 2.108/1996, and Interministries Ordinance 651/1999.

251. Community TVs provide broadcasting services without profit purposes founded on the importance of allowing different social groups to access and actively participate in mass communications through their own channels. As it will be further discussed, these are mostly local grants, and their services are supposed to focus on the public interest of specific communities. In this sense, Community TVs are a diversity-enhancing mechanism implemented in different jurisdictions, anchored in the goal of promoting external pluralism, particularly by allowing the participation of varied cultural and socio-economic background actors in the media field.[175] Community channels are usually operated in a modulated frequency, at low power and with coverage restricted to a certain region, and they can only be awarded grants by non-profit community foundations and associations, with headquarters in the locality where the service is provided.

252. In Brazil, they are regulated by the CBT, Decree 236/1967 and in particular through Law 9.612/1998 and Ordinance ANATEL 4.334/2015. According to Law 9.612/1998, Article 3, the main purpose of community broadcasting in Brazil is to benefit local communities, namely by giving the opportunity for dissemination of ideas, cultural elements, traditions and social habits of the community. Other

174. Jonas Valente, *Regulação Democrática dos meios de comunicação*, 38 (Coleção O Que Saber 2013).

175. United Nations Educational, Scientific and Cultural Organization – UNESCO, *Defining Community Broadcasting*, UNESCO Community Media Sustainability Policy Series (2019). Available at: https://en.unesco.org/community-media-sustainability/policy-series.

goals of these services include offering mechanisms for community formation and integration, leisure, culture and social interaction; providing public utility services, through the integration of its programming with local government services, whenever necessary. These operators shall also contribute to the professional improvement of local journalists and broadcasters, as well as enable the training of citizens in the exercise of their right to freedom of expression.

II. Types of Technology: Analogue and Digital

253. The implementation of digital broadcasting in Brazil lasted for several years, and one can argue that the delay in establishing technical parameters and enacting efficient regulation has affected the potential benefits and relevance of these services. The debate started in the 1990s, when the Ministry of Communications implemented working groups with the goal of studying and choosing a technical support system.[176] During the following years, this group would expand and incorporate members from outside of the Ministry of Communications, such as the Association for Radio and TV Broadcasters (ABERT) and ANATEL (created in 1997). Some of the key debates led by this group were around the digital television system to be adopted (by then, the main choices were between the American, the Japanese and the Brazilian system, which would be a hybrid alternative) and the possibility of allowing multiprogramming, to ensure the extra bandwidth would be used to improve service quality.

254. As a result of these discussions, Decree 4.901/2003 established the Brazilian System of Digital Television (SBTVD), an organ (no longer in place) formed by three commissions, whose goals included: promoting social inclusion, cultural diversity, and the native language through access to digital technology; promoting the democratization of information; enabling the creation of a universal distance-education network; stimulate research aimed at the expansion of Brazilian technologies and of the national industry related to information technology and communication; to plan the process of transition from analogue to digital television so as to ensure the gradual adhesion of users at costs compatible with their income; stimulate the evolution of the analogue television service explorers, as well as the entry of new companies, propitiating the expansion of the sector and enabling the development of countless services resulting from digital technology, according to specific legislation; and to improve the use of the radio frequency spectrum, among others.

255. Further regulation of digital broadcasting was implemented by Decree 5.820/2006, which defined SBTVD as the 'set of technological patterns to be adopted in the transmission and reception of digital broadcasting signals' (Article 2, I). After years of debate, Brazil adopted a modified version of the Japanese system

176. OECD Telecommunication and Broadcasting Review of Brazil 2020, 211 (2020).

(now known as the Brazilian one), which enables digital transmission in high-definition TV (HDTV) and standard definition TV (SDTV), as well as simultaneous digital transmission for fixed, mobile and portable reception.

256. Some of the most significant policy choices consolidated in Decree 5.829/2006 were: broadcasters will receive a radio frequency channel with a bandwidth of 6 MHz for each analogue channel they own; granting of at least four digital channels for direct exploitation by the Federal Government; and simultaneous transmissions in digital and analogical signals for ten years, so as to facilitate the transition process. In this sense, the original date for the switch-off of analogical signals was 2016, later postponed to 2018. In fact, some cities in rural areas are still receiving both signals, and the current plan is to have a final complete switch-off by 2023. By August 2013, only digital broadcasting licences were granted, and bidders for broadcasting grant processes had to ensure the successful completion of the digital switchover by carrying out different activities.[177]

257. Overall, the digital transition can be interpreted as 'a missed opportunity to transform the sector',[178] or as yet another media concentration policy that allowed for 'the occupation of the radio frequency spectrum to prevent the entry of new competitors'.[179] That is in great part due to the fact the regulation ensured the use of new bands by broadcasters reproducing 'the same economic and institutional structures'[180] that already characterised the broadcasting sector as an economically concentrated one.

III. Types of Service: Radio and TV

258. In the Brazilian legal framework, broadcasting services are the ones transmitted through electromagnetic spectrum, which includes both radio (sound broadcasting) and television services (sound and image broadcasting). Even though each of them is ruled by specific regulation that fits its scope and characteristics, overall radio and TV services are threaded by a similar logic. First, they are both regulated by the same constitutional provisions regarding purpose, editorial responsibility and ownership limitations. They both can be object of the three types of grants already described (commercial, educational and community), provided with national, regional or local scope; and in both cases, their operation stations are classified according to their reach and functions (even though the classifications that apply are different). The CBT (Law 4.117/1967) is the main applicable legal instrument, and specific obligations and technical requirements are established in regulatory instruments enacted by the Ministry of Communications and the ANATEL.

177. *Ibid.*
178. *Ibid.*, 212.
179. Jonas Valente, *Regulação Democrática dos meios de comunicação*, 62 (Coleção O Que Saber 2013).
180. OECD Telecommunication and Broadcasting Review of Brazil 2020, 212 (2020).

259. Since Part III of this monograph is focused on audiovisual media, for the purposes of this section, the description of the private broadcasting framework focuses on television services. Nevertheless, we will highlight some of the main characteristics of the radio broadcasting system in Brazil, below.

260. Grants to exploit radio services last for ten years, and the legal instrument that formalizes the grant can be a concession, a permission or an authorization – this varies according to the scope of provision (i.e., national, regional, local)[181] and the type of transmission.[182] Radio broadcasters are divided into frequency modulated (FM), which has superior quality and shorter reach; amplitude modulation (AM, also referred to in Portuguese as onda media – OM), with slightly lower quality and medium reach; and short wave (OC) and tropical waves, with greater reach and reduced quality. Each type of operation requires a different type of grant (concession or permission), and each station can be considered individually for the purposes of technical inspection and fiscal contributions (which means that some of these contributions are collected by station, and not by company). This category is only applicable to radio broadcasting stations; TV stations are divided into generators, retransmitters and repeaters, as we will approach next.

261. Radio broadcasters are authorized to perform services either twenty-four hours of the day or for more limited hours. In both cases, broadcasters must maintain a minimum regular work programme of two-thirds of the hours they are authorized to operate.

IV. Types of Broadcasting Stations: Generators, Retransmitters and Repeaters

262. In order to perform television broadcasting activities, each type of broadcaster (commercial, educational or community) operates a physical infrastructure formed by three different types of stations: generators, retransmitter stations (RTV) and repeater stations (RpTV). Usually, every broadcaster has licences to operate all three types of services, and this is what allows them to build networks to ensure that their signal reaches a wider part of the population.

263. Overall, these three types of broadcasting stations can be summarized in the following way: generators directly broadcast their own programming; retransmitters channels transmit programming that they receive from a generator to the public or to RpTV (simultaneously or not); repeaters are merely connecting infrastructure intended for the transport of signals from one station to another (either generators

181. Miriam Wimmer, *Direitos, Democracia e Acesso aos Meios de Comunicação de Massa,* 247 (2012).

182. National Telecommunications Agency – ANATEL, *Básico de Radiodifusão*, available at: https://www.anatel.gov.br/Portal/verificaDocumentos/documento.asp?numeroPublicacao=213645&assuntoPublicacao=null&caminhoRel=null&filtro=1&documentoPath=213645.pdf (accessed 20 Dec. 2020).

or retransmitters). Generator stations are the primary transmitters of the content that is organized in their own studio, which includes programming and advertisement insertions.

264. Combined, RTV and RpTV allow the generator's signal to reach a wider territory, and they are also known as services that are 'ancillary to television broadcasting'. The main difference between the two of them is that repeaters merely replicate signal carried in-between stations, while retransmitters can also deliver transmissions to the public. While generator stations are broadcasters, for all legal purposes RTV and RpTV are considered telecommunications services, even though they also use the electromagnetic spectrum and are received free of charge by the general public. Relevant legal statutes for these services are the Telecommunications Act – CBT and Decree 5.371/2005 (which is the reference for the legal provisions referred to below).

265. Regulatory supervision is performed by the Ministry of Communications and the ANATEL, with the former performing content and licence grants related supervision and the latter performing technical requirements enforcement (this is actually the case for most of the broadcasting-related competences division between these two bodies, as it will be further noted in Part V). The Ministry of Communication is responsible for: enacting complementary rules for RTV and RpTV Services; granting authorization for their deployment; approval of projects for installation, and use of equipment for RTV and RpTV stations as well as issuing the respective licences for operation; monitoring and enforcing legal compliance in the execution of the RTV Service throughout the national territory; and instituting administrative procedures to investigate infractions of any nature regarding RTV and RpTV services and imposing sanctions. In turn, ANATEL is responsible for preparing and updating the plan for distribution of television channels; granting authorizations for the use of radio frequencies for RTV and RpTV services; and inspecting stations with regard to technical aspects.

266. RTV and RpTV services can be performed by the same entities that are allowed to obtain broadcasting licences of all kinds – i.e., federal, state and local governments; public and private foundations and associations; private corporations or private and public entities (that are legally allowed to be awarded broadcasting grants). In order to obtain this authorization, legal entities that detain broadcasting grants may, at any time, request authorization from the Ministry of Science, Technology, Innovations and Communications to perform the RTV Service. Before approving such a request, the Ministry will evaluate its technical feasibility, including a consultation to ANATEL in order to evaluate the inclusion of the respective RTV channel.

267. In general, RTV and RpTV are not allowed to transmit their own programming and advertisements, and should only broadcast the content coming from generators (Article 31). This means that advertisements aimed at a particular region must be inserted by the television generator associated with this retransmitter, provided that there is no other generator installed in the locality. There is one exception to this rule, which concerns regions that are considered the 'country's borders of development' (to be defined as such by the Ministry of Communications – a recent example of which was defining the states that make up the 'Legal Amazon').[183] Retransmitters authorized to operate in these localities can insert local programming and advertising, as long as: the insertion of local programming does not exceed 15% of the total programming transmitted by the television generating station to which the retransmitter is linked; the programme has educational, artistic, cultural and informational purposes, for the benefit of the general development of a local community; the insertions of advertising have a maximum duration equal to and coinciding with the time slots allocated to the advertising transmitted by the generating station providing the signals; and advertising insertions are carried out by entities authorized to perform the RTV Service for signals originating from generator stations (Articles 31–33).

V. TV Networks: The Affiliate System

268. From this tangle of generators, repeaters and retransmitters accrues a concept called 'affiliated stations network'. Affiliated stations are institutions that, through contractual arrangements with the network owner, deliver to the general public the content generated by a television network.

269. Affiliated networks are the result of a commercial practice whereby broadcasters with grants to operate in different regions form commercial agreements in order to share the same programming. These networks are usually structured around a main broadcaster, responsible for the commercial operation and branding of the affiliates' network, as well as for the programming attracting advertising funds. Besides saving costs, these arrangements allow for broadcasting companies to form partnerships that will allow them to gain national scope, despite the legal limits on ownership imposed by Decree 236/1967 (*see* Part IV):

> We seek to make it, in fact, a powerful instrument for consolidating national unity. Reaching practically the entire country, I believe Globo Network's contribution to the intensification of the dissemination and exchange of those concepts and data of a cultural, social and moral nature – not to mention information, pure and simple – that constitute the basis of national development in all fields and at all levels.[184]

270. These are the words of Roberto Marinho, founder of Globo TV, as he explained the development of his affiliated networks system in a nationally popular magazine (*Veja Magazine*) in 1976. In fact, his company was the forerunner of the affiliates system in the early 1970s, and it has implemented it masterfully until the

183. ANCINE – Brazilian Film Agency, *TV Aberta no Brasil: aspectos econômicos e estruturais*, https://oca.ancine.gov.br/sites/default/files/repositorio/pdf/Estudo_TVAberta_2015.pdf (accessed 20 Nov. 2020).
184. Carlos Eduardo Lins da Silva, *Muito Além do Jardim Botânico*, 32 (Summus Editorial 1985).

present time, covering 98.38%[185] of the Brazilian territory as of 2020. This massive coverage relies upon 120 stations and a national signal distribution for satellite dishes (Band C / Ku). Sistema Brasileiro de Televisão (SBT), the second-largest network in terms of the number of stations, has the national signal transmitted by a station located in São Paulo city, and it owns another 8 stations called 'regional stations' in the company's structure, and it covers the rest of the territory through 104 third-party-owned affiliated stations.

271. Structurally, affiliated networks in Brazil rely on generators and RTV stations. The ability to insert locally relevant programming, such as news programmes, is one of the advantages of deploying generator stations instead of RTVs within a network. In certain situations, the local insertion may represent something commercially irrelevant (due to specific characteristics of the area covered by the grant), situations in which the RTV model is more likely to be adopted.

272. To better understand the programming grid of an affiliated station network, one can visualize a system composed of concentric circles. In the centre, a circle with audiovisual contents understood to be relevant nationwide, or commercially more relevant, is the so-called national broadcast – which in terms of Brazil means the regions in the south and southeast.[186] This national broadcast is the signal made available for reception by satellite dishes. Just beyond this first circle, a second circle is occupied by regional 'network head stations', responsible for generating relevant content for a given macro-region and other grid adjustments related, for example, to time zones and local soccer matches. Finally, the third and largest circle comprises affiliated generator stations, which insert local programming in the grid ranges available for local insertions.

273. Content generated by affiliates is, for the most part, of a journalistic nature (hard news), followed by special reports (documentary format on a microscopic scale) and sports content.

274. Due to their importance, network head stations are entities linked to the same economic group as the main generator station responsible for the national broadcast. To circumvent legal restrictions on concentration of ownership, the concessions are usually held by members of the same family.

275. The agreements between affiliated stations and network owner will define, for example, exhibition rights from network to affiliates, timeframes when the affiliated station can insert local programming into the grid, technical and editorial quality criteria of the locally produced content, licences from the affiliated station to the

185. As reported by Globo TV on December 2020, the total percentage of Globo TV Network coverage through broadcasters (120 in total) is a staggering 92.87% of the country territory, the rest is covered by satellite dishes that capture the available signal, available on https://negocios8.redeglobo.com.br/Paginas/Brasil.aspx (accessed 22 Dec. 2020).

186. Marilena Chaui, *Simulacro e Poder: uma análise da mídia* (Editora Fundação Perseu Abramo 2006).

head station regarding the locally produced content, non-competes, as well as advertising insertion parameters such as local insertions and revenue share. Depending on the network, these contracts can be as simple as a programme licensing agreement or as complex as a chain of contracts framed by a comprehensive affiliation agreement.

276. Affiliates are chosen carefully by the networks, and once these contracts are firmed, these networks are also closer to politically and economically influential families. For instance, the 'clan' of the Sarney family, whose patriarch Jose Sarney is a former president of Brazil, former senator, federal deputy and former Governor of Maranhão State, owns a network of four Globo TV affiliates in the state of Maranhão. Similarly, the family of former president Fernando Collor, who is currently a senator, owns Globo TV affiliates in the state of Alagoas; the dominance of the Magalhães family prevails in Bahia, whose patriarch, Antonio Carlos Magalhães, held positions of Communications Minister, State Governor, Senator, Mayor and Federal Deputy – now Magalhães family owns six Globo TV Network stations in Bahia.[187]

277. The model of affiliated network is a key element for the 'electronic coronelism',[188] and Globo TV's alleged relations with regional politics under the affiliated network umbrella are a recurring headline. In 1994, newspapers reported[189] that a soap opera had investments from the state government of Ceará to promote the natural beauty of the state and certain enterprises associated with a family influential in local politics, who at the time owned a Globo TV affiliated station. Twelve years later, these practices were still well established, the point of broadcasts running exposures of a candidate linked to the company's owner during the electoral period – which is forbidden by the electoral legislation. Therefore, an electoral court determined that a Globo TV affiliated station should go twenty-four hours without transmitting programming.[190]

§2. Licensing Requirements

278. There are a series of ownership and procedural requirements for obtaining a broadcasting licence, starting with the conditions imposed by the Federal Constitution.

---

187. Reporters Without Borders and Intervozes, *Political Affiliation*, Media Ownership Monitor Brazil (February 2019), https://brazil.mom-rsf.org/en/findings/political-affiliation/ (accessed 20 May 2022).
188. As briefly mentioned in Part I, the 'electronic coronelism' refers to the practices of granting broadcasting licences to elected politicians. We will describe these practices in more detail in Part IV.
189. Xico Sá, *Novela custa US$ 700 mil a CE*, Folha de São Paulo (26 May 1994), https://www1.folha.uol.com.br/fsp/1994/6/26/brasil/32.html (accessed 12 Jan. 2021).
190. João Carlos Magalhães, *Afiliada da Globo no RN sai do ar, mas é autorizada a veicular debate*, Folha de São Paulo (28 Oct. 2006), https://www1.folha.uol.com.br/fsp/brasil/fc2810200637.htm (accessed 14 Jan. 2021).

279. With reference to requirements for operating in the market, Article 222 of the Charter prescribes that journalistic and broadcasting companies can only be owned by Brazilians (born as such or with acquired citizenship for no less than ten years), or by a legal entity constituted under Brazilian law and with headquarters in the country. For further details and requirements on ownership and control regulation, refer to Part IV of this monograph.

280. The same precondition is expanded to 'electronic media, regardless of the technology used to provide the service' (Article 222, paragraph 3), which, in practice, means that Pay-TV operators (i.e., telecommunications services that engage in audiovisual activity) must comply with the same principles. In order to allow for monitoring of compliance with these rules, the Constitution also establishes that any changes in corporate control of journalistic and broadcasting companies must be communicated to the National Congress (Article 222, paragraph 4).

281. Another constitutional restriction refers to a specific veto provided by Article 54, according to which congressmen and senators are not allowed to control or direct companies which have contracts with public-law entities. This includes a wide range of companies that have formed agreements of all sorts with the federal, regional or local governments, and among them are broadcasters. Regardless of this clear provision, the practice of elected representatives owning journalistic and broadcasting companies is ongoing and the object of great political dispute, as it will be further discussed in Part III, Chapter 5.

282. The Constitution also provides the general guidelines for the broadcasting licensing processes. In order to move away from the concentration of power in the head of the executive branch of government, it added a parliamentary competence to validate the acts that grant or renew such licences. In this sense, Article 223 states that the executive branch is responsible for granting and renewing concessions, permissions and authorizations for broadcasting services. Once the competent authority enacts the grant, both houses of Parliament must analyse and approve such an act. The non-renewal of these grants requires approval of a minimum of two-fifths of the National Congress, in a nominal vote. The cancellation of the concession or permission, before the expiry of the term, depends on a judicial decision.

283. Within this framework, the procedural aspects that rule these grants are set out in different applicable legislation, like Decrees 236/1967, 52.795/1963 and 2.108/1996 (that regulate broadcasting services), Law 8.666/1993 (which set the rules for public administration bidding procedures and contracts),[191] and a series of normative instruments that may apply to specific types of private broadcasters. Even though the overall procedure is similar, commercial, educational and community grants processing can have a few differences.

191. Soon to be replaced with a new text already approved by Parliament and awaiting presidential enactment (Bill of Law 4.253/2020).

284. Commercial grants are awarded after bidding procedures, intended to guarantee isonomic participation to all agents interested in providing the service and bound by the constitutional principles applicable to the public administration's activities – i.e., legality, morality, impersonality, publicity and efficiency (Federal Constitution, Article 37). The decision to start a bidding process is at the discretion of the Minister of Communications, but interested parties can formally provoke this decision by manifesting their interest in a specific channel.[192] The Minister's decision on starting a bidding process or not, as well as an interested part's manifestation, must be based on the 'National Grant Plan' – a document to be produced yearly by the competent authorities, mapping the available channels in the country's different locations. Once the decision to start a bidding process is taken, the Ministry of Communications must publish a call for interested parties in the official gazette, indicating: the exact object of the bidding; the minimum value grant; payment conditions; list of documents necessary for the qualification; and the criteria according to which technical and price proposals will be judged. Interested parties will have sixty days to present their documentation, including a technical project, a content proposal and a price bid. The proposed price will only be considered at a later stage once the candidates have had their technical and content proposals approved.

285. Once the bidding procedure reaches its end and one candidate is declared as the winner, the National Congress is officially notified of the grant licensing, which is then analysed by both the House of Representatives and the Senate. If both houses approve it, the grant is then formalized in an administrative agreement signed by the Minister of Communications and the grantee entity. The following steps include approvals of installation sites and equipment (also issued by the Ministry of Communications) and issuance of an authorization to use the radiofrequency channel (ANATEL).

286. The term of television broadcasting grants is fifteen years, after which they can be renewed for the same period of time. In order to get this renewal, broadcasters that already operate the service must present a request to the Ministry of Communications, which must then analyse and assess it. In the case of approval, the grant renewal is also sent for parliamentary approval, and final renewal requires a nominal vote of at least two-fifths of Parliament members. In practice, these renewal processes are often criticized for lasting years (grant renewals have waited up to seven years to be finalized), which also allows for the licences to remain longer in the hands of the same agents, without much consideration for how they have been making use of them. The lack of civil society participation in this process is also a matter of concern, as no public hearings of any kind is required for renewal.[193]

192. Cristiano Aguiar Lopes, *Regulação das Outorgas de Radiodifusão no Brasil – uma breve análise*, Consultoria Legislativa, Câmara dos Deputados (2009).

193. Jonas Valente, *Regulação Democrática dos meios de comunicação*, 17 (Coleção O Que Saber 2013).

287. Broadcasting grants can also be transferred to other agents, according to the procedures established in Decree 52.795/1963. Request for transfer shall be authorized by the Ministry of Communications regarding radio broadcasting services and by presidential decree for television broadcasting. After issuing an authorization for transfer, the competent authority must notify the National Congress. The grant transfer can be authorized only after the term of five years, counted from the date of expedition of the definitive licence certificate for the operation of the station.

288. As per the process for educational broadcasting, this type of grant must be claimed in accordance with their legally binding purposes (i.e., the diffusion of cultural, informative, educational and pedagogical content), by private or public entities, including universities, foundations and associations. The legislation does not provide a specific granting procedure for educational broadcasting, but Article 13 of Decree 2.108/1996 exempts the Ministry of Communications from establishing a bidding process in these cases. Some phases of this process are similar to the ones that apply to commercial broadcasting; for instance, the National Grant Plan shall also depict the channels that are available for educational broadcasters, and even interested parties must present technical studies and content programming plan. However, specific requirements might also apply, like the declaration of compliance with cultural and educational purposes, as required by Ordinance 651/1999.

289. The main distinction in relation to commercial broadcasting granting lies in the fact that the Ministry is not mandated to start a bidding process previous to granting the licences (even though, in theory, they could). While this exemption can be seen as a way to facilitate the licensing of educational grants and excluding the price element, it can also be interpreted as way of maintaining the use of these grants as political bargaining chip (which also happened with commercial grants, before the mandatory bidding process was implemented).[194]

290. Renewal of educational grants will only be approved if the broadcaster complies with the legal requirements for these services. Grant transfers are also allowed, as long as they do not affect the purpose of the programming and that grants awarded to public entities are not transferred to private companies.

291. Community broadcasting grants also abide by similar procedures that are particularly shaped by specific rules (as per Law 9.612/1998 and Ordinance ANATEL 4.334/2011). As mentioned previously, the community broadcasting service can only be provided by non-profit associations or foundations that are based in the area where the service is provided. There are a few requirements that apply to these entities' bylaws and institutional documentation. Beyond being legally instituted and duly registered, they must: allow free association of all people and legal entities that reside or have their headquarters in the community grant's respective area; they must allow for democratic and equal participation of members in deliberation forums, including through the broad guarantee of the right to speak and vote; there

194. Cristiano Aguiar Lopes, *Regulação das Outorgas de Radiodifusão no Brasil – uma breve análise*, Consultoria Legislativa, Câmara dos Deputados (2009).

must be an alternation of members of its governing body; and they cannot be under any sort of supervision or subordination to another public or private entity. Also, their directors must be residents in the area of the community served.

292. Community broadcasters must establish a Community Council, composed of at least five people representing entities of the local community (such as class associations, benefactors, religious or residents, as long as legally established). This body shall be responsible for following up on the broadcaster's programming, in view of assuring that it meets the exclusive interest of the community and the principles that found the existence of community broadcasters.

293. When an entity that meets these criteria wants to provide community broadcasting services, it must address a petition to the Ministry of Communications indicating the area where they intend to provide the service, along with a technical study on the local infrastructure conditions. Once this documentation has been analysed, the Ministry can publish an open call for all entities interested in providing the service in the same area. Candidates must present: their constitutive documentation; declarations of each director, committing to the faithful fulfilment of the norms established for the service; manifesto in support of the initiative, formulated by community associations and entities, legally constituted and headquartered in the area intended for the provision of the service, and signed by natural or legal persons that have residence, domicile or headquarters in that area. If only one entity qualifies for the provision of the service and the presented documentation is in order, the Ministry of Communications will grant the authorization; if there are more qualified entities, the same authority shall support and promote an understanding between them, aiming at an association. If this initiative is not successful, the Ministry shall proceed with the choice of the entity, taking into account the criterion of representativeness, as per the manifestations of support sent by members of the community. Community broadcasting license cannot be granted to entities providing any other modality of broadcasting service or electronic communications (or to entities whose members and directors participate in such companies).

294. Authorization for the exploitation of community broadcasting services cannot be transferred under any circumstances. The entity holding this authorization may promote changes to its constitutive acts and modify the composition of its Board of Directors, without prior consent from public authorities (as long as the conditions initially required for the granting are maintained). The formation of networks for exploitation of the community broadcasting service is prohibited, except in situations of war, public calamity and epidemics, as well as the mandatory transmissions of the Executive, Judiciary and Legislative Powers defined in laws.

§3. Programme Standards

295. With regard to programming standards, once again the applicable legal framework varies according to the different types of grants (commercial, educational, community). These differences accrue in great part from two factors: the legal nature of each type of broadcaster and the Brazilian tradition of regulating freedom of expression.

296. In the first place, each type of broadcaster is established with different purposes and ruled by specific principles, which can be linked to the nature of the content they transmit. Educational and community broadcasters are bound by special legal regimes and constitutional requirements that are translated into content standards – that is to say, the content they transmit must abide by the public interest that justified the grant of the electromagnetic spectrum to these broadcasters in the first place. As per commercial broadcasters, the free-market competition logic that marks its grant-awarding process is also reflected in content regulation standards, since, as we will further discuss, these agents are not bound to the same sort of requirements as are applicable to the other ones. Even though in other experiences this sort of commercial grant does not necessarily exclude the possibility of programming standards regulation, this is how the Brazilian framework was deployed (despite overarching constitutional rules that also encompass these services). In this sense, this regulatory tendency can also be interpreted as a reflection of the country's free speech tradition (*see* Part I above), based on the constitutional prohibition of previous control over content and *ex post* remedy of speech abuses (enshrined by the 1988 Constitution after decades of authoritarian control over journalistic and broadcasting companies due to institutionalized censorship imposed by the military regime).

297. The most significant content requirement for commercial broadcasting refers to the limits for advertisement slots (which cannot occupy more than 25% of the airtime) and the stipulation that at least 5% of the grid must be filled with news programmes and five hours per week of educational programmes. For radio broadcasters only, there is also a daily obligation to air the 'Voz do Brasil'.

298. For educational broadcasters, the nature of their activities inspired stricter legal obligations regarding content. According to Inter-ministries Ordinance 651/1999, their programming must be fully dedicated to 'educational-cultural content', understood to mean the works that represent or complement educational systems (including basic and higher education, as well as job training), and that promote educational, cultural, pedagogical activities, as well as professional guidance. Article 2 of the Ordinance expressly provides that recreational, informational or sports-related programmes may be considered educational-cultural if they are presented through instructive elements, or other sorts of educational or cultural approaches.

299. Community broadcasters' programming is also subject to specific requirements, notably the ones provided by Law 9.612/1998 and regulated in Ordinance

ANATEL 4.334/2015. The latter's Article 103 establishes that in order to comply with these conditions, community broadcasters must: disseminate and stimulate the production of local content; promote cultural, sporting, leisure or any other events related to the formation and integration of the community; give preference to or prioritize programmes that allow the participation of listeners; report facts of local public interest, such as traffic, weather conditions or warnings and reports from public authorities; create internship and voluntary service programmes; promote debates and lectures on topics of local public interest; develop activities that allow integration between the local community and the community broadcaster, encouraging the adhesion of new members; inform the community, notably during its programming, of its condition of community broadcaster; and inform the listeners of the right that assists any citizen of the benefited community to issue opinions on any matters addressed in the broadcaster's programming, as well as expressing ideas, proposals, suggestions, complaints or claims, upon request forwarded to the entity's management.

300. Overarching constitutional provisions that apply to all three types of broadcasters include the freedom of expression guarantees (Article 5, IV and IX) and Article 221 of the Constitution that binds them to educational, artistic and cultural purposes, promotion of regional and independent content and respect for 'family and ethical values'. These provisions remain unregulated in great part, especially in what applies to commercial TV. Legislation does not provide concrete parameters for the fulfilment of these requirements, even though compliance with these demands is one of the conditions for grant renewal. In this sense, Jonas Valente highlights that not only there is no regulation that translates these principles into measures to be taken by broadcasters but also the whole process of grant renewal does not include any assessment of these standards (as it could, for instance, promote public audiences where civil society and different actors could contribute to the analysis of compliance with these constitutional standards).[195]

301. Other extensive requirements can be found in national legislation, including, e.g., juvenile and child protection-related duties (item Part III, Chapter 1, §3, III below) and the accessibility rules established in Law 13.146/2015 (whose Article 67 states that television broadcasting services must allow the use of accessibility resources, which may consist of hidden subtitles, side window with sign language interpreters and audio-description).

I. Impartiality

302. There are no statutory obligations expressively requiring that commercial and educational broadcasters present information impartially. Even though they are bound to the right to reply regulation (as well all types of broadcasters – *see* Part III, Chapters 1–3), which provides obligations and standards when presenting alternative versions of a fact, this right only produces information pluralism effects when

195. Jonas Valente, *Regulação Democrática dos meios de comunicação* (Coleção O Que Saber 2013).

somebody expressly exercises it. This means that there is no obligation to follow impartiality standards within the programming organically.

303. For Community TVs, Ordinance ANATEL 4.334/2015 sets out a few standards that relate to impartiality, mostly expressed by the prohibition of 'proselytism' – a term that in Brazilian Portuguese broadly refers to the employment of efforts and argumentation with the goal of converting individuals to a certain religion, ideology, cult, or political view (among others). Article 102 forbids community broadcasters 'any kind of proselytism', stating that their programming must reflect the plurality of ideas and opinions through the dissemination of different interpretations on controversial topics. For the purposes of this rule, the term is defined by Article 7, IV, according to which it encompasses 'any activist efforts that, through the programming of the community broadcaster, aims to get followers for a doctrine, philosophy, religion or ideology'.

II. Cultural Diversity

304. Cultural diversity is an overarching constitutional requirement (as per Article 221's guideline regarding the promotion of national and regional culture and encouragement of independent production), which is often replicated by legislation as a principle or purpose to be pursued. Nevertheless, there is little to no regulation detailing how private broadcasters should comply with it, i.e., what is it that national and regional culture means and in what proportion or form should it be promoted (this regulation is far more advanced for national funding and development purposes and for Pay-TV regulation, as it will be further described).

305. Among the three types of private broadcasters, the commercial and educational are the furthest from a concrete framework that in fact embraces cultural diversity, as no concrete obligations of such apply. As per their nature, community broadcasters are bound by stronger obligations regarding the transmission of content that is particularly relevant to the region they serve (as mentioned above). At the same time, they do not have any obligations for assuring external diversity, in the sense that they are not obliged to present content produced in other regions that reflect diverse cultural values.

306. This critique can be better understood once we consider the model for cultural diversity regulation implemented by the Pay-TV regulation. As depicted herein below, these obligations go beyond principle-based rules, and are materialized in specific obligation to air a minimum amount of independent and regional content, within a specific timeframe.

III. Protection of Minors

307. Law 8.069/1990 (Children and Juveniles Protection Act – ECA) is the legal instrument that provides a series of norms regarding the protection of minors, among which are the procedural and substantive requirements for parental rating in different cultural and artistic manifestations (which includes not only audiovisual services but also, e.g., public spectacles and events). According to Article 76, radio and television stations will only show programmes with educational, artistic, cultural and informational purposes at the recommended time for children and juveniles, and no TV show can be presented or announced without notice of its classification. Furthermore, Article 254 established an administrative sanction of 'fine of twenty to one hundred reference wages; duplicated in the event of a repeated offense' and the possibility of a judicial authority suspending the broadcaster's programming for up to two days if they 'transmit, through radio or television, a show at a time different from that authorized or without notice of its classification'. Even though the obligation of parental rating remains applicable, this provision regarding sanctioning was declared unconstitutional by the STF and is no longer valid, as we will later describe.

308. The governmental authority responsible for enforcing parental ratings is the Ministry of Justice, which does so through its Ordinance 1.189/2018 and its 'Practical Guide on Parental Rating' (containing recommendations and instructions for different agents on how to rate the content they produce). According to these rules, TV shows must present parental rating in two forms during a work's transmission: the first one is at the beginning of the programme, in the form of what the norms calls a 'complete display' (consists of the presentation of the indicative rating information at the bottom of the projection area or in full screen before the programme starts, containing age group symbol, respecting the colour and format specified in the guide). The second form is a summary display that must take place on the return of the intervals (consisting of the presentation of the classification symbol indicative, for at least five consecutive seconds, in the first thirty seconds after the break). The guide also establishes content classification according to each age range.

309. According to the Ministry of Justice's instructions, parental rating in broadcasting services can be previously determined by the Ministry of Justice upon request of the television channel, or broadcasters can proceed with self-rating its content, in which case it can later be verified by the Ministry. Regardless of the chosen method, the broadcasters must submit a registration petition with the Ministry regarding content rating, which can be done electronically. This petition must include a digital video copy and a synopsis of the work, proof of tax payments, and the broadcaster's documentation. Ratings done upon request shall be enacted by the Ministry of Justice between 30 and 120 days, depending on the extension of the product, according to Ordinance MJ nº1.189/2018, and publish in the *Brazilian Official Journal.* Self-rating will be confirmed or altered up to 60 days after the show airs.

310. As per the original provisions of the ECA, broadcasters that do not comply with parental rating guidelines could be subject to financial sanctions and even suspension of broadcasting; however, Brazil's Constitutional Court invalidated this provision. Lawsuit ADI 2.404[196] was filed at STF (the Constitutional Court) by the Brazilian Workers Party (Partido Trabalhista Brasileiro – PTB) in 2001, arguing the unconstitutionality not of the obligation to abide by parental rating, but of the sanctions provided in Article 254 in case the TV show is transmitted at a time other than the authorized. As per their claim, the Constitution does not authorize legislation to turn what is an indicative or informative classification into an act of permission or authorization, by creating prohibitions on airing content and imposing penalties.

311. The Justices started deliberating on the case in 2011, with rapporteur Justice Dias Toffoli and other three Justices voting in favour of the unconstitutionality claim, only for the trial to be then interrupted for almost five years. The trial was resumed in 2016, when the STF held the original claim and declared this provision unconstitutional. The decision was anchored on a literal interpretation of the constitutional texts that reads 'indicative' or 'informative' as a characteristic of parental rating. According to the decision's wording, the Constitution itself outlined the rules for weighing between the values of freedom of expression in the media and the protection of children and adolescents, by laying out the Federal Government's competence to 'exercising the classification, for indicative effect, of public spectacles and of radio and television programs'.

312. According to the Court's interpretation, the Charter established a mechanism capable of offering viewers of public entertainment and of radio and television programmes the necessary indications, information and recommendations about content. In this sense, the classification of audiovisual products seeks to clarify, inform and indicate to parents the existence of inappropriate content for children and teenagers. Since the exercise of freedom of programming by broadcasters prevents the prohibition of showing a particular content or conditioning it to state approval, the submission to the Ministry of Justice was interpreted by the Court as an administrative competence, i.e., to classify content for indicative purposes (an act not to be confused with licences or authorization). Thus, there would be no such thing as a time-schedule that was authorized, but only a recommendation.

313. Furthermore, the Court's decision highlighted that eventual abuses would always be under judicial scrutiny and that verified infractions or damages to the children's rights are still subject to civil and criminal prosecution, as well as damage reparations. In this sense, the Constitution also provides that federal legislation shall 'establish legal means that guarantee the person and family the possibility of defending themselves against programs or radio and television programs that contradict the provisions of Art. 221' (Article 220, §3, II).

314. While the parental rating obligations are still in place (i.e., content must still be rated according to a recommendation related to age), the decision gave broadcasters more freedom to show programmes at different times schedules, as long as they abide by the classification standards.

---

196. STF, ADI 2.404, tried on 31/08/2016. Available at: https://portal.stf.jus.br/processos/detalhe.asp?incidente=1902202 (accessed 15 Apr. 2022).

315. The National Child and Juvenile Rights Council referred to the ruling as 'a serious setback', which 'violates the guarantee of absolute priority for the rights of children and adolescents, as well as international commitments assumed by the Brazilian State'.[197] In its statement, the Council defends the schedule limitation of audiovisual content according to the parental rating system for a series of reasons, among which are: the fact that this mechanism guarantees the effectiveness of the parental rating policy system, since parents and guardians are not always at the side of children and adolescents to recommend or not the audience for a certain radio or television programme; and the difference in time zones in the Brazilian territory should also have been taken into consideration, as there is a risk that the media will stop adjusting their schedules to local time, resulting in children from states located in different time zones would be under greater vulnerability; audiovisual content, especially aired through broadcasting services, have a special influence on their development, which is why the attention and concern with such aspects is extremely relevant; and the indicative classification policy and its mechanism of time slots are in accordance with the pillars of the rights of children and adolescents, insofar as they recognize the peculiar stage of development of this public in favour of their best interest, emphasizing their full protection and putting their rights first.[198]

316. In addition, the Council also registered the importance of dissociating parental rating public policies from mechanisms of violation of freedom of expression that have long allowed for the implementation of institutional censorship – a claim that has also been made by the specialized literature.[199] To that effect, these policies are not aimed at prohibiting the transmission of content, or even submitting it to previous control; their main goal is to indicate an appropriate time for display, considering the requirements of child protection legislation and of the Constitution itself. Even though the interpretation of the constitutional provision can vary – and in this sense, the STF has decided for a different one – express and detailed regulation in this sense should not be mistaken for arbitrariness (especially considering that communication vehicles themselves can also self-classify their content, with monitoring by society and the competent authorities).

317. It is worth highlighting that, outside programming and parental ratings, another important issue concerning the *intersection minors v. media* is children's artistic participation in the production of content. As 'child labour' is prohibited by Brazilian law,[200] the performance of children in audiovisual works, shows and spectacles, cannot have features of a work relationship, but as mere 'participation'.

---

197. Conselho Nacional dos Direitos da Criança e do Adolescente, *Nota pública sobre a decisão do STF que pôs fimà vinculação horária da classificação indicativa*, available at: https://www.gov.br/mdh/pt-br/sdh/noticias/2016/setembro/nota-publica-sobre-a-decisao-do-stf-que-pos-fim-a-vinculacao-horaria-da-classificacao-indicativa-artigo-254-do-eca (accessed 10 Feb. 2021).
198. *Ibid.*
199. Jane Reis Pereira, *Classificação indicativa e vinculação de horários na programação da TV: a força das imagens e o poder das palavras*, 38 Revista da SJRJ, 169–197 (2013).
200. ECA, Art. 60.

While this relationship type does not prevent such participation from being paid, it does have a number of practical consequences, such as reduced daily availability, and compatibility with school routines.

318. There are several provisions in the Brazilian legislation that aim to protect and safeguard children in view of their physical and psychological maturity stage – this is the so-called principle of integral protection of minors adopted in Brazil.[201] From this substrate, the ECA determines that there are places and situations, including participation in film shootings, in which the child's participation needs to be previously assessed by the children's court. Thus, in the form of Article 149 of the ECA, children's participation in audiovisual works must be submitted to the scrutiny of the children's court with territorial jurisdiction over the area in which the filming will take place, under penalty of a fine. Once the request has been made, the public prosecutor's office and the children's court judge will assess, in the manner outlined in II, §1 of the aforementioned Article 149, the risks to the child's physical and psychological integrity. If the request is approved, a 'child participation permit' will be granted. According to regional rules applicable in the territory of the competent court, if the participation is paid, all or part of the remuneration due must then be credited to a savings account in the name of the minor.

IV. Human Dignity

319. Regarding the protection of human dignity, all broadcasters are submitted, first and foremost, to the mechanisms aiming at fighting abuses of the right to freedom of expressions that are in place in the Brazilian legal order. This system speaks to the constitutional prohibition of censorship or previous control over content, from which accrues the maxima that abuses to freedom of expression will be addressed *ex post.*

320. As described in Part I of this monograph, these mechanisms encompass civil and criminal liability in the face of conducts pre-established in the legislation (e.g., libel and defamation). This is particularly relevant for fighting abuses regarding human dignity since the sanctions applicable to such conducts can be increased in the face of predetermined circumstances – such as content directed at one's race, ethnicity, religion, origin, elderly or disabled condition.

321. Until 2017, Decree 88.066/1983 expressly prohibited the transmission of programmes that attack the public sentiment, exposing people to situations that, to different degrees, result in embarrassment, even if the original programme had journalistic characteristics. The Decree was revoked in 2017, but before that, it served as the basis for judicial actions against commercial broadcasters for harming human dignity in aired TV shows. One famous case is the 2005 collective action filed by the public prosecution of São Paulo and a series of civil society organizations that

201. ECA, Art. 1.

challenged the commercial broadcaster 'RedeTV!'. The channel was accused of airing an afternoon TV show marked by misogyny, homophobia and prejudice against people with disabilities.[202] After disobeying a series of decisions that ruled in favour of the plaintiffs (determining measures like financial compensation, rights of reply to human rights and LGBT rights advocacy organizations and even the ceasing of transmissions), the broadcaster formed an agreement with the public prosecution.[203] As per the agreement's terms, the broadcaster had to air thirty editions of a programme produced by human rights organizations, containing educational and cultural content. The broadcaster was forbidden to sell advertisements during these transmissions and forced to pay BRL 200,000 for the production of these programmes. In addition, the company committed to depositing BRL 400,000 in a fund for the Defence of Diffuse Rights. The daily fine for non-compliance with the agreement was set at BRL 50,000. In addition, RedeTV! Committed to no longer airing 'pranks' with homophonic, racist and misogynist content, or directing offences at the elderly, children or people with disabilities. Eventually, the agreement resulted in the termination of the afternoon TV show that had given rise to the legal action.

202. Bel Mercês, Cristina Charão, Daniele Ricieri, Diogo Moyses, Michelle Prazeres, *'A Sociedade ocupa a TV: o caso de Direitos de Resposta e o controle público da mídia'*, Intervozes (2007). Available at: https://www.intervozes.org.br/arquivos/interliv005asotvdr.pdf. Accessed on: 17 Dec. 2020.

203. Leonardo Fuhrman, *Ministério Público faz acordo com RedeTV! e encerra litígio*, Conjur (2005). Available at: http://www.conjur.com.br/2005-nov-16/acordo_entre_mpf_redetv_livra_joao_kleber. Accessed on: 17 Dec. 2020.

Chapter 2. Public Service Broadcasting

§1. The Concept and Mission of Public Service Broadcasting

322. The EBC (in English 'Brazilian Communications Company') is a federal public company created by Law 11.652/2008, which also established the principles and objectives for public service broadcasting in Brazil. Since the promulgation of the 1988 Federal Constitution, there had been no further implementation or considerable investment in public broadcasting services, which means that EBC was a long-awaited regulation of the triparty broadcasting constitutional system. In 2017, its structure was significantly modified by Law 13.417/2017, through a reform process that many argue altered its public character, notably by altering governance mechanisms.

323. EBC was created with an intent similar to that of public broadcasting systems implemented in other countries. Specifically, it sought to strengthen democracy in Brazil by adding another voice to the public discourse.[204] Even though it is owned by state entities, EBC is rooted in the idea of an independent public broadcaster – that is, one whose activities and governance are guided by the public interest, and not by the governmental one. In this sense, its creation is commonly referenced as a way to fill an existing gap in constitutional norms that assured the complementarity between the public, the private and the state-owned systems of communication.[205] That is because commercial and state broadcasting had long been implemented and regulated, which was not the case for a public system of broadcasting, driven by institutional independence and the duty to reflect society's plurality. As will be further described, the key institutional aspect for the pursuance of the public interest was originally the participation of society in its governance structure, combined with financial independency and programming requirements.

324. Until the 2017 reforms, its creation was deemed to be the inauguration of a new stage in the public communication system. Unlike in previous times, now the institutional framework included a platform marked by management, financing, production and diffusion of content meant to expand the public debate and the participation of society in mass communications.[206]

325. According to Article 2 of Law 11.652/2008, the Brazilian public service broadcasting must abide by the following principles: complementarity between the private, public and state systems; promoting access to plural information; content production and programming must seek educational, artistic, cultural, scientific and informational purposes; promotion of national culture, stimulation of regional and

204. OECD, *Telecommunication and Broadcasting Review of Brazil*, 215 (2020).
205. Media Ownership Monitor – Brazil, Empresa Brasil de Comunicação – EBC | Media Ownership Monitor (mom-rsf.org).
206. Diolinda Madrilena Feitosa Silva & Maria Cristina Gobbi, *Cenários e desafios da digitalização para as TVs públicas*, in Maria Cristina Gobbi & Maria Teresa Miceli Kerbauy, *Televisão digital: informação e conhecimento*, 186 (Scielo Books 2010).

independent production; respect for the ethical and social values; non-discrimination regarding religion, political party, philosophy, ethnicity, gender or sexual orientation; autonomy (in relation to the Federal Government) in decision regarding production, programming and distribution of content; and participation of civil society in controlling the observance of these principles and the respect for plurality.

326. As per its objectives, Article 3 establishes a series of overarching obligations to such public broadcasters, such offering mechanisms for public debate on topics of national and international relevance, developing people's critical awareness through educational, artistic, cultural, informative, scientific and citizenship-promoting programmes and promoting the construction of citizenship, the consolidation of democracy and participation in society. They are bound to cooperate with educational and training activities, support processes of social inclusion and socialization of knowledge production, guarantee spaces for the exhibition of regional and independent content. Obligations regarding production activities include: seeking excellence in content and language and developing creative and innovative formats; becoming a centre for innovation and talent training; directing production and programming towards educational, artistic, cultural, informational, scientific and citizenship-promotion purposes (without waiving its competitive character in the search for the interest of the largest number of listeners or viewers); promoting partnerships and national audiovisual production; stimulating the production and ensure the transmission, including on the world wide web, of interactive contents, especially those aimed at universalizing the provision of public services.

327. EBC describes its mission as commitment to public communication, expressed in 'content independency, ethics, transparency and participatory management', along with 'defence of human rights, freedom of expression and the exercise of citizenship', 'value [of] people and Brazilian cultural and regional diversity'.

328. The creation of EBC can be interpreted as an attempt to democratize the Brazilian broadcasting system, which has been traditionally marked by economic concentration and privilege of private interests. As narrated by Jonas Valente, the initiative was one of the products of the discussions that took place at the National Forum for Public TVs that happened between 2006 and 2007. After participants strongly flagged the necessity of balancing the broadcasting landscape, the Federal Government (then headed by President Luís Inácio Lula da Silva) approved Executive Order 387/2007, which combined three already existing broadcasting companies operated by the Federal Government. This reunion created what is now EBC, and the Executive Order was later ratified by the National Congress and sanctioned as Law 11.652/2008.[207]

---

207. Jonas Valente, *Regulação Democrática dos meios de comunicação*, 50 (Coleção O Que Saber 2013).

329. EBC encompasses all public broadcasting services that are provided by the Federal Government (which includes radio and television services), as well as competences related to federal government communications. The public broadcasting services include TV Brasil (a public broadcasting television network formed by the merger of TV Educativa do Maranhão, TV Nacional de Brasilia, and TV Educativa do Rio de Janeiro), Radioagência Nacional, Rádio Nacional AM do Rio de Janeiro (1,130 KHz), Rádio Nacional AM de Brasília (980 KHz), Nacional FM de Brasília (96.1 MHz), Rádio MEC AM do Rio de Janeiro (800 KHz), MEC FM do Rio de Janeiro (99.3 MHz), Rádio Nacional da Amazônia OC (11,780 KHz e 6,180 KHz), Rádio Nacional AM do Alto Solimões (670 KHz) e Rádio Nacional FM do Alto Solimões (96.1 MHz).[208]

330. Despite being a public service broadcaster, since the beginning of its operation, EBC also encompasses federal government communication channels – namely, the NBR (a cable channel reporting on the actions and policies of the Federal Government) – and it operates the radio programme 'A Voz do Brasil'[209] (earlier referenced as the mandated slots for governmental content in radio services). As it will be further described in the next section, the public broadcaster's proximity to governmental interests has always given cause for concern regarding the company's claimed independency. In fact, the mix of its public and governmental function became even more controversial as a 2017 law changed its governance structure and more recently, the NBR channel was shut down and merged with TV Brasil.

331. Regarding these entities and their services, EBC is responsible for operating all their broadcasting activities, which includes (Article 8 of Law 11.652/2008): managing their use of infrastructure; establishing cooperation and collaboration initiatives with public or private entities that operate communication or public broadcasting services, aiming at forming the National Public Communication Network; and producing and disseminating informational, educational, artistic, cultural, scientific, citizenship and recreation programmes. Furthermore, EBC is also responsible for promoting and stimulating the training of specialized personnel that is necessary for radio broadcasting, communication and related services, providing services in the field of broadcasting, communication and related services (including the transmission of official events and communication from the Federal Government); airing legal advertising of public bodies and entities of the federal administration; and to guarantee the minimum of 10% of regional content and 5% of independent content during its weekly broadcasts.

§2. The Organization of Public Service Broadcasting

332. EBC is organized as a state-owned corporation of closed capital, represented by ordinary nominative shares, of which at least 51% must be owned by the

208. As listed in EBC's website on April 2022. Available at: https://www.ebc.com.br/.
209. Ivonete da Silva Lopes, *Political Culture and the Democratization of Communications in Brazil*, 198 Latin American Perspectives, 5, 129–140 (2014).

Federal Government. Entities of the federal indirect administration, as well as of states, the Federal District and Municipalities (or entities of their indirect administration) shall participate in owning the remaining 49%.

333. State-owned companies are conventionally part of the indirect public administration. But regardless of being state owned, EBC was meant to be an independent broadcaster, which would be assured by a governance system driven by the public interest through societal participation, as well as programming in accordance with constitutional standards.[210] This system was altered by Law 13,417/2017, in a sense that affects its original characteristics. In the following paragraphs, we will describe both the system that was approved at first and the one that is currently in force.

334. Law 11,652/2008 originally provided one Administrative Council (formed by representatives of federal government entities, appointed by the President) and one Curator Committee – where civil society participation was secured. The latter was formed by twenty-two members, four of which were appointed by federal ministers, two representatives of Parliament, one representative appointed by EBC's employees, and fifteen members were representatives of civil society (to be nominated by the President). The competences of the Curator Committee were intrinsically related to editorial and governance guidelines. These guidelines include: deliberating on the educational, artistic, cultural and informational guidelines included in the communication policy proposed by the EBC Executive Board; to ensure compliance with the principles and objectives provided in Law 11.652/2008 and provide opinions on matters related to the principles; to deliberate on the editorial line of production and programming proposed by the EBC Executive Board and express its opinion on its practical application; to forward its resolutions to the Social Communication Council (*see* Part V); and to deliberate on 'confidence votes' regarding the members of the Executive Board. Members of the Curator Committee had either two- or four-year fixed mandates.

335. Law 11.652/2008 also laid out the rules for a Board of Directors, headed by the President of EBC, all with four-year fixed mandates (which meant they could only be removed from their position in cases previously provided by the legislation and according to a voting process that involved the Curator Committee).

336. By the time of EBC's creation, this arrangement was already criticized for its deference to the Presidency. Miriam Wimmer, for instance, highlighted the independency limitations accruing from the fact that representatives of civil society were supposed to be appointed by the President.[211] In a similar sense, Eugenio Bucci stressed that the administrative link to the Presidency's press office also diminished EBC's independency from government, inappropriately mixing it with

210. Miriam Wimmer, *Direitos, Democracia e Acesso aos Meios de Comunicação de Massa*, 245 (2012).
211. *Ibid.*

state propaganda institutions[212] – a concern that would prove to be ever more pertinent as EBC's structure started to be altered.

337. In 2016, shortly after succeeding impeached President Dilma Rousseff, President Michel Temer led a series of changes to the EBC governance structure, initially implemented through Executive Order 744/2016, and later sanctioned by National Congress into Law 13.417/2017.[213] The new rules included the possibility of the President dismissing the Director of EBC without any constrictions, and the replacement of the Curator Committee with an Editorial and Programming Committee.

338. As per the terms of Law 13.417/2017, EBC's Editorial and Programming Council (which replaced the Curator Council) is a technical body of consultative and deliberative nature, formed by eleven members, to be shortlisted by representatives of sectors and appointed by the President, including: a representative from broadcasting companies; a representative of higher education courses in Social Communication; a representative of the independent audiovisual sector; a representative of the legislative means of communication; a representative of the cultural community; a representative of the scientific and technological community; a representative of entities that defend the rights of children and adolescents; a representative of entities that defend human rights and minorities; a representative of civil society entities defending the right to Communication; a representative of higher education courses; a representative of EBC employees. The remarkable difference here is the reduction of civil society participation in the body that deliberates over content guidelines – while the former Curator Council had twenty-two seats, fifteen of which were occupied by civil society representatives, the present Editorial and Programming Council has eleven seats, of which only one is reserved for a representative of said entities.

339. The role played by this Council was also shrunk. While the Law provided eight lines of action for the former Council, the present one is based on only three, namely: to propose the expansion of space, within EBC's programming, for content focused on the role and importance of public media; to develop a mechanism that allows the permanent assessment of EBC's audience, through the construction of indicators and metrics consistent with the nature and objectives of public broadcasting (all while considering the peculiarities of the reception of signals and regional differences); and to prepare and approve its internal regulations and elect its President.

340. The new law also increased presidential control over EBC's corporate administration bodies. It extinguished the guarantee of a four-year tenure to the

212. Eugênio Bucci, *O Estado de Narciso: a comunicação pública a serviço da vaidade particular*, 114 (Companhia das Letras 2015).

213. *See* Luciene Pazinato da Silva & Vera Michalany Chaia, *A descaracterização da Empresa Brasileira de Comunicação – EBC com o fim do Conselho Curador*, in Edwaldo Costa, *Tecnologia e Estéticas da Comunicação no Brasil* (Atena 2020).

director-president position, a position that under current rules is freely nominated and can be dismissed by the President of the Republic (which harms the company's autonomy and management continuity). It also increased the participation of the government in EBC's administration Council. It now has six seats occupied by government representatives, instead of the former four nominations, which increases the subordination of the company to the interests of government.

341. Furthermore, in 2019, Decree 9.660/2019 submitted EBC to the supervision of the Special Secretary of Communications of the Presidency – bringing the company and its apparatus even closer to the centre of federal government. In the same year, EBC had already merged its main TV channel (TV Brasil) with TV NBR (the Federal Government's cable channel). It should be noted that this merger was challenged by the Federal Prosecutor's Office (Ministério Público Federal – MPF) regarding its constitutionality. The institution argued that this move was likely to harm the separation between commercial, public and governmental broadcasting regimes, as provided by the Federal Constitution, along with social participation and plurality of views displayed through the Public Service Broadcaster.[214]

342. The OECD Report 'Telecommunication and Broadcasting Review of Brazil' reinforces the interpretation that these changes reduced the independence of EBC, placing it directly under the control of the Presidency.[215] Civil society stakeholders, journalists and EBC employees criticized these measures for undermining the editorial autonomy of company and thus eroding the independency from government, a public interest prerogative that inspires the foundations of public service broadcasting all over the world.

§3. The Financing of Public Service Broadcasting

343. Overall, one can assume that EBC's financing model relies mostly on the Federal Government's budget, institutional advertising and on the Contribution for the Promotion of Public Broadcasting (CFRP).[216] CFRP is a federal tax of the species CIDE (Contribution for Intervention in the Economic Domain), whose objective it to finance the improvement and expansion of public broadcasting services. As we will describe, this Contribution plays a pivotal role in assuring the means to sustain EBC's financial independence – which in turn is an essential condition for freedom of programming and independent journalism.[217]

214. OECD, *Telecommunication and Broadcasting Review of Brazil*, 216 (2020). *See also*: http://pfdc.pgr.mpf.mp.br/atuacao-e-conteudos-de-apoio/oficios/oficio-127-2019-pfdc-mpf/view.
215. OECD, *Telecommunication and Broadcasting Review of Brazil*, 216 (2020).
216. Jonas Valente, *Regulação Democrática dos meios de comunicação*, 55 (Coleção O Que Saber 2013).
217. Murilo César Ramos, *A Contribuição para o Fomento da Radiodifusão Pública e o paradoxo de financiar o NBR* (17 Apr. 2019), https://teletime.com.br/17/04/2019/a-contribuicao-para-o-foment o-da-radiodifusao-publica-e-o-paradoxo-de-financiar-o-nbr/.

344. Article 11 of Law 11.652/2007 details a series of different sources of income that are a part of EBC's budget. They include: governmental budget allocations; the exploitation of public broadcasting services referred to in this Law; provision of services to public or private entities, content distribution, programming models, licensing of brands and products and other activities inherent to its communication services; donations, subsidies and other resources allocated to it by individuals, public or private entities; cultural support from public and private law entities, in the form of sponsorship of programmes, events and projects; institutional advertising by public and private entities (while advertisement of products or services remains prohibited); resources obtained through legal mechanisms for cultural and audiovisual funding and development; funds from agreements and covenants concluded with public and private national and international entities; financial investments; other sources of income, provided that they do not compromise the principles and objectives of public broadcasting. Last and foremost, EBC shall be funded by at least 75% of the values collected through the CFRP (as per Article 32).

345. The CFRP is due on an annual basis by the service providers listed in Law 11.652/2008 which includes mobile and other telecommunications operators, different sorts of radio broadcasters (medium, short and modulated frequency waves), television broadcasters and Pay-TV operators, among others. The law also provides that the totality of resources collected through this contribution should be used exclusively for the improvement of public broadcasting services and the expansion of its penetration through the use of telecommunications services (something which is not entirely done through EBC). The Telecommunications Federal Agency (Agência Nacional de Telecomunicações – ANATEL) is responsible for planning, enforcing, monitoring and evaluating taxation, inspection and collection of the contribution (for which is entitled to 2.5% of the amount collected).

346. The constitutionality of this Contribution was under dispute for several years. In 2013, the Association for Telecommunication Operators (Sinditelebrasil) filed a lawsuit against its collection by arguing that such category of tax should directly benefit the economic sector which bears its cost. That is to say, according to Sinditelebrasil, telecommunications operators submitted to the CFRP do not benefit in any way from the improvement and expansion of public service broadcasting. The eighth Panel of the first Federal Court of Appeals (Tribunal Regional Federal 1 – 8a Turma) has decided against this reasoning, stating that: the CFRP's ultimate goal is to guarantee 'the right of access to educational information, as a corollary of freedom of expression of thought';[218] telecommunication operators do benefit from carrying the content that is generated by EBC; and that CFRP aims to assert the educational nature of the broadcasting media, to be guaranteed through state intervention and funded by the resources collected from companies that benefit from the broadcasting system. This decision can be interpreted as a validation

218. Gustavo Schneider Fossati, *Public Broadcast contribution: an Analysis in the light of the recent decision of the German STF*, Revista do Direito, 1, 57, 22–42, 32 (2019).

of the importance of public broadcasting, as well as of the possibility of funding it via CIDE, as a way to justify state intervention in media-related economic sectors.[219]

347. Although the Contribution is still in place, it is worth noticing that the recent changes to EBC's structure might add different layers to this legal dispute and shift the preponderant legal interpretation. As highlighted by Murilo Cesar Ramos, as EBC becomes more and more entrenched in the Federal Government, its public interest character shifts further into that of a governmental institution. This could potentially weaken the public interest claim that sustains its collection of the Contribution, as there is little to no legitimate justification for the private sector to fund a governmental media operation.[220]

348. Against this background, the recent OECD Report on the Brazilian Telecommunications framework has also stressed that EBC lacks stable funding and that 'the public service broadcasting system should not be subject to inappropriate financial or political pressures in its editorial decisions'. Among other governance limiting aspects, the absence of stable funding is considered by the OECD as one of the reasons why EBC 'has never been resourced at the level needed to fulfil its full potential'.[221]

349. In fact, OECD's final assessment of the Brazilian public broadcasting system is highly influenced by both the recent changes in governance mechanisms and in the absence of consistent and independent funding. The report states that:

> [i]n comparison to OECD countries, Brazil lags behind in terms of funding, staffing and editorial independence of its public broadcasting system. A strong national public broadcaster can promote media pluralism and can help provide national, regional and municipal content that may not be commercially viable. As in many countries, trustworthy public journalism is at risk. Public service broadcasting could provide an important, independent voice in FTA broadcasting. However, two factors have weakened the public service broadcasting system in the country. First, Brazil lacks a co-ordinated public policy concerning FTA broadcasting. Second, the governance and structure of the principal public system broadcaster in Brazil – EBC – have recently changed. Ensuring the full editorial independence of EBC from the government would entail reversing the 2016-17 reforms. More funding would allow Brazil to guarantee the independence of EBC (or an equivalent new entity).[222]

---

219. *Ibid.*
220. Murilo César Ramos, *A Contribuição para o Fomento da Radiodifusão Pública e o paradoxo de financiar o NBR* (17 Apr. 2019), https://teletime.com.br/17/04/2019/a-contribuicao-para-o-fomento-da-radiodifusao-publica-e-o-paradoxo-de-financiar-o-nbr/.
221. OECD, *Telecommunication and Broadcasting Review of Brazil*, 216 (2020).
222. *Ibid.*, 47.

§4. Programme Standards

350. Law 11.652/2008 established a few requirements for EBC's programming, which is also regulated by Decree 6.689/2008.[223] Both of those legal instruments reiterate constitutional provisions by stating that EBC's programming will be stirred by the public interest and thus is driven by educational, cultural, informative, artistic and pluralistic purposes. Specifically, Article 3, §1 prohibits any form of proselytism from being displayed in the programming.

351. Article 8, IX establishes that 10% of the weekly broadcasts that take place between 6AM and 12AM must display regional content, while 5% must display independent production content. The definitions for regional and independent content are further depicted in paragraph 4, I (regional content is 'content produced in a given state, with a technical and artistic team composed mostly of local residents') and II (independent content is 'content whose production company, the majority holder of the patrimonial rights on the work, does not have any association or link, direct or indirect, with sound and image broadcasting service companies or providers of electronic communications'). Moreover, paragraph 5 stipulates that EBC shall air content from the different regions of Brazil in the same proportion; while EBC's 2016 Work Plan clarifies that, for such purposes, regional content for television services encompasses productions originated outside of Brasília and the states of Rio de Janeiro and São Paulo. The 2016 Work Plan also highlights that independent content does not encompass works mostly owned by EBC, and recommends that, while determining whether a content is independent or not, the company also take into consideration proportionality of investment in the content production and participation equity.

352. EBC can air institutional publicity for public and private entities, which shall not exceed 15% of its programming (Article 11, §2); any sort of services and products advertisement is strictly forbidden (Article 11, VII). Another of its competences is to air institutional advertisement for the Federal Government's entities (Article 8, VII) – which shall be understood as publication of announcements, notices, balance sheets, reports and other forms of communication which the federal public administration is legally required to provide (Article 8, §1).

353. Furthermore, EBC's programming must transmit information contained in the database of the National Register of Missing Children and Adolescents referred to in Law No. 12.127, of 17 December 2009, including photographs of missing persons, daily, for at least one minute, between 6 PM and 10 PM.

223. For consistency purposes, in this section we will keep referencing provisions contained in Law 11.652/2008.

Chapter 3. State Service Broadcasting

§1. The Concept and Mission of State Service Broadcasting

354. The third and last part of the broadcasting system provided for by the 1988 Constitution is state broadcasting, which consists of the television channels operated by governmental institutions in all the three republican branches – executive, legislative and judiciary. Most notable examples are TV Câmara (the channel of the House of Representatives), TV Senado (Senate's channel) and TV Justiça (the channel of the judiciary branch). As we already mentioned in Chapter 2, the Federal Government broadcasters are in theory also state broadcasters, even though they are currently operated by what should be the public broadcasting structure. Within their programming, state channels can also air sessions of deliberative bodies (e.g., TV Justiça airs STF trials, and TV Câmara and TV Senado air parliamentary sessions). Even though these three notable state broadcasters are within the Federal Government, it is also possible for state and local government institutions to hold this type of licence. In this sense, regional and local legislative bodies can also have their own TV channels, which along with the federal ones (TV Câmara and TV Senado) are commonly referred to as 'legislative TVs'.[224]

355. As it is the case for many sectors of broadcasting services, state channels also suffer from the lack of a unified and consistent public policy. As mentioned previously, Article 223 of the Federal Constitution provides the complementarity among private, public and state broadcasting systems, but more specific regulation of this division is still missing. There are no express provisions on the scope and characteristics of the state broadcasting systems, which has led to some discussions about its legal treatment and distinction from the public system. Cláudia Regina Fonseca Lemos et al. *see* these discussions stemming from the fact that, for decades, public and state broadcasting in Brazil meant similar things (i.e., strongly centralized in the state).[225]

356. This muddle should no longer have a place in the Brazilian legal order, notably due to the express provision of three broadcasting systems in Article 223. Despite the lack of detailed regulation, the best interpretation of the media law instruments in force is the same as that found in specialized literature, according to which a state-run TV system is one that provides a private service for the state, with

---

224. Fernando Oliveira Paulino, *As TVs Legislativas como instrumento de promoção do pluralismo e da diversidade*, E-Legis – Revista Eletrônica do Programa de Pós-Graduação da Câmara dos Deputados, 12, 29, 21–28 (2019); Cláudia Regina Fonseca Lemos, Cristiane Brum Bernardes & Antonio Teixeira de Barros, *TV Câmara, TV pública: As TVs legislativas brasileiras na transição para a plataforma digital,* 5 (2) Observatorio (OBS*), 1–22 (2011).

225. Cláudia Regina Fonseca Lemos, Cristiane Brum Bernardes & Antonio Teixeira de Barros, *TV Câmara, TV pública: As TVs legislativas brasileiras na transição para a plataforma digital,* 5 (2) Observatorio (OBS*), 1–22 (2011).

the objective of offering the citizen informative, cultural, and educational content.[226] In this context, the state authority in charge of the grant is responsible for financing it, appointing managers and exercising control over programming,[227] from which it follows that these TV channels are not to be presumed impartial, organically diverse or necessarily reflective of civil society. On the other hand, public broadcasters are to be understood as the ones that have a greater degree of independence from the state, where editorial choices are made or influenced by civil society or multi-stakeholder decision-making processes. The idea behind it is that public broadcasting should prioritize impartial and diverse public interest agendas while being anchored in governance models that allow plural participation. In this sense, there is strong agreement that public broadcasting should be implemented independently of the government, which should not be able to interfere in the appointment of directors, nor in programming.[228] This does not mean that state broadcasters are not subject to usual constitutional requirements, or that they will not include any form of societal participation – the main factor of distinction to be considered here is the institution that controls its operation. In fact, the very creation of state broadcasters in Brazil, especially legislative channels, can be deemed as pluralism-friendly[229] or associated with social pleas for the democratization of communications.[230]

357. Even though this distinction is clearly in tune with the Federal Constitution, it should be highlighted that it is currently weakened by the changes made to EBC's structure since 2019, changes which have strengthened its relationship with and dependency on the head of the Federal Government (*see* Part III, Chapter 2 herein above).

§2. The Organization of State Service Broadcasting

358. State broadcasters are created and operated by the respective state authorities (whether federal government, judiciary or legislative bodies). Granting procedures are similar to the ones for private broadcasting, in the sense that the Ministry of Communications and the National Parliament are the main state authorities involved in the authorization process (*see* Part III, Chapter 1, §2). Correspondingly,

226. Ericsom Meister Scorsim, *O controle dos serviços públicos de radiodifusão (Rádio e Televisão) no Brasil*, Revista da Faculdade de Direito da UFPR, 34, 161–175 (2000).
227. Cláudia Regina Fonseca Lemos, Cristiane Brum Bernardes & Antonio Teixeira de Barros, *TV Câmara, TV pública: As TVs legislativas brasileiras na transição para a plataforma digital,* 5 (2) Observatorio (OBS*), 1–22 (2011).
228. *Ibid.*; Ericsom Meister Scorsim, *O controle dos serviços públicos de radiodifusão (Rádio e Televisão) no Brasil*, Revista da Faculdade de Direito da UFPR, 34, 161–175 (2000).
229. Ericsom Meister Scorsim, *Ibid.*
230. Cláudia Regina Fonseca Lemos, Cristiane Brum Bernardes & Antonio Teixeira de Barros, *TV Câmara, TV pública: As TVs legislativas brasileiras na transição para a plataforma digital,* 5 (2) Observatorio (OBS*), 1–22 (2011).

authorization to exploit equipment and spectrum exploitation is handled by the ANATEL. Most of the state TVs currently also transmit their signal onto online audiovisual platforms.

359. Management and editorial decisions are also led by employees of these authorities, who can be either hired or selected from publicly selected civil servants. In the latter case, selection of journalists and other employees through public competition processes (open to the general public and resulting in job stability) can be seen as a way to promote plurality and independence of the journalistic contents aired by these channels.[231]

§3. The Financing of State Service Broadcasting

360. Each state broadcaster is financed by the budget of the government authority responsible for its operation.

§4. Programme Standards

361. State broadcasters are submitted to the same constitutional programme requirements as private broadcasters (*see* Part III, Chapter 1, §2 herein above), as well as to overarching national legislation (e.g., minor protection and accessibility requirements). Beyond this, there is no regulatory framework generally applicable to all state broadcasters providing content standards.

362. It is interesting to notice that, originally, some state broadcasters – namely judiciary and legislative channels – had the main mission of transmitting these bodies' deliberative sessions, as a way to improve transparency in the public decision-making processes.[232] Even though these sessions are still transmitted, their programming also encompasses educational, journalistic and cultural content.

---

231. *Ibid.*
232. *Ibid.*

Chapter 4. Pay-TV

363. Pay-TV services in Brazil encompass a variety of activities that take place within the Conditional Access Service ecosystem (as in the expression in Portuguese Serviços de Acesso Condicionado (Conditional Access Services) – SeAC). SeAC is a term created by the legal diploma that unified the regulation of Pay-TV services – Law 12.485/2011. This term refers to telecommunications services intended to distribute audiovisual content to consumers against payment, employing any technology, process, electronic means and communication protocols. This includes cable, FTTH, TVA, satellite, MMDS waves and any other infrastructure that falls into this definition – except for the Internet. Throughout this monograph, the terms Pay-TV and SeAC refer to this same set of services.

364. SeAC differs from OTT distribution services, which are provided through the Internet's infrastructure. SeAC are essentially telecommunications services, which OTT services are not; in the current Brazilian framework, OTT services are considered Added Value Services (from Serviços de Valor Adicionado – SVA) and thus submitted to a different set of regulations.[233] SeAC services shall also not be confused with 'broadcasting'. As mentioned previously in this monograph, in Brazil, this term refers only to transmissions over the air, by means of radio waves, a synonym for the activities developed by concessionaires of FTA television and radio stations. None of Pay-TV operators, regardless of the infrastructure that supports their services, are considered broadcasters for any purposes.

365. The Pay-TV production chain consists of programming, packaging and distribution services. This division is provided in Article 4 of Law 12.485/2011, and it reflects the way these services have been organized since their expansion in Brazil. Overall, programming activities refer to the organization of television channels and encompasses direct production and/or acquisition of audiovisual content produced by third parties; packaging refers to the organization of channels in bundles, in order to sell them to distributors; and distribution refers to transmission to the consumers (performed by the telecommunication services operators).

366. All of these activities are addressed by the legislation in different degrees, and their main characteristics and legal obligations will be addressed in the following sections.

---

233. Brazilian Federal Law 9,472/1997 (General Telecommunications Law): Art. 61. Value-added service is the activity that adds value to the telecommunications service that supports same, and with which new features related to the access, storage, presentation, handling or recovery of information are not mistaken:

§1° Value added service is not a telecommunications service, however, the provider thereof is classified as user of the telecommunication service providing support thereto, with the rights and obligations inherent to this condition.

§2° Access to the utilization of telecommunications service networks for rendering value added services is assured to interested parties, for which the Agency shall regulate the conditions as well as organize the relationship between *same and the telecommunications service providers.*

§1. SeAC Distribution

367. According to Article 3, X of ANATEL Res. 581/2012, the distribution activity consists of 'activities of delivery, transmission, dissemination or provision of packages or audio-visual content to subscribers through any electronic means, either their own or through third parties, with the distributor having the ultimate responsibility for complementary marketing activities, customer service, billing, collection, installation and maintenance of devices, among others'. At the present moment, the telecommunications infrastructures that support the distribution of Pay-TV services in Brazil are: DTH, FTTH, TVA, cable and MMDS.

368. All of these Pay-TV distributors can be subject to technical-specific rules, depending on the type of infrastructure they are authorized to explore. Resolution ANATEL 581/2012 brings a more nuanced set of rules that considers technical differences between these infrastructures and how they can or should affect services provision. Nevertheless, there are a number of obligations accruing from the unified framework (Law 12.485/11) that apply to all of these players, notably: providers' obligation to be registered as such before ANCINE; complying with content quotas; must-carry obligations; applicable taxes; ownership limits; parental rating; and provision of blocking and filtering tools. In the next topics, we will approach the key aspects of these provisions:

(i) SeAC distributors must register with ANATEL in order to obtain an authorization to provide telecommunication services. Article 29 of Law 12.485/2011 determines that:

> Art. 29. The distribution activity through the SeAC is free for companies incorporated under Brazilian laws, with headquarters and administration in the Country, being governed by the provisions outlined in this Law, in Law nº 9.472, of July 16, Art. 1997, and in the regulation issued by the National Telecommunications Agency – Anatel.
>
> Sole paragraph. Anatel will regulate and supervise the distribution activity.

In the form of the sole paragraph of Article 29 above, ANATEL issued Res. 581/2012 (today in force under the changes introduced by Res. 717/2019 and 720/2020). Res. 581/2012 determines, among others, technical definitions related to the reception and decoding of signals, and, in particular, the parameterization for obtaining authorization from ANATEL to provide the distribution service. Specifically regarding authorization, the rules are parameterized in Res. 720/2020.
It should be highlighted that Res. 720, in its Article 3, corroborates that 'authorisations, to which the public bid is not required, will be indeed granted, as long as required in the form and conditions provided'.
As seen in Article 29 above, there is no limitation on foreign capital in the activity, nor is it necessary for SeAC distributors to participate in public bids

or to be chosen by the public administration, to the detriment of other companies, based on the qualification presented.

(ii) SeAC distributors are subject to quotas for Brazilian channels. Law 8.977/1995 and its regulatory decree 2.206/1997 had already established, in a very modest structure, quotas for the presence of channels containing Brazilian content, a specific type of content in the programming packages offered to Pay-TV subscribers. This regulation was revoked entirely by Law 12.485/2011, which established a complex quota system, under the grounds of strengthening the national audiovisual industry and promoting the Brazilian cultural diffusion and contents produced in Portuguese language. If before 2011 the quota consisted of a single channel, which could be licensed exclusively to a single distributor, as of 2011 the system became more robust, including the provision of content quotas within channel quotas, and of independent content quotas within national content quotas. It also implemented Pay-TV dictionary concepts such as 'independent Brazilian programmers',[234] 'qualified space',[235] 'qualified space channels – CAEQ',[236] 'Brazilian qualified space channels – CABEQ',[237] and 'Brazilian qualified space channels programmed by an independent company CABEQ-I' (for the definitions, please refer to the footnotes).

Under Law's 12.485/2011 quotas regulation (as per the provisions featured in the list below), distributors must observe in their programming packages minimum proportions of channels that exhibit specific characteristics:

(1) Article 16 and Article 19 §1: In CAEQ, including those offered in the separate programming mode, at least three hours and thirty minutes per week of the contents aired in the primetime[238] must be Brazilian and integrate qualified space, and an independent Brazilian producer should produce half.

(2) Article 17: For each three CAEQ in the same package, one of them must be classified as CABEQ, and such quota must be fulfilled up to (a) the

234. Law 12.485/2011, Art. 2, XXII: Brazilian programmer who meets the following requirements, cumulatively: (a) not be a parent, subsidiary or affiliated company to the packaging entity or to the distributor; (b) not maintaining an exclusive bond that prevents it from selling, to any packaging company, the exhibition rights associated with its programming channels.

235. *Ibid.*, Art. 2, XII: total airtime space of the programming channel, excluding religious or political content, sporting events and advertising, telesales, infomercials, electronic games, mandatory political propaganda, journalistic content and anchored auditorium shows.

236. *Ibid.*, Art. 2, II: programming channel that, in the primetime, exhibits mostly audiovisual content that constitutes a qualified space.

237. *Ibid.*, Art. 2, III: qualified space channel that meets the following requirements, cumulatively: (a) be programmed by a Brazilian programmer; (b) broadcast mostly, in prime time, Brazilian audiovisual content that constitutes qualified space, half of which produced by an independent Brazilian producer; (c) not be subject to exclusive agreements that prevent the programmer from selling to any interested packaging entity, its exhibition rights.

238. The regulation (IN 100, Art. 13) defines primetime as follows: (I) for the programming channels directed to children and adolescents: seven hours between 11 am and 2 pm and between 5PM and 9PM considering the official time in Brasilia; and (II) for the other programming channels: six hours between 6PM and 12AM considering the official time in Brasília.

absolute limit of twelve CABEQ or (b) three CABEQ concerning distributors that, due to technological restrictions, can only distribute up to thirty-one programming channels.

(3) Article 17, §1: For every three CABEQ in the same package, one of them must be programmed by an independent Brazilian programmer (CABEQ-I).
(4) Article 17, §4: For CABEQ distributed in the same package, at least two must transmit at least twelve hours a day of content produced by independent Brazilian producers, with a minimum of three hours in prime-time.
(5) Article 17, §5: An independent Brazilian programmer must programme 1 of the two channels mentioned in item 4 above.
(6) Article 18: In packages where a programming channel is programmed by a Brazilian programmer that mainly exhibits journalistic content during prime time, at least one additional programming channel with the same journalistic characteristics, but programmed by a different company, must be offered in the same package or on standalone sale mode (off-packages).
(7) Article 19, §2: In the programming channels offered standalone, at least 10% of the contents offered that integrate qualified space must be Brazilian.
(8) The following will not be considered for the fulfilment of quotas (Article 19): channels distributed due to must-carry obligations; FTA broadcasters' programming; channels under the responsibility of the public authorities; channels whose programming grid has not undergone any modifications to adapt to the Brazilian public, including subtitling, dubbing for Portuguese or specific advertising for the Brazilian market; channels dedicated primarily to the delivery of erotic content; standalone channels; on-demand content.
(9) Article 20: For computation purposes, at least half of the audiovisual content must have been produced in the seven years before its broadcast; the content produced by a Brazilian-born or naturalized citizen for more than ten years will be assimilated to that produced by a Brazilian producer, or an independent Brazilian producer, as the case may be.

In situations such as financial incapacity, technical limitations, scarcity of supply, among others, upon proven impossibility to comply with quotas, the distributor may submit a discharge request to ANCINE (Article 21). Quotas will be mandatory only until September 2023 (Article 41). Since the beginning of its application, undeniably, the national audiovisual production has been positioned at another level. Before the quotas, 1,707 Brazilian audiovisual works were registered with ANCINE, of which independent Brazilian producers produced only 532; one year after the quotas, 3,297 works were registered, of which independent Brazilian producers produced 1,525:[239]

---

239. Source: Observatório Brasileiro do Cinema do Audio-visual – https://oca.ancine.gov.br/mercado-audio-visual-brasileiro.

(iii) Distributors *must carry* specific TV channels, such as non-digital channels transmitted by local broadcasting services providers, state broadcasting (e.g., legislative channels), public service television, educational channels programmed by the Federal Government, university channels, and channels reserved for the executive branch (the details and extensions of these rules are further detailed in Part III, Chapter 9 below).

(iv) In terms of taxes, SeAC distributors are subject to a myriad of costs such as ICMS,[240] FUST[241] and FUNTTEL.[242] The total tax burden for telecommunications activity can reach more than 40% in some Brazilian states, besides the mandatory collection of CONDECINE (a contribution particular to audiovisual services, further approached in Part III, Chapter 9 below). On the other hand, OTT is subject only to ISS tax, which the applicable rate in some municipalities is as low as 2%.

(v) SeAC distributors are subject to ownership, control and certain rights acquisition restrictions, such as the prohibition of holding more than 30% of equity interest in broadcasting services providers, pay-TV programming entities or audiovisual producing companies, and to acquire exploitation rights concerning events of national interest (*see* Part IV for further details).

(vi) SeAC distributors will be held accountable before ANATEL if the programming entities are not exhibiting parental rating warnings before each content of their programming grids (Law 12.485/2011, at Article 11, §2).

(vii) SeAC distributors must provide tools to their subscribers in order to permit them to block any content (Law 12.485/2011, Article 11 §3).

369. Due to this regulatory framework, current discussions on the regulation of OTT services in Brazil are greatly fuelled by allegations of regulatory asymmetry. Even though there have been a few policy debates led by former governments on the regulation of VOD services, as of now, they are still unregulated, and the application of pre-existing obligations (specially CONDECINE collection and registration of agents and work before the authorities) is questionable.

§2. SEAC PACKAGING

370. The packaging activity is usually integrated with the distribution; that is, the distributors themselves are in charge of organizing the distribution packages that will be offered and distributed to the subscriber. A constraint to be observed in the integration between the activities is that the management, editorial responsibility, selection and direction activities inherent to packaging are exclusive to Brazilian-born or naturalized citizens for more than ten years (Article 10, Law 12.485/2011). The same requirement does not apply to the distribution activity.

---

240. Value-added state tax levied on sales and telecommunication services, which rate, depending on the state, varies from 25% to 37% of the good or service price.
241. Federal tax levied on telecommunication services providers' gross revenues, at the rate of 3%.
242. Federal tax levied on telecommunication services providers' gross revenues, at the rate of 0.5%.

§3. SeAC Programming

371. In addition to registering each audiovisual work (and therefore, obtaining a CRT[243]) and eventual payment of CONDECINE, works exhibited on Pay-TV must follow a specific procedure for declaring content rating with the Ministry of Justice, and the appropriate age rating for such content must be announced prior to its exhibition.[244]

243. Title Registration Certificate (from Portuguese Certificado de Registro de Título) is an official document issued by ANCINE to authorize the exhibition and exploitation of audiovisual works in television, movie theatres and other market segments. In certain legal conditions (e.g., journalistic and sports contents), obtaining the CRT is not necessary. Associated with obtaining the CRT, it will be necessary to pay the CONDECINE tax as further detailed in item Funding and development mechanisms.

244. Article 12 Law 12.485/2011 e Portaria MJ 1.189/2018.

Chapter 5. Political Broadcasting

372. For the purposes of this chapter, we understand the regulation of political broadcasting as the rules that to the different ways elected or campaigning politicians appear on or make use of broadcasting or telecommunications services. These rules are usually grounded on a series of democratic principles meant to assure, for instance, that different politicians will have equal access to communication with the public. They are also inspired by the idea that the people elected to manage public interest decisions regarding access to public communication will not take personal advantage of such position. As simple as it sounds, assuring these fundamental principles has proven to be a challenging task in different democracies. In Brazil's case, there are a series of sociopolitical peculiarities, as described in the previous chapters, that further challenge this landscape, notably: (i) the regulatory framework of the broadcasting services provision; and (ii) the historical path that led to the emergence of commercial television in Brazil, and especially how this process allowed for the concentration of grants in the hands of privileged political groups.[245]

373. In Brazil, the rules that apply to political broadcasting are strongly dependent on (and therefore influenced by) the judicial assessment of concrete situations – this entails the integrative role played by the resolutions of the Superior Electoral Court (TSE), which is the primary source of consultation to anyone who faces electoral periods, political candidates and parties. The Electoral Justice has broad competence in Brazil since, besides judging the effectiveness of the electoral process, any abuses committed during the electoral campaign, the allocation of financial resources by the parties, the Electoral Justice is also competent if, for example, during electoral propaganda, a party violates a television station's copyrights.

374. A handful of mechanisms in the electoral legislation seek to induce greater equality and a balance of forces in the electoral process, regulating the coverage of pre-candidates and candidates by the media. Many of these mechanisms were implemented by Law 9.504/1997, which provides rules for the elections. However, the rules that form electoral legislation are for the most part only applied during electoral periods. The timeframe to which different electoral regulations apply may vary, coming into force during different periods of the electoral year. For instance, political parties must be registered with the electoral authorities by 2 April, and crowdfunding initiatives to be led by the candidates can be registered from 5 May.

375. Concerning broadcasting, specifically, electoral restrictions range from prohibition of viewing to the showing of TV shows presented by candidates, to exposure rules during interviews in journalistic programmes. However, outside of the electoral period, the state's presence is eclipsed by the business machine that forges, at will, the editorial guideline of broadcasters, covered by the shadow of freedom of expression and economic freedom.

---

245. During the military dictatorship (1964–1985), only 40 commercial broadcasting licences were assigned (including Globo TV's in 1964). For example, 1,028 grants were assigned only in 1990, and in the period between 1994 and 2002, 886 grants were assigned.

376. From 15 August on,[246] broadcasters are bound to air 'electoral propaganda'. Electoral propaganda is 'the advertising in which political parties and candidates disclose, by means of messages addressed to voters, their candidacies and political proposals, in order to show that they are the most suitable to assume the elective positions they are running for'.[247] Electoral propaganda is regulated by the electoral legislation, with the goal of preventing abuse of economic and political power and preserving equality among candidates.[248] The applicable rules include specific time parameters for exposure of candidates, parties, alliances, government branding[249] and candidacies.

377. From 6 August to the day before the elections, radio and television broadcasters are not allowed to:[250] broadcast, even if in the form of a journalistic interview, images of a survey or any other type of popular consultation of an electoral nature in which it is possible to identify the interviewee or in which there is data manipulation; broadcast political propaganda (that does fit into the 'electoral propaganda requirement'); give privileged treatment to a candidate, political party, federation or coalition; broadcast or disseminating films, soap operas, miniseries or any other programme that alludes to or criticizes a candidate, political party, federation or coalition (even if covertly and with an exception for news programmes or political debates); disclose the name of the programme that refers to the candidate or candidate chosen in convention, even when pre-existing, including if it coincides with his name or name chosen to appear on the ballot box, in which case it is forbidden to disclose, under penalty of cancellation of registration.

378. Furthermore, until 31 August of the electoral year, radio and television broadcasters, and other communication vehicles, must submit to the Electoral Justice the name of the person in charge for receiving notices and other communications related to the elections, including the respective email address and mobile phone number; and from the end of September on, propaganda is authorized. One of the challenges for political broadcasting in Brazil accrues from the territoriality of the broadcasting service concession areas. As such concessions are referred to municipalities, there will eventually exist only repeaters and retransmitters of programming (*see* Part III, Chapter 1 above) in certain locations. Consequently, there will be no programming generators with regulatory and technical capacity for inserting electoral propaganda referring to local candidates. In this case, political

246. Law 9.504/1997 at Art. 36.

247. TSE, *Politic-electoral Propaganda.* Available at: https://www.tse.jus.br/o-tse/escola-judiciaria-eleitoral/publicacoes/revistas-da-eje/artigos/propaganda-politico-eleitoral (accessed 15 Apr. 2022).

248. *Ibid.*

249. There is another peculiarity in Brazil called 'government branding'. Usually, a logo followed by a slogan associated with a particular administration formed by political representatives. Such branding is associated by mandataries with the achievements and works of their administration and is even used on official websites. For example, in the administration of President Luis Inácio Lula da Silva the official slogan, used as a government brand, was 'Brasil: um país de todos' (Brazil: a country of everyone); and in the administration of President Jair Bolsonaro 'Pátria Amada Brasil' (Beloved Homeland Brazil).

250. As per Law 9.504/1997, Art. 45, I, III, IV, V and VI; also Res TSE nº 23.610/1, Art. 43.

broadcasting will not be mandatory for repeaters and retransmitters,[251] and there will be 'electoral network generation' (one entity providing the signal carried by the other broadcasters), in a manner previously communicated and authorized by the Electoral Justice. Once the heads of the electoral networks are appointed, they will receive from the political parties, through the Electoral Justice, media plans with the spots to be inserted in their programming grid.

379. As a consequence of this territorial structure and specificities of grants and considering the affiliates model (Part III, Chapter 1 above), the programming generators of the affiliates network must send their signals to their ordinary affiliated entities clear of non-national-wide electoral campaigns (e.g., candidates for the Presidency). A card shall replace any non-applicable electoral insertion with the words 'Reserved for Free Electoral Propaganda'.

380. Finally, elections in Brazil use the electronic voting system, which makes it possible to monitor, in real time by the press, from 5PM on, on election day, the results of the ballots.

381. Electoral propaganda differs from official public administration propaganda. The federal public administration, through the special secretariat for social communication (in Portuguese: Secretaria Especial da Comunicação Social – SECOM), an arm of the Presidency of the Republic, can purchase advertising space to promote campaigns related to the Federal Government. For example, campaigns shown on FTA television in 2020 were backed by the Federal Government: the subjects were the then-new BRL 200 bill, awareness of violence against women, and drivers' education.

§1. Rules on Political Independence of Broadcasters

382. Broadcasting has long been the primary source of information for the Brazilian population, with staggering numbers of penetration and great impact on Brazilian culture, habits, and life. This influence can be illustrated by many different episodes, but one holds special importance for the matters pertaining political broadcasting. In December 1989, the first democratic direct elections after decades of dictatorship took place. During the electoral campaign period, Globo TV showed a debate among the then candidates who were running for the first place in the voting preferences in the election polls: Luiz Inácio Lula da Silva, former machinist and union leader affiliated to the Workers' Party, and representative of the left wing, and Fernando Collor, rich heir to a media empire, which among his possessions, had an affiliate that retransmits Globo TV's programme in the Northeast of the country. The day before the second round of the election, to be decided between these two candidates, Globo TV aired a 'best moments edition' of this debate during its daily

251. TSE Resolution 22.915.

prime time news show. This 'best moments' edition was extremely biased,[252] and it highlighted the moments of the original debate that suggested that candidate Fernando Collor had won the debates with a vast advantage.

383. As a result of several criticisms that suggested that the broadcaster had deliberately supported its business partner and would not prefer to have a representative of the left as the President, Globo TV, thirty years later, officially recognized its fault,[253,254] declaring that the editing was an attempt to demonstrate only 'best moments' just as someone who transmits the goals of a soccer match might do. Although the edited broadcast might have influenced the result of the election (won by candidate Fernando Collor), Globo TV did not admit that on that occasion the company had intentionally benefited a candidate, as it happened due to following an objective artistic guideline that it should not have applied to the elections. Nowadays, Globo TV no longer broadcasts 'highlights' of electoral debates.[255] This incident illustrates the intricate power dynamics entailed in broadcasting activities (and even mass communications as a whole) in Brazil, where despite the terms of a democratic constitution, political oligarchies are often favoured by formal and informal elements.

384. As seen in Part III, Chapter 1 above, it is part of the executive branch's competence to grant and renew sound and image broadcasting services concessions, always in favour of the complementarity of private, public, and state services. However, such an act by the executive branch is submitted for approval by the National Congress through voting. As seen in our General Introduction, National Congress is composed of federal deputies and senators elected by the people. It happens that there are countless cases in which grants and renewals are claimed by companies linked to these same deputies and senators, which may favour the use of these grants according to their political interests (*see* Part IV below).

385. This is a problem because the volume and quality of a particular candidate's exposure on FTA television will be decisive for their polls' performance. Thus, understanding that broadcasting concessions held by lawmakers represent a risk to freedom of expression, which may cause a severe threat to democracy and citizenship, in 2011 the Socialism and Freedom Party filed a constitutional action aimed at questioning the granting and maintenance of broadcasting concessions to

252. Da Redação, *Edição de debate pelo 'JN' em 1989 causou polêmica*, Folha de São Paulo (30 Sep. 2006), https://www1.folha.uol.com.br/fsp/brasil/fc3009200622.htm (accessed 16 Feb. 2021).
253. Memória Globo, *Debate Collor x Lula,* Globo Group, https://memoriaglobo.globo.com/erros/debate-collor-x-lula/ (accessed 16 Feb. 2021).
254. Mercado, *'Jornal Nacional' faz mea-culpa sobre edição de debate Lula-Collor*, Folha de São Paulo (23 Apr. 2015), https://www1.folha.uol.com.br/mercado/2015/04/1619986-jornal-nacional-faz-mea-culpa-sobre-edicao-de-debate-lula-collor.shtml?cmpid=menupe (accessed 16 Feb. 2021).
255. *See* Alexsandros Cavgias, Lucas Novaes, Luís Meloni & Raphael Corbi, *Edited Democracy: Media Manipulation and the News Coverage of Presidential Debates* (14 May 2019), https://www.insper.edu.br/wp-content/uploads/2019/05/Edited_Democracy_v2.pdf.

politicians elected by the people (elected representatives). In this lawsuit, the political party questions the granting and renewal of broadcasting permissions to companies that have as owners or associates, directly or indirectly, politicians holding an elective mandate; and the reason for the Federal Government's failure to supervise the granting and maintenance of broadcasting licences to elected politicians. The ADPF also specifically questions Ordinance 517/2011 of the Ministry of Communications, which renewed the broadcasting licence for the benefit of a company that at that time had a Senator of the Republic (Sen. José Agripino Maia) as a partner, as well as the Legislative-Decree 48/2014 that approved the renewal subject matter of the Ordinance 517/2011.

386. On a different tack, the Federal Attorney General's Office (in Portuguese Advocacia Geral da União – AGU) has a different interpretation of the same legislation, arguing that politicians' mere participation in the capital of broadcasting companies, for example, is not prohibited by the Constitution. Interestingly, Article 54, I, a, of the Federal Constitution prohibits contracts between lawmakers and the public administration or public service concessionaires (such as the broadcasting service concessionaires). While the AGU argues that the Article would only apply to agreements by lawmakers 'as an individual' and not as 'legal entity' in ADPF 379, the antithesis to this is supported by adding that the articles of association will represent, directly or indirectly, a contract executed by individuals.[256]

387. The Federal Senate sustains that prohibiting senators, i.e., its own body of senators, and deputies from having a certain property right would be a violation of Article 5, II of the Federal Constitution ('no one shall be obliged to do or refrain from doing something except by virtue of law'). In addition to that, the Brazilian Telecommunications Code (Law 4.117/1962) had the opportunity to regulate the matter, and it only set out one restriction, in its Article 38, §1, that a person who holds parliamentary immunity or specific jurisdiction rights cannot be a director or officer of broadcasting companies.

388. Finally, the same National Congress has the exclusive competence to appreciate the acts of granting and renewing the concessions[257] (Part III, Chapter 1 hereinabove) and the exclusive competence to create laws on broadcasting.[258]

§2. Fair Representation in Election Periods

389. During a period of thirty calendar days, ending three days before the voting day, radio and FTA television broadcasters must broadcast mandatory[259] free

256. Brazilian Civil Code, at Art. 981: the contract of society is executed between persons who reciprocally obligate themselves to contribute, with goods or services, to the exercise of economic activity and to share the results.
257. Brazilian Federal Constitution, at Art. 223, §§2 and 3.
258. *Ibid.*, Art. 22, VI.
259. Law 9.504/1997 at Arts 47 and 51.

electoral advertising regarding the first round of elections. If there is a second round, the advertisement will last for one more week, ending on the date corresponding to two days before the voting day.

390. From 31 August of the election year, television and radio stations are prohibited from broadcasting any shows presented or commented on by a pre-candidate (or candidate), even if the person does not perform this activity in a professional and remunerated manner. They must also refrain from providing privileged treatment to a candidate, party or coalition, or showing paid electoral propaganda.

391. During the electoral period, radio and television stations may broadcast debates between candidates. These debates must follow the rules previously established between broadcasters and representatives of political parties and candidates (the legislation uses a minimum approval quorum), with subsequent filing with the Electoral Justice. In the debates, broadcasters are obliged to invite at least all candidates whose parties have representation in the Chamber of Deputies. In the first round, the debates can occur until 48 hours before the beginning of the voting day, and in the second round, they must end until 00 hours of the voting day (respecting the time zone[260] of the place where the voting will take place).

392. The privileged treatment of candidates during normal programming is an offence under Article 45, IV of Law 9.504/1997 and the broadcaster will be subject to the payment of fines.

§3. News and Current Affairs Programmes

393. Also, as a tribute, above all, to freedom of expression and the right to information, radio and television can at any time show journalistic programmes that contain allusion to or criticism of a candidate or political party, according to Article 43, IV of Resolution 23,610 of TSE.

394. The rules of non-censorship, freedom of expression, and pluralism of ideas are also applicable in the expression of opinions on politics during electoral campaigns. Abuses will be judged by the competent courts since there are no public authorities with any prerogative of defining previously what could be said by the individuals. This position was reinforced when the STF ruled on ADI 4451.

395. In ADI 4451, the Brazilian Radio and TV Association (ABERT) challenges certain Electoral Law provisions (Article 45, II, III and §§4 and 5 of Law 9.504/1997) that prevented their associated entities from producing content involving montages and satires with candidates during the election period. ABERT further argued that the legal provisions were causing a severe silencing effect over the

260. Brazil has four different time zones.

media, as it prevented them from addressing any controversial political issue, injuring the following fundamental rights inscribed in the Federal Constitution: freedom of thought,[261] freedom of expression and prohibition of censorship,[262] right of access to information,[263] and freedom of the press.[264]

396. The STF unanimously declared the provisions of the Electoral Law that prevented radio and television stations from producing and exhibiting satirical programmes involving candidates unconstitutional, recognizing that it is also of the essence of freedom of expression the freedom for dubious, exaggerated, reprehensible, satirical, humorous opinions and ideas that are not shared with the majority.

§4. Political Advertising on Radio Broadcasters and FTA Television

397. ANCINE describes audiovisual works aimed at political advertising as those 'intended for the propaganda of political parties or their candidates, including audio-visual works for parties' free institutional advertising campaigns, pursuant to Law 9.096/1995, and the audio-visual advertising work intended to promote candidates during the electoral period (electoral propaganda), as provided for under Law 9.504/1997'.[265] As per the legislation, such political advertising pieces are exempted from prior registration with ANCINE[266] and collection of CONDECINE,[267] but they must still be registered before ANCINE with the indication of a specific code pertinent to that type of work.[268]

398. In Brazil, radio and television operators must form a simultaneous network and broadcast propaganda produced by political parties during the electoral period, plebiscites, referendums and at any time required by the Electoral Court for relevant communications. The election propaganda airtime was introduced in Brazil in 1950 and was only applicable to radio stations. From 1962 onwards, it became free of charge to political parties and candidates. It began to cover, in addition to radio, the FTA television – the time reserved for mandatory broadcasting does not apply to Pay-TV channels, Internet, or any means other than FTA television and radio broadcasters.

399. Currently, the legislation applicable to free electoral advertising is parameterized through Federal Law 9.504/1997. Articles 44–57 establish the rules applicable to free advertising on radio and television. Although free of charge to parties, broadcasters receive compensation due to the programming grid airtime occupied by electoral propaganda. Such compensation consists in a reduction in Income Tax

261. Brazilian Federal Constitution at Art. 5, IV.
262. *Ibid.*, at Art. 5, IX.
263. *Ibid.*, at Art. 5, XIV.
264. *Ibid.*, at Art. 220.
265. ANCINE IN (Normative Instruction) 95, at Art. 1, IX.
266. *Ibid.*, at Art. 16.
267. *Ibid.*, at Art. 28, IV.
268. *Ibid.*, at Art. 16, II.

due by broadcasters; the amount is calculated from an equation that considers such airtime if converted into advertising inserts according to the prices actually practised by the broadcaster (i.e., it shall be observed the usual discount policies over public prices, subject to inspection by the IRS). The rules for calculating the amount and deduction in Income Tax are found in Federal Decree 7.791/2012 and Normative Instruction 1.700/2017 of the Brazilian IRS. According to estimates, the compensations granted by the Federal Government to radio and television stations due to the electoral propaganda for municipal elections in 2020 totalled approximately BRL 540 million[269] (or approx. USD 100 million at the exchange rate then applicable); it is important to bear in mind that within the framework of electoral legislation, network advertising in municipal elections occupied ten minutes in the afternoon (1 PM to 1:10 PM), ten minutes in the evening (8:30 PM to 8:40 PM), plus inserts of a few seconds during programming.

§5. Political Advertising on the Internet, Pay-TV and Other Media

400. According to Article 1 of TSE Resolution 23,679/22, media vehicles other than FTA television and radio stations are not obliged to run mandatory free electoral propaganda. However, in common with FTA television and radio, Internet portals, Pay-TV, and other media, they also cannot sell space for political advertising on pain of criminal and civil sanctions, in addition to a fine.

401. In conjunction with Article 38 of Law 9.504/1997, Law 13.488/2017 and TSE Resolution 23.457/2015 regulate electoral advertising on the Internet. Under certain specific rules, candidates and political parties are allowed to:

- produce and promote electoral content on online platforms, on candidate's, party's or coalition's websites;
- produce mailings to registered addresses;
- produce and post content on blogs, social networks, and instant messaging sites.

402. Article 57-C of Law 9.504/1997 (whose current wording was introduced in 2017 by an amendment), as an exception to the absolute prohibition against any paid or free electoral advertising on the Internet, allows the 'promotion' of content, since unequivocally identified, hired and paid directly by the political parties, coalitions, candidates to be promoted or their representatives, directly with the respective platform. It is important to note: the content promotion must be contracted directly within the social media platforms, without any media bureaux, brokers, or intermediaries. That is an effort to prevent inauthentic and covert mechanisms that could be used in social media or private messaging apps. Article 26 of the same law defines

269. Folha Press, *Propaganda eleitoral gratuita custará R$ 538 milhões em renúncia fiscal*, Valor Econômico (6 Oct. 2020), https://valor.globo.com/politica/noticia/2020/10/06/propaganda-eleitoral-gratuita-custara-r-538-milhoes-em-renuncia-fiscal.ghtml (accessed 16 Feb. 2021).

promoted content as 'the paid prioritization of content resulting from Internet search applications', allowing the purchase of keywords in search engines, such as Google AdWords.

403. It is important to note that these advertisements must be contracted on a date before the voting day;[270] otherwise, any person responsible for such transaction will be subject to criminal sanctions.

404. Application providers will only be liable for contents if such providers do not meet the Electoral Justice's removal determination.[271] Law 9.504, in its Article 57-D corroborates that the expression of thought is free, however, prohibiting anonymity during the electoral campaign. The law also provides for the right to respond.

---

270. Law 9.504/1997, at Art. 39, §5.
271. Law 9.504/1997, at Art. 57-F.

Chapter 6. Advertising Rules

405. According to a research led by the Interactive Advertising Bureau, it is estimated that in 2017 company expenditures on advertising in Brazil were BRL 44.4 billion (approx. USD 13 billion at the time).[272] The same report revealed that, of this amount, BRL 14.8 billion (approx. USD 4.35 billion at the time) were directed to digital media, equivalent to one-third of the total, representing a 25.4% growth compared to the previous year.

406. Brazilian advertising is framed within a private sectorial self-regulating system, which encompasses two organizations: first, the National Council for Advertising Self-Regulation (CONAR), founded in 1980, as the guardian of ethics in advertisement messaging; second, the Executive Council of Standard Norms (CENP), founded in 1988, as the guardian of the commercial relations between market players. Both are private, non-governmental entities, constituted under Brazilian law in the form of a 'non-profit civil association'. While CONAR focuses on the materials produced and exhibited, CENP focuses on the relationship between market agents.

407. Self-regulation does not, however, override any statutory law, such as public laws and official decrees. Even though CONAR is a famous benchmark for successful self-regulation in Brazil, it does not hold legitimacy to rule on any abuse, damage, or legal violation – assessments that remain under the courts' competences (*see* Part I above). Nevertheless, CONAR's self-regulation system is often perceived by agents in the media sector as more effective than legal adjudication, even though it lacks any power to impose sanctions on those found guilty, or rule on indemnifications to any injured party.

408. Within the Brazilian legislative system, several laws directly impact the advertising activity, either in general or through provisions that address specific issues.

409. In general, if someone causes any damage to the image of another person due to the content of advertisement material or makes improper use of materials owned by third parties such as copyrights and trademarks, they will be subject to general legal statutes applicable to the duty to indemnify, crimes against the honour and violation of intellectual property rights (as per the applicable legal diplomas).

410. More specifically, the Code for Consumer Defence and Protection (Law 8.078/1990) and the ECA, although aimed at specific rights protection, also bring many provisions that are applicable to advertisement. In the face of infraction to these provisions, CONAR does not have the authority to compel a communications

---

272. Research Carried by IAB Brasil, *Digital representa R$ 14,8 bilhões de investimento publicitário no Brasil em 2017* (21 May 2018), https://iabbrasil.com.br/digital-representa-r-148-bilhoes-de-investimento-publicitario-no-brasil-em-2017/ (accessed 17 Feb. 2021).

vehicle to remove a certain part of an ad from its programming grid, or to compel an agency to change the content of an ad.

411. Under the Code of Consumer Defence and Protection, consumers have protections against misleading or abusive[273] advertisement and the right to be informed that specific material or content is an advertisement.[274] According to its Article 37, §1, misleading advertising shall be understood as 'any type of information or communication of an advertisement nature, wholly or partially false, or, in any other way, even by omission, capable of misleading the consumer regarding the nature, characteristics, quality, quantity, origin, price and any other information related to products and services'. In turn, 'misleading by omission' is understood to be a misleading piece added by the circumstance of 'failing to report on essential aspects of the product or service'[275] and the term 'abusive', means among others, 'discriminatory advertisement of any nature, which incites violence, exploit fear or superstition, takes advantage of children's lack of judgment and experience, disrespects environmental protection, or can induce consumers to behave in a way harmful or dangerous to their health or safety'.[276,277]

412. Furthermore, the Code for Consumer Defence and Protection determines that the entity that pays for the advertisement is the one responsible for proving the aired or published information's veracity and correctness. In addition, a product or service supplier who becomes aware of their commodity's dangerousness after placing them on the market must use advertisements to inform consumers of the risk related to the commodity.[278] These provisions apply to advertisement published or aired on any media.

413. With the expansion of online advertisement, CONAR has recently acted vigorously concerning pieces exhibited in digital media, pointing out the lack of clarity in identifying to the general public the advertisement character of particular contents – an understanding that is applicable for any media or format, from *publiposts* (which is how social media advertisement posts are usually referred to in Brazil) to *podcasts.*

414. From February to October 2018, CONAR started forty-six ethical processes related to the lack of clarity of the advertisement nature of certain materials.

---

273. Code of Consumer Defence and Protection, at Art. 6, IV: 'The following are basic consumer rights: (…) protection against misleading and abusive publicity, commercial methods based on coercion or in any other way unlawful, as well as against practices and causes that are abusive or imposed as part of the products and services being supplied.'
274. *Ibid.*, at Art. 36: publicity must be shown in such way that the consumer will easily and immediately identify it as such.
275. *Ibid.*, at Art. 37, §3.
276. *Ibid.*, at Art. 37, §2.
277. In particular, Arts 6, 10, 30, 31, 33, 35, 36, 37, 38, 60, 63, 67, 68 of the Code of Consumer Defense and Protection shall be observed.
278. *Ibid.*, at Art. 10, §1: the products or services supplier who gains knowledge of harm or danger presented by a product or service previously placed in the consumer market must immediately communicate this fact to the proper authorities and to consumers, through the use of advertisements.

Recently, CONAR summoned several digital influencers about the need to indicate in their posts that certain content is or encompasses advertisement, even though the legislation provides no parameters for such identification. Nevertheless, CONAR has declared itself in favour of the use of hashtags and descriptors such as '#advertisement', '#anuncio' and '#publi', as it understands, above all, that they express sufficient clarity to identify the advertisement bias. CONAR's stance is for transparency, as the law determines that advertising must always be clearly identified as such. Furthermore, CONAR also stated that, depending on the public, #ad will not be effective in identifying a clearly identifiable ad, just as #publi will not be. If the public is not trained in English language, the hashtag '#ad' will not mean much to them. In the same vein, some parts of the audience (e.g., elderly populations) might be unable to identify 'publi' as a paid advertisement. In addition, the place where the text is indicated is relevant for clarifying the purpose of the piece. The CONAR guide itself indicates that the platform's own features should preferably be used to identify the advertising character.

415. In 2020, CONAR released 'Guidelines for Publicity by Digital Influencers'[279] presenting an array of definitions and recommendations for clarifying and guiding advertising initiatives implemented in digital media by digital influencers. In the document, CONAR defines advertising by an influencer as 'the third-party message aimed at stimulating the consumption of goods and/or services, carried out by so-called digital influencers, after being contracted by the advertiser and/or agency'. Such messages, in general, are characterized by three cumulative elements: (i) the promotion of the product, service, cause or other form of association; (ii) a compensation or commercial relationship, even if not financial, with the advertiser and/or agency; and (iii) the interference by the advertiser and/or agency within the content of the message (editorial control in the influencer post). On the other hand, CONAR does not encompass, under the definition of advertising, messages of gratitude to gifts and courtesies, but recommends that such messages contain explanations about what motivated the relationship (e.g., thanks and compliments to the hotel that offered free lodging).

416. In addition to laws and codifications not aimed explicitly at advertisement communication (as highlighted in the paragraphs above), Law 4.680/1965 provides for the exercise of the profession of advertiser and advertising agent, and institutes, in its Article 11, the controversial 'standard discount'. This financial amount consists of a commission due by the media vehicles to the advertising agencies for their intermediation in the purchase of media by the advertiser, which fact as a kind of incentive plan. This provision is highly controversial because it holds conflicting interests. Moreover, this type of reward would be unethical, conflicting, and inexorable in the light of the legal system without this provision.

417. Law 12.232/2010 establishes general requirements for contracting of advertising services by the public administration. An important point of this Law is

---

279. *See* CONAR *Digital Influencer Advertising Guidelines* at http://conar.org.br/pdf/CONAR_Digital-Influencer-Advertising-Guidelines_2021-03-11.pdf (accessed 24 Mar. 2021).

the express recognition through its Articles 18 and 19 of the sector's self-regulation system, including the controversial 'standard discount'.

§1. The Self-Regulation Framework

418. The Brazilian advertising market's self-regulation consists of rules freely adopted by the market agents themselves, and it is divided into two pillars: Market (CENP) and Content (CONAR). Although affiliation to these institutions is not mandatory,[280] being an affiliate can bring two main advantages. The first one comes with the primacy of self-regulation, preserving the market, to a certain degree, from statutory regulation (even when self-regulation, especially in terms of content, has proved to be efficient and rigorous). The second one relates to economic benefits, as affiliation comes with access to business models where the media vehicles themselves, if also affiliated to CENP, are obliged to grant the controversial 'standard discount' to the agencies.

I. CENP

419. The rules imposed on CENP affiliates take shape through the codification called 'Standard-Norms for advertising activities', sometimes complemented by other norms, referred to as 'regulatory communications' (also issued by CENP). The standard discount, whose rates are defined by CENP regulation, is defined as follows in the Standard Norms:

> Art. 1.11: (…) the remuneration of the Advertising Agency for creating the concept, executing and distributing advertisement, demanded by and on account of client advertisers, and follows a percentage format as established by the Standard Norms calculated over the Negotiated Amount.

420. The standard discount can be paid to the agency once the advertiser pays the amount equivalent to advertisement space to the communications vehicle.

421. Although the agencies have the legal duty to negotiate with communication vehicles for the most favourable viewing conditions for their clients, the agency will be entitled to the standard discount calculated based on these same negotiated amounts.

422. Another peculiarity of the system is that agencies can collect payments for the advertising space, on behalf of the vehicles, against their own clients. It is important to reinforce: that the agency, in this relationship, has a contract with the advertiser (the client) and provides services to it, and yet it charges the client on

280. Brazilian Federal Constitution, at Art. 8, V: no one shall be required to join or to remain a member of a union.

behalf of the vehicle. The self-regulation framework also provides the agency with the possibility of giving up the standard discount.

423. An attempt to balance this equation is the imposition, by the same Standard Norms, to cause the associated vehicles to publish their practices' price list. However, the market rarely discloses this price list, and agencies mostly provide only their so-called full price (without clarifying the percentage of it equivalent to the Standard Discount). Media vehicles always offer discounts on the announced values.

424. The discussion around whether or not the advertising professionals need to register in advance has not yet been judicially challenged before the STF. Another argument that weighs against the bureaux is that services such as FTA television must be the object of a concession granted by the government, and the activity of filling in the programming grid is part of editorial responsibilities. Thus, transferring this activity to a third party could be, in addition to a flagrant violation of the terms of the concession contract, an illegal provision of broadcasting services. However, there seems to be a certain elasticity in interpreting the rules that assign rights and duties related to programming activities, given the frequent commercialization of airtime for independent producers and religious institutions to exhibit their shows and services.

425. Finally, it is important to highlight that the Standard Rules determine cross-ownership rules and that the ideas, plans, pieces, and advertisement campaigns rights cannot be assigned to the advertiser. When interested in obtaining an extension for exhibition rights, the advertiser must negotiate a new licence with the agency, which is likely to act once again in the intermediation of the acquisition of advertisement space with the vehicles, and may be entitled to the standard discount related to such negotiation.

II. CONAR

426. While CENP is responsible for the market and commercial relations between the industry players, CONAR focuses on the content of advertisement pieces. Currently, the entity has 180 counsellors who may act based on third-party accusations or on its own initiative. The CONAR rules are materialized in the 'Brazilian Advertising Self-Regulation Code', which among other requirements, determines that ads must be clearly identified as such, regardless of the format or means of dissemination (except for the pieces characterized as 'teasers'); or prohibition of any form of incitement to social differentiation resulting from greater or lesser purchasing power; and the prohibition to exploit fear or superstition.

427. The Code's parameterization on comparative advertisement (addressed in its Article 7), which consists of comparing competing brands and products, has been used as a guideline by the STJ (highest appeals court for federal legislation)[281] when analysing a comparative campaign's legality related to intellectual property violation and anticompetitive behaviour accusations.

428. To better understand CONAR's practice, it is interesting to review the historical decisions that shaped the market's ethical behaviour.

429. For example, in 1988, a prominent publisher considered itself offended by comparative advertisement, where several of its periodic magazines were compared to just one weekly magazine. The advertiser affirmed that his weekly magazine would be much more advantageous to the consumer since he could have in one publication the different thematic of several others. CONAR considered the products non-comparable, as it was a magazine, and, in contrast, the others were specialized magazines. CONAR recommended that the advertisement should no longer be exhibited. In 1992, a consumer understood that a campaign that advertised Mickey and Minnie children's scissors carried a message that children who did not have the scissors would be socially inferior. Throughout the ad, the children wielded the artefacts and hummed to those who did not have them, 'I have it, you don't have it.' CONAR understood that the ad could inspire antisocial behaviour and understood further that the campaign should be terminated. CONAR justified the decision by arguing that children are human beings under development, with significant weaknesses and vulnerabilities, and not having the artefact in question could make children feel frustrated and inferior.[282]

430. In 1994, CONAR recommended that the exhibition of an ad that incited fear should be suspended. The ad carried a message that it would be better to bet on the lottery to have enough money to leave Rio de Janeiro to avoid urban violence.[283]

431. In 1995, in response to a request from the Public Relations Advisor of the United States Information Service, CONAR analysed an advertising campaign in which Mrs Hillary Clinton appeared seated in a real photo that depicted her thighs and underwear pieces. The campaign extolled a particular underwear brand's attributes, stating that the US President should know what that brand was capable of doing. CONAR understood that, in addition to using the image of the first lady of the US without prior authorization, the campaign revealed disrespect for dignity, intimacy, and family values, and therefore recommended that the exhibition should be suspended.[284]

---

281. CONAR representation 131/92. Available at http://www.conar.org.br/processos/detcasohistorico.php?id=135 (accessed 12 Feb. 2021).
282. CONAR representation 131/92. Available at http://www.conar.org.br/processos/detcasohistorico.php?id=135 (accessed 12 Feb. 2021).
283. CONAR representation 133/94. Available at http://www.conar.org.br/processos/detcasohistorico.php?id=229 (accessed 12 Feb. 2021).
284. CONAR representation 223/95. Available at http://www.conar.org.br/processos/detcasohistorico.php?id=186 (accessed 12 Feb. 2021).

§2. VARIOUS FORMS OF COMMERCIAL COMMUNICATIONS

432. There are many commercial communication forms in the industry, all adopted by the Brazilian market, from modern branded content in line with the currently famous storytelling, to public communication actions in audiovisual works. A curious fact is that, in Brazil, the general public refers to 'merchandising' or 'merchan' when addressing certain actions that consist of the insertion of brands in audiovisual works (also known as product placement).

433. An administrative rule delivers the definition of audiovisual advertisement. According to ANCINE's Normative Instruction 95 (the IN 95), audiovisual advertisement is defined as 'audio-visual work whose purpose is advertising, exhibiting or offering products, services, companies, public or private institutions, political parties, associations, public administration, as well as material and immaterial goods of any nature'.[285] Audiovisual advertisement must be registered before ANCINE prior to their exhibition, and such registration requires the payment of a specific tax (CONDECINE-ad) applicable to each market segment in which the ad will be exhibited (e.g., FTA television, Pay-TV).

434. As per IN 95, only companies previously registered with ANCINE with corporate purposes compatible with audiovisual production or advertising agencies' activities may obtain advertisement registration.

I. Product Placement

435. In product placement, a certain product, service, or brand is embedded in the script of an audiovisual work or in the story of any other type of work, such as literary, for example, so that its nature is not transformed into an ad piece. Therefore, the purpose of the work is not an advertisement, although the promotion of a particular brand will take place within the work, but it will be organically positioned in the structure of the plot. Authors such as Miguel Baños-González and Joaquin de Aguilera[286] argue that the differentiation between formats is based on the intentionality in creating the content that conveys the brand's message.

436. When an audiovisual work presents a product placement, the specific regulation of advertisement works requiring prior registration with ANCINE does not apply (since it will not be considered an audiovisual advertisement work). However, other rules related to advertisements are still applicable, such as the consumer protection code rules, as seen in this chapter's introductory paragraphs.

---

285. ANCINE, IN 95, at Art. 1, XVIII.

286. J Aguilera & M. Baños, *Branded entertainment: cuando el branded content se convierte en entretenimento* (ESIC 2016), in K. Avelar & N. Prata, *O branded content como modelo de negócio*, 10 71–88 (Revista Geminis 2019).

II. Branded Content

437. Sometimes called infotainment, advertainment, branded entertainment, or brand experience, branded content is an ad combined with content or experiences, in which the brand, ultimately, ends up guiding the development of the content. In other words, the content without the brand identity printed into it would either have no reason to exist or would be completely different. It is important to highlight that ANCINE understands that the audiovisual branded content is an audiovisual advertisement, also subject to prior registration.

III. Contests and Sweepstakes

438. It is a common practice worldwide that marketing campaigns to promote certain products involve distributing free samples. In Brazil, such campaigns, if involving random selection of recipients, or a limited number of rewards (e.g., 'buy and win' limited to the first 10,000 purchases), or the need for the prior purchase of a product or service to participate in the campaign, must necessarily be registered with the competent public body, which is the Secretariat of Assessment, Planning, Power, and Lottery (SECAP), under the Ministry of Economic Affairs. Failure to comply with the legislation is subject to a series of sanctions, such as fines and a ban on undertaking new actions of this type during a specific period of time.

439. Among a handful of applicable rules, advertisers must register the contest with SECAP, the entity must collect taxes calculated based on the market price of the goods offered as rewards, and the advertiser must afterwards report to the public authorities the reward delivery at the end of the contest. There is a set of applicable rules, which are currently: Law 5.768/1971 and its regulatory decree, 70.951/1972; SECAP Ordinance 20.749/2020; MF Ordinance 41/2008; MF Ordinance 422/2013; and MF Ordinance 215/2006.

§3. Restrictions on Content

440. The Brazilian Federal Constitution in its Articles 220, §3, II, and §4 establishes the need for parameterization, through infra-constitutional rules, of means for the defence of the population and the family against harmful advertising, expressly citing the need for protection against the advertising of tobacco, alcoholic beverages, pesticides, medicines and therapies. As we will describe below, the infra-constitutional legislation performs its duty by fulfilling such constitutional rules with limits and parameters.

441. Law 6.360/1976 brings a list of restrictions related to advertising communication involving medicines and pharmaceutical supplies. Such rules are also complemented by the National Health Surveillance Agency (Agência Nacional de Vigilância Sanitária – ANVISA) regulation, which holds the legal power to regulate the matter (*see* RDC 96/2008 published by ANVISA).

442. Law 9.294/1996 sets parameters for advertising communication involving products derived from tobacco, alcoholic beverages, medicines, and pesticides. As for the advertising of alcoholic beverages, for example, the law determines that the pieces cannot associate the use of the product with the practice of sports activities and shall bring alerts and specific information about the harm caused by consuming alcoholic beverages. As for tobacco derivatives, the law expressly prohibits its advertising, including indirect forms, except for exposure at points of sale. The law further stipulates that the transmission or retransmission, on TV, of cultural or sporting events with images generated abroad sponsored by companies linked to smoking products requires the free broadcast by TV stations, during the event's transmission, of warning message on the perils of smoking.

443. Law 10.826/2003 prohibits the offering of guns, ammunition, and accessories through commercial communication, except in specialized publications.

444. Law 11.265/2006 regulates the publicity of food for infants and young children and childcare products, bringing a series of rules applicable to advertising communication related to these products. This includes an express prohibition, in its Article 4, of the announcement of infant formulations, formulations for high-risk newborns, and pacifiers, in addition to the imposition of text alerts for other products.

445. In 1992, a complaint was filed with CONAR against a particular campaign that featured animals and women breastfeeding. In this case, one of CONAR's advisors offered representation at its own initiative for understanding that the campaign was advertising that milk formulae would be better for infants than breastfeeding. At the end of the process, CONAR recommended the inclusion of a lettering in the advertisement stating that the advertised product was not indicated to replace breastfeeding.[287]

446. In its Advertising Self-Regulation Code,[288] CONAR includes specific exhibits for ruling the advertising related to certain varieties of products:

- alcoholic beverages;
- education, courses, and teaching;
- jobs and opportunities;
- real estate sales and rental;
- investments, loans, and capital markets;
- stores and retail;
- physicians, dentists, veterinarians, massage therapists, nurses, hospital services, paramedics, prosthetic products and treatments;
- food products;

---

287. CONAR representation 177/92. Available at http://www.conar.org.br/processos/detcasohistorico.php?id=143 (accessed 12 Feb. 2022).

288. Brazilian Advertising Self-Regulation Code in English available at http://www.conar.org.br/pdf/Brazilian_Advertising_Self-Regulation.pdf (accessed 18 Feb. 2022).

– pharmaceutical products;
– tobacco products;
– smoke-inhibiting products.

I. Children

447. Advertising materials aimed at children are not considered illegal per se, except if they fall under abusive content.

448. There are restrictions on ads placement and their content. They must not, among other limits, address an imperative consumption message directly to the child, promote or cause discrimination. There are even limitations on using elements from the children's particular universe. Although CONAR has in its code of self-regulation rules applicable to advertising aimed at children, imposing ethical boundaries considered sufficient by the market, the National Council for the Rights of Children and Adolescents (CONANDA), an organ connected to the Ministry of Women, Family and Human Rights, tried to set some rules applicable to children's advertising through its Resolution 163/2014. There is currently a discussion about such Resolution's constitutionality, mainly due to an alleged violation of the Federal Union's exclusive power to legislate on advertising. Compliant with the Federal Constitution or not, Resolution 163 has been serving as a guideline for numerous court decisions. Resolution 163 is aimed to combine abusive practices prohibited by the Code of Consumer Defence and Protection with the integral protection of children.

449. Resolution 163 defines abusive advertising as (Article 2):

> the practice of directing advertising and marketing communication to children, to persuade them to consume any product or service and use, among others, the following aspects:
>
> I – children's language, special effects, and excess of colours;
> II – soundtracks composed of children's songs or songs sung by children's voices;
> III – child representation;
> IV – people or celebrities with an appeal to children;
> V – children's characters or hosts;
> VI – cartoon or animation;
> VII – dolls or similar;
> VIII – promotion with the distribution of prizes or collectible gifts or with appeals to children; and
> IX – campaigns with competitions or games appealing to children.

450. Resolution 163 also brings general principles to communication targeting adolescents, such as not inducing feelings of inferiority if they do not consume a particular product or service.

451. Nonetheless, since 2013, CONAR, through its self-regulation code, prohibits indirect advertising communication aimed at children, maintaining that the advertising spaces suitable for the exhibition of the pieces should only consist of programming breaks.

§4. Time and Frequency Restrictions

452. Law 4.117/1962[289] and Law 12.485/2011[290] impose a limit of 25% of the total channel programming time on FTA television and Pay-TV channels to be allocated to advertisements. As an exception, channels registered with ANCINE as exclusively dedicated to commercial advertising are not subject to advertisement time limitations.[291]

453. Institutions that hold authorizations to perform 'educational broadcasting services' are prohibited from selling advertising spaces.[292] However, these entities regularly announce funding partners and institutional partnerships in their programming grid.

289. Law 4.117/1962, at Art. 124: 'The time allocated by programming broadcasting stations, to commercial advertising, may not exceed 25% (twenty-five percent) of the total [programming grid].'
290. Law 12.485, at Art. 24: 'The maximum time allocated for commercial advertising on each programming channel must be equal to the limit established for the broadcasting service of sounds and images. [i.e., the time limit set above].'
291. *Ibid.*, at Art. 24, sole paragraph: 'The provision in the caput of this Article does not apply to the channels referred to in Art. 32 of this Law and the exclusive channels of commercial advertising, sales and infomercials.'
292. Decree-Law 236/1967, at Art. 13, sole paragraph: 'Educational television is not commercial in its nature, and it is forbidden to transmit any advertising, directly or indirectly, as well as sponsorships for the broadcasts, (…).'

Chapter 7. Right to Information

§1. Access to Major Events

454. Major events access rules are statutory requirements regarding the licensing and transmission rights of 'major events', i.e., events over which there is a notorious and relevant public interest. These rules are often implemented in order to ensure that broadcasters or other audiovisual media services do not hold exclusive rights over this type of content, thus assuring the majority of the public the possibility to follow these events and allowing for fair competition in the sector. Some examples of what constitutes 'major events' are international, national and regional sports events, elections, speeches by heads of state and cultural events. Major events include 'simple components of democratic and cultural processes',[293] and regulating access to them is a way of ensuring audiovisual media fulfils its democratic role in society.

455. There is no structured regulatory framework regarding licence and the transmission of major events, and dispersed legislation applies in different degrees. For instance, speeches by heads of government abide by the requirements of political broadcasting (*see* Part III, Chapter 5 above); there is no statutory rule regarding social and cultural public interest events. Intellectual property legislation also applies to all the cases where institutes such as copyrights, brand protection, sports media rights must be considered.

456. Nevertheless, regarding the transmission of sports events, competition law enforcement performed by CADE has played a significant role in reshaping long-lasting licensing practices, notably regarding the rights over transmission of soccer championships.

457. Football competitions are widely popular across the territory, and a world-renowned emblem of the Brazilian culture. Even though sports events do not qualify as works of authorship under Brazilian legislation, the audiovisual recordings of such events can eventually enjoy copyright protection and entitle the rights holders of the first recording of the event to the right of reproduction, distribution, licencing and communication to the public.[294] In Brazil, it is common that the television channel that records images of a given sporting event will not have rights to re-exhibit such event since its subsequent rights of use are limited due to the so-called direito de arena. In Brazil, the legislation provides for a neighbouring right referred to as 'direito de arena' (literally translated as 'arena right' but also referred to English language as 'sports media rights' or 'sports broadcasting rights'), and it is provided by Article 42 of Lei Pelé, as follows:

293. *See* Max Schoenthal, *Major Events and Reporting Rights,* IRIS Plus: IRIS Legal Observations of the European Audiovisual Observatory (2016), https://rm.coe.int/16807833ca (accessed 24 Mar. 2021).

294. *See* Broadcasting of major sports events in the EU (2018), https://www.europarl.europa.eu/RegData/etudes/ATAG/2018/621900/EPRS_ATA(2018)621900_EN.pdf (accessed 24 Mar. 2021).

> Sports practice entities are entitled to arena rights, which consists of the exclusive prerogative to negotiate, authorize or prohibit the capture, fixation, emission, transmission, retransmission or reproduction of images, by any means or process, of sports events in which they participate.
> Paragraph 1 – Except for collective labour agreement to the contrary, 5% (five percent) of the revenue from the exploitation of audio-visual sports rights will be passed on to the professional athletes' unions, and these will distribute, in equal parts, to the professional athletes participating in the show, as a civil nature instalment.

458. As per this provision, sports broadcasting rights rest with the entities that perform sports activities, i.e., sports cubs, associations, etc. Regarding national football competitions, these rights are negotiated by an entity called 'Club of the Thirteen' ('Clube dos Treze'), which reunites the biggest Brazilian football teams and has long-headed negotiations regarding the transmission of the national championship and the partition of royalties among its members.

459. For decades, these rights were negotiated exclusively with Globo TV, leaving all other broadcasters and Pay-TV channels out of the conversation. This gave ground to an investigation and administrative process started by CADE in 1997, when it accused both Globo TV and the Club of the Thirteen of: limiting, distorting or harming free competition or free enterprise in any way; dominating relevant markets of goods or services; limiting or preventing new companies of accessing a certain market; creating difficulties to the Constitution, operation or development of competition; creating difficulties to the establishment, operation or development of a competing company or of a supplier, purchaser or financer of goods or services; preventing competitors' access to sources of inputs, raw materials, equipment or technology, as well as to distribution channels; discriminating purchasers or suppliers of goods or services; and discriminating purchasers or suppliers of goods or services through the differentiated fixing of prices or of operational conditions of sale or provision of services.[295] All of these practices were referred to the joint negotiation of the broadcasting rights of the Brazilian Football Championship together with clauses of exclusivity and preference, favouring Globo TV. In its analysis of this case, the OECD Telecommunication and Broadcasting Review of Brazil paints an accurate picture of what this negotiation meant, in terms of advantages and profits acquired by Globo:

> In Brazil, football is extremely popular. It has the power to attract and maintain broadcasting audience share not only for football matches, but also across all programming. Therefore, it is a major source of competition among broadcasters. Moreover, Globo held almost half of all audience share and earned about 75% of all advertising revenue in the FTA sector. The amounts paid by Globo to the participating clubs are indicative of the Brazilian Football

295. CADE, *Mercado de TV Aberta e Paga*, Cadernos do CADE (2020). Available at: https://telaviva.com.br/wp-content/uploads/2021/01/mercado-de-tv-aberta-e-paga-2020.pdf. Accessed on: 5 Jan. 2021.

League's importance. In 2005, Globo paid more than 3.5 times the combined total paid for FTA rights to the São Paulo State Championship, the National Football Cup (Copa do Brasil) and the South American Cup. A preference clause may have helped Globo to remain the lone broadcaster of the Brazilian Football League from 1997 to 2011. Under that clause, rival broadcasters had to submit every bid to Globo. If Globo matched the bid within 30 days, it won the contract. Accordingly, the overarching antitrust issue in the case was whether and to what degree the contract between Globo and the Club of 13 foreclosed competition from rival broadcasters.[296]

460. This administrative process lasted for thirteen years, during which CADE and other competition authorities' recommendations skirted around the creation of two separate packages for broadcasting rights and unbundling of rights under negotiation. The process ended in 2010, when CADE settled with both Globo and the Club of the Thirteen. Globo's agreement demanded that the broadcaster: waived its rights of first refusal related to the transmission of the national championship for the 2009, 2010 and 2011 seasons in FTA television, Internet, Pay-TV, pay-per-view and mobile transmissions; and that it did not exercise its preference rights regarding the 2012 and all of the following seasons. In its turn, the agreement with the Club of the Thirteen bound the entity to: refrain from using the preference clause in the commercialization contracts of the national championship's broadcasting rights; sell these broadcasting rights separately (according to championship's modalities) in order to make it easier for interested parties to propose isolated or joint proposals for the modalities; define clear and objective criteria for the processes of bidding national championships' transmission rights; allow third parties to sublicense the rights acquired, in the open TV media; provide CADE with certified copies of these contracts, within thirty days of signature, as well as a report explaining how the sale process took place, and to publish a 'market report'.

461. Despite the settlement being registered and made 'compliant' by CADE, it proved ineffective since the football clubs openly circumvented it by selling these rights directly to Globo, instead of through the Club of the Thirteen – even though the other two broadcasters also offered to buy these rights from the teams. The favouritism of Globo can be interpreted as a sign that 'Globo's offer is well beyond its competitors' capacities in terms of audience share, quality of the broadcasts and ability to generate advertising revenues.'[297]

462. Another administrative process with similar claims was initiated due to a claim from the Federal Public Prosecution received in 2014. After its analysis, CADE opted to close down the process, given that the settlement with Globo and the Club of the Thirteen was still valid. Also, in 2016 the authority started an investigation over anticompetitive practices in the same sector. The Enquiry was closed

---

296. Organisation for Economic Co-operation and Development – OECD, *Telecommunication and Broadcasting Review of Brazil*, 228–229 (2020).
297. *Ibid.*

and archived in 2019, due to lack of sufficient evidence of violations of the economic order regarding the negotiations and contracts of broadcasting rights of national soccer championships.[298]

§2. SHORT NEWS REPORTING

463. The Brazilian Copyright Law holds a few exceptions for conducts related to news reporting, as long as the report abides by a few requirements. As per Article 46, the following conducts, among others not directly related to news reporting, do not infringe copyright protection: (a) the reproduction in the daily or periodical by the press of journalistic or informative content (as long as the author's and original publication's names are mentioned); (b) the reproduction, in newspapers or periodicals, of speeches performed in public meetings of any nature; (c) the quotation in books, newspapers, magazines or any other medium of communication of passages from a work for the purposes of study, criticism or debate, to the extent justified by the purpose, provided that the author is named and the source of the quotation is given; and (d) the reproduction in any work of short extracts from existing works, regardless of their nature, or of the whole work in the case of a work of three-dimensional art, on condition that the reproduction is not in itself the main subject matter of the new work and does not jeopardize the normal exploitation of the work reproduced or unjustifiably prejudice the author's legitimate interests.

298. Conselho Administrativo de Defesa Econômica – CADE, *Mercado de TV Aberta e Paga*, Cadernos do CADE (2020). Available at: https://telaviva.com.br/wp-content/uploads/2021/01/mercado-de-tv-aberta-e-paga-2020.pdf (accessed 5 Jan. 2021).

Chapter 8. Access to Networks

§1. Must Carry Rules

464. The rules known as 'must carry' are a type of regulatory mechanism used to oblige audiovisual service providers to include in their programming certain channels elected by the legislature, or by the regulator, according to legal stipulation.

465. The logic behind must-carry obligations may involve different aspects, such as, for example: (i) the restriction of vertical integration between Pay-TV operators and programmers, by establishing a percentage of channels to be offered by the operator that are programmed by companies or entities not controlled by or related to it; (ii) the protection of open, local and national television networks whose competitiveness was threatened by Pay-TV services; and (iii) the facilitation of access to certain channels due to their importance for serving the public interest (such as those reserved for the legislative and judicial powers, or in the case of educational and community channels). Infiltrated in all these aspects is the pluralistic essence of the must-carry rules, which guarantee a minimum level of diversity of content and sources of information in the channel packages offered by Pay-TV operators.

466. The first law to implement must-carry mechanisms in Brazil was Law 8.977/1995, which regulated cable TV services (and hence commonly referred to as the 'Cable Law'). Its original provision 23, I mandated cable TV operators to offer, without any extra charge to consumers: (i) channels offered by local commercial broadcasters; (ii) one a municipal or state legislative channel, reserved for shared use between the City Councils located in the municipalities of the service provision area and the Legislative Assembly of the respective state; (iii) a channel reserved for the House of Representatives and another for the Federal Senate, for the documentation of their work, especially the live broadcast of the sessions; (iv) a university channel, reserved for shared use among the universities located in the municipalities of the service provision area; (v) an educational-cultural channel, reserved for use by the bodies that deal with education and culture in the Federal Government and in the state and municipal governments with jurisdiction over the service provision area; (vi) a community channel open for free use by non-governmental and non-profit entities, and (vii) a channel reserved for the Federal STF, for broadcasting the acts of the Judiciary and the services essential to Justice. Also, added to these is the obligation to carry the signal of the channel offered by the EBC, created by Law 11. 652 of 7 April 2008 (for further details on EBC creation and operation, *see* Part II, Chapter 2).

467. When the Cable Law was enacted, Brazil still had a fragmented legal framework for Pay-TV services, which were regulated separately, according to the means used for signal distribution – cable, DTH (Distribution of Television and Audio Signals by Subscription via Satellite) and MMDS (which uses microwave bands). The fact that only cable TV operators were bound to must-carry obligations gave ground to a debate that questioned the isonomy of this rule, given that other competitor services did not bear any cost regarding the distribution of public interest channels.

468. Despite these discussions around its legitimacy, the must-carry provisions contained in the Cable Law are often named as a key factor for the creation of public interest channels – including the institution of state broadcasters (specially legislative and judiciary channels) and community broadcasters (as the provision created a demand for these channels and potentialized their distribution). In fact, the original wording of Article 23, I, b actually shaped legislative channels, as it read that municipal or legislative channels were to be 'dedicated to the documentation of parliamentary work, especially the live broadcast of the sessions'. Fernando Oliveira Paulino highlights that this transparency characteristic (i.e., enabling access to official sessions and public interest information) was an essential feature of this must-carry rule, essential to justify the existence of channels connected to the Chambers, Assemblies and Congress.

469. The must-carry framework was unified by Law 12.485/2011, Article 32. According to this provision, a SeAC distributor must provide, in its area of service provision, without any burden or additional cost to its subscribers, in all packages offered, programming channels of mandatory distribution for the following destinations:

- the FTA television channels available in that area (which the ANATEL in 2017 ruled that does not apply to high-definition channels, but only analogical ones[299]);
- a channel operated by the federal House of Representatives;
- a channel operated by the Federal Senate;
- a channel operated by the Federal STF (STF);
- a channel for public broadcasting services provided by the executive branch;
- a channel reserved for the executive branch's official broadcasting station;
- one educational channel;
- one community channel;
- one citizenship channel (to be organized by the Federal Government and destined for broadcasting local community programmes, for publicizing acts, works, projects, sessions and events of the federal, state and municipal public powers);
- one municipal or state legislative channel, reserved for shared use between the City Councils located in the municipalities of the service provision area and the Legislative Assembly of the respective state or for use by the Legislative Chamber of the Federal District; and
- one university channel (reserved for shared use among higher education institutions located in the municipality or municipalities in the service provision area).

299. National Film Agency – ANATEL, Procedure nº 53500.008950/2014-11, 31 Oct. 2017. Available at: https://sei.anatel.gov.br/sei/publicacoes/controlador_publicacoes.php?acao=publicacao_visualizar&id_documento=2094849&id_orgao_publicacao=0 (accessed 10 Jan. 2021).

470. Pay-TV operators cannot alter the transmission of these channels in any sense. And if a Pay-TV operator finds themselves unable to comply with these obligations for technical reasons, they can request a partial or total release from them to the ANATEL (the agency will have ninety days to rule on). Law 12.485/2011 also brings a series of other requirements to these obligations, which are further regulated by Resolution ANATEL 581/2012. In this secondary norm, the agency further regulated the flexibility of this obligation, stating, e.g., that Pay-TV operators supported by MMDS infrastructure are not subject to the obligations.

Chapter 9. Funding and Development

471. Brazil has had a volatile history of state funding policies towards audiovisual content, with different funding and development institutions having been created and later extinguished throughout the XX century.[300] The last time these policies were extinguished was during the government of President Fernando Collor (1990), under a liberal justification in the sense that it was not up for governments to intervene in cultural sectors. The decision tanked the country's audiovisual production: two years later, in 1992 only three Brazilian movies were produced in the country.[301]

472. The institutional mechanisms currently in place are a result of a process that followed this crisis in the production sector, a process referred to in Brazilian Portuguese as 'Retomada' (translatable as 'resumption'). The reactions to the non-intervention policy started shortly after the extinction of funding mechanisms, in 1991, and resulted in one funding and development mechanism approved in 1991 (Law 8.131/1991, which applies to a series of cultural activities). In 1993, the 'Audio-Visual Law' was enacted, with focus on the development of audiovisual national content, and from the second half of the 1990s, the resumption process indeed took off, during the government of President Fernando Henrique Cardoso. During his second presidential term, the ANCINE was created with the main objective of developing and regulating the audiovisual sector[302] (MP 2.228-1/2001). This was a turning point in assuring a structured public policy that was key in developing the industry. Another pivotal moment was the approval of Law 12.485/2011, which regulated Pay-TV services and further enabled the audiovisual sector by increasing tax collection, incentive mechanisms and assuring a demand for national and independent content through the establishment of screen quotas.[303] With time, the policies for the audiovisual sector started to be justified not only under their cultural relevance (i.e., as a means of affirmation of national and regional identities) but also under economic reason, as an industry that generates jobs and foreign exchange.

§1. Funding and Development Mechanisms

473. The Federal Union's legitimacy to regulate and promote the audiovisual activity derives from the Article 174 of the Federal Constitution, according to which, '[a]s a normative and regulating agent of economic activities, the State shall

300. For more details about this process, *see* Marcelo Ikeda, *Cinema Brasileiro a partir da retomada: aspectos econômicos e políticos,* Ch. 1 (Summus Editorial 2015).
301. Marcelo Ikeda, *Cinema Brasileiro a partir da retomada: aspectos econômicos e políticos,* Ch. 1 (Summus Editorial 2015).
302. More details on ANCINE will follow in Part V below.
303. As described in Part III, Ch. 3 herein above.

exercise, according to the law, the functions of inspection, incentive and planning, the latter being determinant for the public sector and indicative for the private sector'.

474. State interference through regulation of the audiovisual sector is justified by the sector's strategic character from cultural and economic perspectives. The regulation will seek to preserve the national content and industry, aiming at the domestic market's growth through the expansion of supply and demand for content produced by independent Brazilian producers.[304,305] As a way of fostering the national industry, the regulation is mostly based on: funding production of audiovisual works; creating demand for audiovisual national and independent content (for instance, through movie theatre and Pay-TV services screen quotas, which require more content to fill them, which will be funded with public resources); providing funding for professional training; providing funding for acquisition and distribution of Brazilian works, as well as for the construction and sustainment of movie theatres. A few mechanisms also aim at ensuring that these policies observe regional and local imbalances and cultural characteristics.

475. Against this background, the promotion of the audiovisual sector in Brazil takes place in several ways, such as tax incentives, public investments derived from an audiovisual fund, tax exemption for investment in movie theatres, and application of minimum quotas for Brazilian audiovisual content in movie theatre and Pay-TV. Such public policies at the federal level are mostly executed by the ANCINE. In the following paragraphs, we will approach the main mechanisms available for funding and development of audiovisual works.

476. Currently, these incentives can take the form of 'indirect' or 'direct' support. Indirect support for audiovisual projects is given through the tax incentive mechanisms provided in Law 8.313/91 (Rouanet Law), in Law 8.685/93 (Audio-Visual Law), and in MP 2,228-1/01. These legal provisions allow taxpayers, individuals and legal entities, to have a reduction or exemption from certain taxes, provided they direct funds, through sponsorship, co-production or investment, to audiovisual projects approved by ANCINE.[306]

477. In its turn, direct incentives refer to the support through funding that is made available by the public treasure, directly to audiovisual projects. The mechanisms are implemented through public calls for proposals and public selections and are led by the Audio-Visual Sectorial Fund (Fundo Setorial do Audio-visual – FSA). FSA policies cover the various segments of the sector's production chain – from production to exhibition, distribution/marketing and service infrastructure. The resources that make up this fund come first and foremost from the collection of the

304. Only companies owned and controlled by a Brazilian person may apply for tax benefit funding on audiovisual productions.
305. ANCINE Guidelines for foreign companies: https://www.ancine.gov.br/en/co-producing-with-Brazil/guidelines-foreign-companies.
306. National Film Agency – ANCINE, *Fomento*. Available at: https://antigo.ancine.gov.br/pt-br/fomento/o-que-e (accessed 4 Jan. 2021).

Contribution to the Development of the Cinematographic Industry – CONDECINE (which will be further approached in the next section), from the Federal Union's Budget, and from telecommunications grants revenues (mainly from FISTEL – the Telecommunications Supervision Fund).

478. The logic of FSA is that of an investment fund. That is to say that, once FSA funds a certain audiovisual project, it becomes one of its investors, and as such, it will receive a share of the profits generated by the project once it is commercialized. The more successful the works funded by FSA become, the more funds return to it, which will later be further available to support other works (and so it goes). In practical terms, this means that, as soon as a project has resources from FSA (regardless of the volume of investment), it must abide by a specific legal regime. Among others, this framework includes obligations such as: guaranteeing that the majority of rights over the work will remain with Brazilian and independent producers; limitations on the negotiation with third parties of the elements that make up the project (e.g., brands. marketing products and works derivatives); and licensing limitations (regarding who and to what extent third parties can have rights over the work).[307]

479. The indirect funding occurs through laws that grant tax incentives to private entities that allocate resources to independent Brazilian audiovisual production. In these mechanisms, the government waives part of the taxes due so that companies shall distribute this amount to individual projects.

480. This sort of incentive mechanisms rests on the interaction of three agents: the proponent, who is the company or individual who can propose a financeable project through a certain mechanism (for audiovisual production, for instance, this would be the Brazilian independent producer); the taxpayer, which is the one who will have the tax benefit if he contributes a portion of the tax payable in a certain mechanism; and the competent government entity, which will register the interested taxpayer and approve projects that can receive financial resources; and, finally. In the project blueprint, its essential characteristics shall be described to figure out how much public money this project can receive, which compensations shall be offered, and deadlines inherent to the presentation, production, fundraising, execution, and accountability, in accordance with the limits and options provided by within the regulatory framework. Depending on the mechanism under use, the taxpayer figures as a co-producer or investor of the work, and similar contractual limitations to those of the directly funded audiovisual projects also may apply.

481. In the next lines, we provide a summary of the characteristics of the three main tax incentive mechanisms currently in place: Article 3 of Law 8.685/93; Article 3-A of Law 8.685/93; and Article 39, X of MP 2.228-1/2001:

307. This legal framework is provided by the PRODAV regulation ('Regulamento Geral do Prodav – Programa de Desenvolvimento do Audio-visual Brasileiro'). Available at: https://fsa.ancine.gov.br/sites/default/files/regulamento-geral-do-prodav/RG_PRODAV_versao_07.11.18___Apos_Resolucoes_178_180_e_182.pdf (accessed 4 Jan. 2021).

(A) Article 3, Law 8.685/93: the mechanism provides that 70% of the amount corresponding to the income tax applicable to the remittance of licence fee resulting from the exploitation of foreign works in Brazil can be directed at the co-production of independent Brazilian works (in association with independent Brazilian producers). Besides that, there will be an exemption benefit from the payment of CONDECINE levied on remittance of royalties – so that the CONDECINE exemption in fact represents a financial advantage:
   - Target: Foreign companies which distribute (or license the distribution of) audiovisual productions for theatrical in Brazil.
   - Tax Benefit: Deduction of 70% of income tax on royalties' remittances from Brazil to foreign companies plus exemption of CONDECINE[308] tax levied on these remittances.
   - Tax benefits must be used to: (a) invest in the development of feature film projects; and/or (b) co-produce (i) telefilms; (ii) miniseries; (iii) series; and (iv) cinematographic productions. Cap for investment per production: BRL 3 million.

(B) Article 3-A, Law 8,685/93: According to the mechanism, foreign taxpayers who receive income related to broadcasting rights on FTA television or Pay-TV can allocate 70% of the income tax[309] to an ANCINE-approved audiovisual project. Unlike Article 3, there is no exemption from CONDECINE – however, this incentive can be combined with the 39, X mechanism below:
   - Target: Foreign companies (e.g., TV channels, producers, events rights holders) which license the transmission of audiovisual contents or events (featuring sports events with the presence of Brazilian athletes) to FTA television or to pay TV channels in Brazil.
   - Tax Benefit: Discount of 70% of income tax on royalties' remittances from Brazil to foreign companies as payment for the acquisition of rights for the transmission of foreign audiovisual contents or events on FTA television or Pay-TV.
   - Tax benefits must be used to: (a) invest in the development of feature film projects; and/or (b) co-produce (i) telefilms; (ii) miniseries; (iii) series; and (iv) feature, medium and short films (cinematographic productions). Cap for investment per production: BRL 3 million.

(C) Article 39-X, MP 2.228-1/01: According to the mechanism, if a Pay-TV programmer applies 3% of the income from the exploitation of foreign works in Brazil in an approved audiovisual project, there will be an exemption from collecting the 11% of CONDECINE-remittance. It will represent a real gain of 8%:

---

308. CONDECINE (MP 2,228-1 Arts 3, 29, 30 and 33–40) is a federal tax which funds are aimed at fostering the Brazilian audiovisual industry's development. These funds are allocated to initiatives such as the Audio-Visual Sector Fund (FSA), which invests in the national audiovisual industry (which comprises the production, development, and distribution of independent Brazilian productions). The type mentioned herein is CONDECINE on remittances, levied on payment, credit, remittance, or delivery abroad to foreign companies of amounts consisting of revenues originating from foreign audiovisual exploitation contents in Brazil or their acquisition or importation. CONDECINE on Remittances is equivalent to 11% of each remittance sent abroad and should be withheld in Brazil.
309. At the rate of 15%.

- Target: Foreign Pay-TV programming companies which programme channels offered in Brazil through Pay-TV.
- Tax Benefit: Exemption of CONDECINE.
- Tax benefits must be used to: co-produce (i) feature, medium and short films; (iii) telefilms; (iii) miniseries; and (iv) TV contents deemed educative or cultural. No cap for investment per production.

482. In addition to any real financial gains resulting from applying the above mechanisms, the foreign taxpayer will have an equity of the audiovisual work's IP. The foreign agent's ownership will be proportional to the financial contribution, up to a limit of 49%.

§2. The Contribution to the Development of the Cinematographic Industry: CONDECINE

483. The Contribution to the Development of the National Film Industry (Contribuição para o Desenvolvimento da Indústria Cinematográfica Nacional – CONDECINE) is a tax species, of the type contribution for intervention on an economic sector (from Contribuição de Intervenção no Domínio Econômico – CIDE). The constitutional basis for this type of tax is Article 149 of the Federal Constitution, according to which CIDEs are to be implemented by the Federal Union, in order to intervene in certain markets with the goal of rebalancing them. CONDECINE plays this role regarding the audiovisual sector, and is levied over transmission, production, and exploitation of cinematographic and video-phonographic works; payment, credit, and remittance of audiovisual works royalties related to producers, distributors, or intermediaries located abroad. The market is balanced by the distribution of the amounts collected through CONDECINE for the benefit of independent audiovisual production, funding an audiovisual sector fund.

484. CONDECINE itself is provided by Article 32 of MP 2.228-1/2001. It assumes different forms, depending on the taxable event. The first one is known as 'CONDECINE remittance', which refers to an 11% fee levied on royalties remittances from Brazil (or less, if part of it is reverted for the benefit of producing independent audiovisual works under certain tax incentives as described above). The second one is 'CONDECINE Title' applicable to the licensing of each audiovisual work in each market segment. Market segments are defined in Article 33, I of MP 2.228-1/2001 (i.e., FTA television, Pay-TV, home video, movie theatres, and other segments). The same law also provides for a table containing fixed values of CONDECINE for each market segment, varying according to the type, nationality, purpose, length and destination of the audiovisual work (this is the CONDECINE that applies to audiovisual advertising, as mentioned above in Part III, Chapter 6).

485. The third type is known as 'CONDECINE Teles' because it is due from concessionaires, licensees, and authorized telecommunications services providers, whose infrastructure is or can be used for the distribution of audiovisual content. The contribution must be collected annually, until 31 March, for the services licensed until 31 December of the previous year, and values are also fixed in the legislation. This modality was not originally intended when CONDECINE was implemented by MP 2.228-1 in 2001; instead, it was established by the Pay-TV regulatory statute, Law 12.485/2011. The alleged logic behind the extension of CONDECINE to the telecommunications sector was insertion of these activities in the audiovisual market allowed by technological convergence. While convergence is an indisputable fact, grounds for the collection of CONDECINE Teles have been exhaustively argued before courts since its creation.

Part IV. Media Ownership and Control Regulation

486. Ownership rules are key mechanisms for media regulation, whose fundamentals rest not only on the fragmentation of economic power that can lead to abuse (as it is for antitrust regulations implemented across different sectors) but also on the necessity of assuring a democratic media landscape. For a long time, spotlight space to diffuse a certain message was conditioned to access to infrastructure – i.e., owning a media platform, be it a newspaper, a magazine, or radio and TV channels. In fact, this is still mostly the case. Even though the Internet's expansion and the emergence of content platforms have amplified the possibilities for content distribution, relevant public debates are still highly influenced by the traditional media, whose long history of building good practices and infrastructure still enjoys great influence. Media ownership regulations aim at limiting this power by limiting property over media vehicles, and thus promote external pluralism and enhance their democratic potential. The assumption here is that the more actors there are in charge of media companies, the more perspectives will be displayed in public debates, and there would be less possibility for one single group of interests to dominate the public agenda.

487. As it is in many constitutional democracies, Brazil has a set of different rules that rest on these foundations. However – as it also happens in other constitutional democracies – there is still a great degree of concentration in the media sector, which in Brazil's case can be referred to both its long history of building economic and political power (that benefited from the dictatorship's approach to the sector), and to the non-enforcement of the constitutional limitations currently in place.

488. In a follow-up study conducted since 2017,[310] NGOs Intervozes and Reporters Without Borders have been performing studies of Brazil's legislative, economic and political landscapes, with particular attention to media ownership. Their contributions are centred on their finding that the media sector in Brazil is still highly concentrated, so that media pluralism is subject to tremendous systemic risk

310. Media Ownership Monitor in Brazil, *Media Pluralism,* available at: https://brazil.mom-rsf.org/en/findings/ (accessed 8 Jan. 2021).

in the country. They point out that freedom of information is at risk due to a lack of sufficient regulatory safeguards on media ownership concentration and cross-media ownership concentration.

489. In the next chapters, we will highlight the main features of media ownership rules provided for in the Brazilian regulatory framework, with focus on applicable constitutional provisions and the specific rules for broadcasting and Pay-TV services. In our last section, we will also provide a brief overview of how these rules influence or relate to the legal treatment of merging media services.

§1. Constitutional Provisions

490. As already described in Part III, the Federal Constitution established a few requirements for the social communications sector, among which are rules regarding ownership of different types of media vehicles.

491. The first set of rules applies to media vehicles in general. Article 220, §5 establishes that 'social communications vehicles cannot be, directly or indirectly, an object of monopoly or oligopoly'. This is an express prohibition of economic concentration in the sector. Despite comprising a significant limitation, this provision has not been properly regulated by legislation and enforced by public authorities, which weakens its adoption in practice.

492. In turn, Article 222 aims at 'broadcasting and journalistic' companies – which includes print media and possibly other platforms that perform press activities. According to Article 222, §1, 'ownership', for the purposes of the ownership regulation, shall mean detaining direct or indirect control over at least 70% of the total capital and the voting capital of the journalistic and broadcasting companies. Besides ownership, editorial responsibility and the activities of selection and direction of the broadcasted programme are also exclusive to Brazilian natives or those naturalized for more than ten years (paragraph 2). This nationality requirement applies to all broadcasting services, of any categories and types of grant. Paragraphs 3 and 4 establish further specific conditions for the implementation of this rule, as we will discuss in the next chapters.

493. Under the Constitution, there is also a prohibition that elected politicians hold participation in companies that have been granted with licences to exploit broadcasting services. This provision is not specific to broadcasting; in fact, Article 54, II, holds that, once they take office, house representatives and senators cannot be the owner, controller or director of a company that enjoys favourable treatment under a contract with a public-law entity, or holding a paid position therein. This includes every public service granted company, and thus is a prohibition that encompasses broadcasting licences.

494. The impossibility of house representatives and senators holding broadcasting grants is in accordance with not only the constitutional text but also a fair democratic standard that relates to a series of other constitutional values. Making sure that politicians in power do not dictate the media vehicle's agenda also favours pluralism, freedom of expression and access to information, as well as the principle of fair elections, to mention a few.

495. Even though this ban is crystal clear in the constitutional text, several broadcasting grants remain in the hands of politicians and their families. The legal justification for this lies on the constitutional provision of Article 54, I, a, which provides that these politicians can hold contracts with public concessionaires if these contracts have 'uniform clauses'. This provision is a clear reference to 'adhesion contracts', commonly implemented in consumerist relationships between service providers and their users, based on a single model of contract with uniform clauses that apply to everyone. This is the constitutional exception that allows house representatives and senators to, for instance, have mobile services and other public utilities contracts. The maintenance of this immoral practice, now under the scrutiny of STF, as detailed below, is thus based on a poor misinterpretation of the constitutional text that is only held due to a political legal framework that is fond of fostering long-acquired political and economic privileges. Due to this specific feature – i.e., allowing long-standing political privileges to survive – this practice is commonly referred to as '*coronelismo eletrônico*'.

496. This is a reference to '*coronelismo*', or in English, 'colonelism', as in a power system dated from the end of XIX to the beginning of the XX century, headed by local leaders also referred to as 'colonels'. The colonels concentrated property and agrarian power and were aligned with the Federal Government. They controlled the vote of the population under their area of economic and political domain, making sure their leadership would always remain in power.[311] The maintenance of broadcasting gives politicians the space to express the bias and political perspective that will favour their maintenance of power; hence, we have the name 'electronic colonialism' (in Portuguese, '*coronelismo eletrônico*') to refer to this practice.[312]

497. There are currently two lawsuits filed in the STF that claim the unconstitutionality of the grants handed to politicians – ADPF 246[313] and ADPF 379.[314] The first one was filed in 2011 and second one in 2015. In August 2016, the Attorney General's Office petitioned in the ADPF 379 case records to file its legal opinion[315]

---

311. For more details on this political moment, *see:* Victor Nunes Leal, *Coronelismo, enxada e voto: o município e o regime representativo no Brasil*, 4ªed (Companhia das Letras 2012).
312. Venício A. de Lima & Cristiano Aguiar Lopes, *Coronelismo eletrônico de novo tipo (1999-2004): as autorizações de emissoras como moeda de barganha política,* Observatório da Imprensa; Instituto para o Desenvolvimento do Jornalismo (2007).
313. It is possible to follow this process directly on the STF website: https://portal.stf.jus.br/processos/detalhe.asp?incidente=4183656.
314. *Ibid.* https://portal.stf.jus.br/processos/detalhe.asp?incidente=4900898.
315. Legal opinion 186.689/2016-AsJConst/SAJ/PGR. Available at https://portal.stf.jus.br/processos/downloadPeca.asp?id=310159920&ext=.pdf (accessed 20 Feb. 2022).

through which it argued that the concession or maintenance of the operation of broadcasting services by legal entities in which holders of elective mandates participate as partners or associates 'collides with the impartiality and independence that should exist in the exercise of these functions'. So far, the STF has not yet tried these cases.

§2. Ownership and Control on Broadcasting Services Concessionaires

498. Decree-Law 236/1962 regulates the concentration of ownership of broadcasting services by imposing grants limits 'by entity' – i.e., by company. According to this statute, each 'entity' can only hold a total of ten television broadcasting grants, out of which only five grants can be in a very high frequency – VHF. Out of the five VHF grants only two can be with a maximum of five grants in VHF and two per state – a rule that is originally meant to avoid the concentration of grants in the same region. For the purposes of this rule, grants are also accounted for in relation to shareholders of the grant's holder – i.e., a shareholder that participates in more than broadcasting companies also cannot accumulate grants, even if through their different companies. In the same sense is the rule that prevents an economic agent from holding more than one broadcasting licence in the same municipality (provided by Article 15, §2, II of Decree 52.795/1963). The Decree exempts from this limits calculation the grants obtained for repeaters and RTV.

499. It is important to highlight that these provisions already existed before the 1988 Constitution was enacted. In fact, some of them were already established under authoritarian governments, and have never proved effective in promoting media pluralism – in great part, due to the 'affiliates network' contractual system, which became the default for commercial broadcasting by circumventing these requirements (as per Part III, Chapter 1, §1). The prohibition of monopoly and oligopoly established by the Constitution was never effectively implemented by a specific regulation, or even by other legal frameworks that are applicable (e.g., antitrust law).

500. The constitutional property limitation of 30% for non-Brazilian citizens has also been further detailed by legislation. The provision is regulated by Law 10.610/2002, which determines that foreigners' participation must take place indirectly, through companies (vehicles) incorporated in Brazil. However, broadcasting companies' directors must be Brazilian natives or naturalized citizens for more than ten years. It is important to note that in the original draft of the provisional measure that gave rise to Law 10.610/2002, there was a provision that sought not to compute for assessing ownership concentration, equity interest equal to or less than 20%, including in the voting capital.

501. For broadcasting services, the legislation does not provide for cross-property regulation or ownership limits based on audience reach.

§3. OWNERSHIP AND CONCENTRATION ON PAY-TV SERVICES

502. Pay-TV services also abide by a particular set of ownership rules, notably regarding vertical concentration and cross-media ownership.

I. Vertical Concentration Rules

503. Law 12.485/2011 has established vertical ownership limits over the chain of production and distribution of audiovisual content in Brazil. These legal provisions are the outcome of a dispute between the lobbying forces that, on one side, dominated the content programming of Pay-TV channels in Brazil and, on the other side, the content distributors. The economic groups that at the time controlled the programming of the Pay-TV channels were also (still are) responsible for FTA television channels, which explains certain limitations, in the law of Pay-TV, to the cross-ownership regulation between Pay-TV distribution and FTA broadcasting services.

504. Law 12.485/2011 restricts in its Article 6:

> Art. 6 – The telecommunications service providers of collective interest, as well as their subsidiaries, parent companies or affiliates, may not, for the purpose of producing audio-visual content for their placement in the conditioned access service or in the audio and audio and video broadcasting service:
>
> I – acquire or finance the acquisition of rights to exploit images of events of national interest; and
> II – contract national artistic talents of any nature, including rights over works produced by national authors.
>
> Sole paragraph. The restrictions referred to in this Article do not apply when the acquisition or contract is intended exclusively for the production of advertising works.

505. What was introduced with the 2011 law in force was a very clear and direct restriction on the verticalization of the audiovisual value chain, by restricting the exercise of audiovisual production and Pay-TV programming activities by Pay-TV distributors and Pay-TV distribution by Pay-TV programming entities. Market agents that fall into this category consider these limitations an affront to freedom of initiative protected by the Federal Constitution, namely in its Article 170, IV.[316] In

316. Brazilian Federal Constitution, at Art. 170: 'The economic order, founded on the appreciation of the value of human work and on free enterprise, is intended to ensure everyone a life with dignity, in accordance with the dictates of social justice, with due regard for the following principles: (…) IV – free competition.'

a lawsuit[317] seeking the declaration of unconstitutionality of this Article 6, the private civil association NEO TV, which represented small Pay-TV content distributors, argued that the Inc. II above could interfere 'unduly in the exercise of the profession of artists who could eventually be hired by the telecommunications companies of collective interest'.

506. On that occasion, the Constitutional Court ruled that Article 6 above is harmonious with the Articles 170, IV and 220, §5[318] of the Federal Constitution, for being in line with the principle of free competition and for representing an apparatus for achieving the freedom of expression and dissipating the concentration of communicative power. In this sense, the Court stated that Article 6 is justified by the Federal Constitution itself since the wording of its Article 173, §4 prescribes that 'the law shall repress the abuse of economic power that aims at the domination of markets, the elimination of competition and the arbitrary increase of profits'.

507. By means of the above rule, telecommunications service providers and their economic groups, including companies that implement the distribution activities of Pay-TV channels (MSOs) programmed by third parties, are prevented from acquiring rights to events of national interest, a definition intended for encompassing primarily sporting events, World Cup and Olympic Games.[319] Besides that, Pay-TV distributors cannot hire any national artistic talents (broadly, including everything from actors to licensing rights to Brazilian works such as adaptation rights of books), with the purpose of producing audiovisual content, except for audiovisual content of advertising nature.

508. This rule, together with the horizontal concentration of ownership, establishes the so-called cut in the value chain of the Pay-TV industry in Brazil. In simple words, the legal limit explained in this item directly aims at preventing distributors (i.e., telecommunications companies) from entering the market by acquiring rights over sporting events. The entry of new highly capitalized players in this market would certainly change the current distribution of sporting events, as well as paradigms and eventually prices until then practised, and only Globo TV has been placing the higher bets on these prices (as per Part III, Chapter 7 above).

509. To better illustrate the influences on the discussions that shaped the rules described here, the first draft[320,321] that gave rise to law 12.485/2011 prescribed:

317. STF ADI 4.923/DF, tried on 8 Nov. 2017.

318. According to the legal provision, 'The manifestation of thought, the creation, the expression and the information, in any form, process or medium shall not be subject to any restriction, with due regard to the provisions of this constitution. (…) §5º social communication media may not, directly or indirectly, be subject to monopoly or oligopoly.'

319. The exact definition of Events of National Interest according to Art. 1, XIII of Law 12.485/2011 is: 'public events of a cultural, artistic, sports, religious or political nature that incite the significant interest of the Brazilian population, notably those in which participate, predominantly, Brazilians or Brazilian teams'.

320. https://www.camara.leg.br/proposicoesWeb/fichadetramitacao?idProposicao=339998.

321. To which three other bills were later joined: PL 70/2007, PL 332/2007 and PL 1098/2007.

'Companies providing telecommunications services covered by Art. 5 of this Law have the right to, in whole or in part, produce, program, provide and distribute electronic content, subject to the regulation of these services.' Such drafts were attempting to revoke the restrictions of foreign capital in the Pay-TV distributors, but not in the concessionaires of broadcasting services. Had this draft turned into law, certainly it would not only have had a significant impact on the market, but would have been a major blow to national media groups, given that there would be a significant risk to the equilibrium of the market inasmuch as an economic group could be able to purchase and produce the supplies (programmed channel or audiovisual content), as well distribute and sell them to the final consumer through a telecommunications service (as Pay-TV distributor). Potentially, the same player would have the means to impose unfavourable commercial conditions on third parties and establish a system based on content distribution discrimination (i.e., less favourable compression rates, response time, allocated bandwidth, lag on third-party contents) threatening network neutrality. Finally, in this scenario, the economic group would have access to commercial conditions practised by its competitors, insofar as, in its distribution operation, it would negotiate the acquisition of content with companies competing in its production and programming operations.

II. Crossed Ownership Limits

510. As a mechanism to prevent the implementation of anticompetitive practices, such as technically and commercially discriminatory practices and restrictions on access to content or networks of distribution, Law 12.485/2011 at its Article 5 sets limits on cross-ownership between the layer of production and programming versus the layer of packaging and distribution, as follows:

> Art. 5 The control or ownership of more than 50% (fifty per cent) of the total and voting capital of companies providing collective interest telecommunications services may not be held, directly, indirectly or through a company under common control, by audio and audio and video broadcasting concessionaires and permissionaires and by producers and programmers based in Brazil, which are prohibited from directly exploiting those services.
>
> §1 – The control or ownership of more than 30% (thirty per cent) of the total and voting capital of concessionaires and permit holders of audio and audio and video broadcasters, and producers and programmers based in Brazil cannot be directly owned, indirectly or through a company under common control, by telecommunications service providers of collective interest, being prohibited to directly exploit those services.
>
> §2 – Concessionaires and permissionaires of audio and audio and video broadcasters and to producers and programmers with headquarters in Brazil are allowed to, directly or through a company over which they have direct, indirect or common control, provide telecommunications services exclusively for concessionaires and permissionaires of audio and audio and

video broadcasting services, or to transport audio-visual content from producers or programmers based in Brazil for delivery to distributors, provided within the scope of their own network.

§3 – Companies providing telecommunications services of collective interest, directly or through a company over which they have direct, indirect or common control, are allowed to control producers and programmers based in Brazil that exercise activities exclusively destined to the commercialization of products and services for the international market.

511. As seen, content producers and Pay-TV programmers cannot hold more than 50% of telecom services providers' capital,[322] nor can they directly exploit telecom activities. It is interesting that, in addition to the Pay-TV players, this legal provision also affects TV broadcasters. That is, the Pay-TV law determined that broadcasters must also respect the limit of ownership and control over telecom activities, except for telecom services provided within the scope of their own networks, such as satellite uplink services, content transmission and others that also need regulatory authorization, but restricted to this private context, as follows:

512. Additionally, as per Part IV, §1 above, in the distribution layer, telecommunications service providers cannot hold more than 30% of broadcasters, producers and Pay-TV programmers, nor can they directly exploit those services, with the exception of control over Brazilian producers that carry out activities aimed exclusively at the international market (Part IV, §3).

513. Like many other countries, Brazil currently witnesses the expansion of streaming services.[323] This can be attributed to increased bandwidth supply enabling a better experience for the consumer, as well as to new consumer habits (on-demand, binge-watching, etc.) and economic crisis forcing citizens to cut costs and consequently cord cutting.

514. All of this strengthens not only newcomers but also direct-to-consumer operations carried by the Pay-TV programmers themselves. The regulation of the Pay-TV distribution service, SeAC, imposes costs that are fatally passed on to consumers, such as a 20x higher tax burden than OTT, or other costs imposed by the regulatory framework. These include the obligation to carry specific channels and the obligation to the inclusion of Brazilian channels and news channels in packages for the purpose of complying with legal quotas, in addition to the costs of maintaining telecommunications infrastructure, which involves the acquisition of satellite capacity, the acquisition of equipment for receiving and decoding signals, headends, etc.

---

322. For definitions adopted by ANATEL for assessing control, controlling and affiliated entity, *see* Res. ANATEL 101/1999.

323. As of January 2021, the most relevant video on-demand subscription platforms in Brazil are Netflix, Amazon Prime and Globoplay, the latter from Globo Group. Months earlier, in November 2020, Disney + made its debut in Brazil.

515. In addition to dealing with regulatory barriers and costs as seen above, Pay-TV distributors currently have to contend with the competition that distributes content through OTT operations. OTT, by its essence, does not have distribution infrastructure costs as Pay-TV distributors (i.e., SeAC), nor is it subject to the same regulation. The flexibility of packaging and costs has put a lot of pressure on the industry and has promoted a significant dispute between SeAC distributors and OTT platforms. With the migration of consumers to streaming,[324] and with the technical means available, the programmers only had to consider possible regulatory obstacles and possible non-compete contractual commitments with the Pay-TV distributors. The first to challenge regulation was Fox, launching Fox+ in 2018, an OTT delivery operation of its linear Pay-TV channels to non-SeAC subscribers, selling them direct-to-consumer. Fox's strategy led to a regulatory and judicial battle with the SeAC distributors, represented by Claro (America Movil) which initiated three administrative proceedings with the federal telecommunications regulatory agency (ANATEL).[325] In such regulatory dispute between Claro, and FOX (but later joined by ABRATEL and ABERT, private associations of radio and FTA broadcasters), Claro argued that (i) the paid linear programming offer must comply with SeAC rules; (ii) Fox by means of such operation is clandestinely providing a telecom service; (iii) under a finalistic interpretation model of the law, differentiation does not derive from the means of distribution but from the purposes and object of the communication, that is, reception of linear content, either OTT or SeAC, being certain that the last consists of providing data packages, content distribution by means of any process, paid subscribers, scheduled content and direct relationship with consumers.

516. Fox argued in its defence that (i) Fox+ is not a telecom service since the distribution means shall be independently contracted with a third-party telecommunication service provider since it is an OTT delivery; and (ii) the use and control of the telecommunications network (proprietary or third party owned) by the service provider is of the essence of SeAC.

517. The imbroglio had several chapters. ANATEL granted in 2019 an injunctive relief requested by Claro to prohibit the offer and commercialization of Fox+. However, this same ANATEL, in September 2020, decided that it could not prevent the OTT Fox+ platform from delivering the same linear channels that are also offered within the SeAC ecosystem, legitimizing the direct-to-consumer offer of linear Pay-TV channels. This opened doors for Globo Group to start selling its Pay-TV channels through its OTT platform (Globoplay).[326] As a reaction, the distributors are since then asking for profound changes in the SeAC law, sometimes

324. *See* Bruno Villas Boas, *IBGE: TV por assinatura perde espaço com crise e serviço de streaming*, Valor Econômico (20 Dec. 2019), https://valor.globo.com/brasil/noticia/2018/12/20/ibge-tv-por-assinatura-perde-espaco-com-crise-e-servico-de-streaming.ghtml (accessed 26 Mar. 2021).

325. Administrative proceedings 53500.056473/2018-24, 53500.057279/2018-66, 53500.022476/2019-45 and 53500.022573/2019-38.

326. Thais Monteiro, *Globo integra canais pagos no Globoplay*, Meio & Mensagem (31 Aug. 2020), https://www.meioemensagem.com.br/home/midia/2020/08/31/globo-integra-canais-pagos-no-globoplay.html (accessed 20 Feb. 2022).

even its complete revocation,[327] so that they can offer a product that could compete with OTT and its total lack of regulatory costs.

518. In addition to legal rules, the market itself implements its own private mechanisms, through contractual means. Most-favoured-nation clauses are common practices in programming licensing agreements whereby there are protections not only in relation to commercial conditions practised with third parties but also against any benefits granted to the party's own interests. Other common mechanisms are: non-compete clauses, which can be extremely impactful in OTT's own content distribution initiatives, outside, therefore, the ecosystem that is under the regulatory framework of Pay-TV; segment holdbacks, which could be a by-product of the two previous mechanisms, where content licensors undertake not to place the contents of linear channel programming grids in on-demand segments until the end of a predetermined period of time counted from its debut on the linear channel; and other sensitive ones from an antitrust perspective, such as channel bundling and packaging rules.

519. In the Pay-TV market, certain attributions are exclusive to Brazilian natives or to those naturalized for more than ten years. Regarding these parameters, Article 10 of Law 12.485/2011 determines that:

> Art. 10. Management, editorial responsibility and the activities of selection and direction inherent to programming and packaging are exclusive to Brazilian natives or naturalized for more than 10 (ten) years.
> §1 – Programmers and packagers must deposit and keep updated, at ANCINE, a list with the identification of the professionals referred to in the caput of this Article, the documents and corporate acts, including those referring to the choice of directors and officers, of individuals and legal entities involved in its chain of control, the information of which must be made available to the public, including through the world wide web, except for those considered confidential by Law and regulation, and the Agency is responsible for ensuring their secrecy.

520. Article 10 of Law 12.485/2011 was also challenged through lawsuits that questioned their compatibility with the Federal Constitution, as it would produce unequal treatment between Brazilians and foreigners, prohibited by the Letter.[328] In the judgment of the ADIs, the STF ruled that it is compatible with the Federal Constitution, which in its Article 222 creates a distinction that aims to protect certain values also advocated by its own text, such as protection of sovereignty and national

327. Tele Síntese, *Claro defende a extinção da lei do SeAC* (9 Jul. 2020), https://www.telesintese.com.br/claro-defende-extincao-da-lei-do-seac/ (accessed 20 Feb. 2022).

328. Article 5: 'all persons are equal before the law, without any distinction whatsoever, Brazilians and foreigners residing in the country (…) combined with Art. 12, §2º: (…) the law may not establish any distinction between born and naturalized Brazilians, except in the cases stated in this Constitution.(…)'.

identity and appreciation of Brazilian culture, citing an excerpt from a book[329] by the professor and today also Minister of the STF, Luís Roberto Barroso:

> if other platforms offer the same services [of mass communication], they automatically raise the same concerns associated with broadcasting, regarding national sovereignty, public opinion, national culture and accountability. It is worth emphasizing, once again, the evident finding that the constituent only made reference to radio and television, as broadcasting companies, because this was the 'state of the art', in terms of mass media, at the time in which the work of drafting the Constitution was carried out.

§4. Media Ownership and New Markets

521. As we have highlighted in different parts of this monograph, the scenario of concentration that marks the Brazilian media sector is indisputable. The unenforced constitutional provisions and the maintenance of economic and political privileges translate themselves as indisputable barriers of entry to new players who need the attention of this same audience.

522. Regardless of that, it can also happen that newcomers challenge consumption habits deeply rooted in local culture. That is to say that new media markets can also gain space and penetration, affecting this *status quo* – even though this particular effect will not do much for national media pluralism or democracy. This is the case, for instance, for OTT audiovisual services that have grown considerably in the last years and disrupted the competition for audiovisual services.

523. Although in 1998[330] they participated in the auctions, the owners of the broadcasting companies were unable to establish themselves in geographic areas of activity when there was a process of privatization of public companies that exercised a monopoly in the provision of telephone services in Brazil. Perhaps due to the fact that, at the time, they did not have technical conditions, or even sufficient clairvoyance, to assess the strategic potential of the business, the broadcasting groups ended up considering that the financial risk involved in insisting on the telecommunications business would not be worth it. The pictorial representation of the current moment would be a liquid-looking substance entering a boiling point, where molecules represented by Pay-TV programmers, streaming platforms, and telecom companies (Pay-TV distributors) are colliding. The current moment has not yet been

---

329. Luís Roberto Barroso, *Temas de direito constitucional*, 103 (Renovar 2003).

330. In 1998, privatization auctions were held for Telebrás, the company then controlled by the public administration that was responsible for providing telephone services in Brazil. The activities of the so-called Telebrás System was divided into geographic blocks and private companies were able to bid and obtain certain blocks. Two of the blocks were bought by a consortium formed between one of the largest Brazilian private banks, Bradesco, and Globo Group, but the shares were sold to Telecom Italia shortly afterwards due to a lack of capital injection to accommodate the business risks, in this regard *see* the news from the newspaper *Folha de S. Paulo* published about six months after the auction: https://www1.folha.uol.com.br/fsp/dinheiro/fi16129806.htm.

translated into legislative changes, but changes to certain understandings of governmental regulatory agencies about the current legislation that originated a complete transformation in the market, as will be seen in detail below.

524. This long parenthesis made a great looping; it starts and ends today: today, the dominant forces in Brazil continue to be the owners of the channels, but not the *stricto sensu* TV channel, as they were until the early 2000s. Globo TV delivered pasteurized[331] content to the entire audience, to everyone and anyone; today Netflix delivers content to all audiences, to each and every one. What was once dominance for delivering and shaping mass culture is now a polite supplication to enter several bubbles, and today, in the early years of the 2020s, what Netflix wants is to enter the bubbles that consume soap operas in Brazil.[332]

---

331. In 2005, the Globo TV newscaster with the highest audience ratings on Brazilian television declared that he strove to always be able to communicate with Homer Simpson on the other side of the screen, in a news article by *Folha de S. Paulo* newspaper – https://www1.folha.uol.com.br/folha/ilustrada/ult90u55778.shtml.
332. Bárbara Sacchitiello, *Como serão as novelas brasileiras da Netflix*, Meio & Mensagem (23 Nov. 2021), https://www.meioemensagem.com.br/home/midia/2021/11/23/como-serao-as-novelas-brasileiras-da-netflix.html (accessed 20 Feb. 2022).

Part V. Supervision: Media Regulator

525. Administrative supervision of the Brazilian media sector is fragmented among a series of governmental bodies, with different organizations, attributions and internal processes. The supervision framework applicable to the media sector has been described as 'complex with several authorities having different powers'[333] – a setting that is challenging in itself, and that grows in complexity in the face of technological convergence processes.

526. Each media sector is submitted to supervision by a set of different governmental bodies. For instance, regarding broadcasting services, the Ministry of Communications 'acts as a public policy maker and a quasi-regulator. To that end, it theoretically monitors and controls the broadcasting sector, directly and indirectly',[334] and the main attribution left outside of the Ministry remit is the authorization for radiofrequency use and technical equipment validation (performed by the ANATEL). In turn, Pay-TV regulation is under the scope of two authorities: ANATEL (notably regarding use of infrastructure such as cable, satellite or MMDS), and the ANCINE (responsible for monitoring content requirements compliance).

527. In terms of federative competences, supervision of telecommunications and broadcasting services are concentrated at the national level (*see* Articles 21, XI and XII in the Federal Constitution). This means that the majority of relevant policies are implemented by the Federal Government's direct and indirect administration. Jonas Valente attributes this arrangement to the administrative reforms led by the government of Fernando Henrique Cardoso (Presidency 1995 to 2003) along with the privatization of public utilities and the creation of regulatory agencies. The administrative model implemented by then was based on the division of functions according to which the formulation of policies is led by ministries, and their execution and monitoring are handled by regulatory agencies. As he highlights, the only exceptions to this are the broadcasting policies given that the Ministry of Communications is also in charge of their implementation.[335]

---

333. OECD Telecommunication and Broadcasting Review of Brazil 2020, p. 130.
334. *Ibid.*
335. Jonas Valente, *Regulação Democrática dos meios de comunicação*, 38 (Coleção O Que Saber 2013).

528. The supervision of media sector legislation is thus divided among three federal administration bodies: the Ministry of Communications, the ANATEL and the ANCINE. In the following sections, we will discuss the main aspects including organization, tasks and the sanctioning powers of each administrator. Together, they encompass the vast majority of supervision attributions prescribed by the specialized legislation. There are, nevertheless, certain other institutions that play relevant roles.

529. For instance, two policy councils have attributions related to the sector: the Social Communications Council (Conselho da Comunicação Social – CCS) and the Senior Film Council (Conselho Superior do Cinema – CSC). In Brazil, policy councils are bodies established by law, with functions related to discussion, formation and counselling of public policies targeted at specific economic sectors. Their organization and format can vary according to the legal statute that created them; it is common, nevertheless, that their members represent different stakeholders involved in the same economic activities.

530. Article 224 of Federal Constitution created the CCS, according to which: '[th]e National Congress shall institute, as an auxiliary body, the Council for Social Communication'. This provision was further regulated by Law 8.389/1991, which in its Article 2 establishes that this Council shall carry out studies, opinions, recommendations, and other requests forwarded to it by the National Congress. These functions are to be exercised with focus on social communications related queries, namely in what concerns to: the freedom to manifest thought, creation, expression and information; commercial advertisement of tobacco, alcoholic beverages, pesticides, medicines and healthcare therapies in the media; public entertainments and public spectacles; production and programming of radio and television stations; media monopoly or oligopoly; educational, artistic, cultural and informative purposes of the radio and television broadcasters' programming; promotion of national and regional culture, and stimulus to independent production; complementarity of the private, public and state broadcasting systems; individual and family's protection from radio and television content that might be contrary to the provisions of the Federal Constitution; ownership of journalistic and sound and image broadcasting companies; and granting and renewal of concessions, permissions and authorizations for broadcasting services. The CCS shall be formed by three representatives of the social communications companies (radio services, television companies, print media), five representatives of professional categories (one engineer with notorious knowledge in the area of social communication, one representative of journalists, one of radio broadcaster; one representative from the professional category of artists, one from the cinema and professional video categories), and five members representing civil society.

531. The CSC was created by MP 2.228-1/2001, the same legal instrument that created the ANCINE and instituted a national film policy. Article 3 describes it as a collegiate body that integrates the structure of the Civil Secretariat of the Presidency, which shall be in charge of: defining the national cinema policy; approving general policies and guidelines for the development of the national film industry, aiming at the sector's self-sustainability; stimulating the presence of Brazilian content in different markets; following up the execution of these policies; and establishing the distribution of the Contribution to the Development of the Cinematographic Industry – CONDECINE for each of its destinations provided by law. According to Article 4, the CNC is formed by seven ministers or their representatives (namely, the ministers of Justice, Foreign Relations, Economy, Culture, Development and Industry, Communications; and the President's Chief of Staff) and by five representatives of the national cinematographic and video-phonographic industry, highly regarded in their field of speciality, to be appointed by decree, for a term of two years, which term can be renewed once.

532. While the Communications Council is an advisory board to the National Congress, the Film Council's competences are combined with the Secretariat of Culture Ministry of Communications' and ANCINE's, in the sense that they elaborate and consult together on public policies to be further elaborated by ministries and executed by regulatory agencies. Both these Councils' operations are still in the realm of legislation specifically directed at the media sector.

533. There are other governmental bodies responsible for supervision regarding overarching legislation that also applies to these activities, to greater or lesser degrees.

534. The Ministry of Justice, for instance, is in charge of anti-piracy governmental programmes and of enforcing parental rating obligations. The latter comprises all rating that is required by the Constitution, a universe that includes public spectacles, concerts, books, videogames and audiovisual content (both in movie theatres and in television). These policies establish age recommendations for all sorts of content, and the detailed procedure for audiovisual services to obtain these ratings as described in Part III, Chapter 1, §3, III.

535. Matters related to the promotion of competition in media and communications markets are handled by both the respective regulatory agency and the Administrative Council for Economic Defence (Conselho Administrativo de Defesa Econômica – CADE). CADE is the Brazilian competition authority, in charge of antitrust law enforcement both through the *ex ante* promotion of competition (e.g., in mergers and acquisitions analysis) and *ex post* investigations related to antitrust violations in all economic sectors (media markets included). These competences are shared with specialized regulatory agencies that can also take the form of cooperation agreements. This is the case, for instance, with ANCINE, that has an agreement with CADE since 2015 defining exchange of documents, information and data basis, as well as of internal analysis and diagnostics related to their shared competences.[336] While ANATEL does not have a formal agreement with CADE, these

336. ANCINE, *ANCINE e CADE assinam convênio de cooperação,* available at: https://www.gov.br/ancine/pt-br/assuntos/noticias/ancine-e-cade-assinam-convenio-de-cooperacao (accessed 1 Dec. 2020).

institutions still interact and exchange information regarding the promotion of competition in the telecommunications sector.

536. Even though the interaction of specialized bodies with other institutions that hold overarching competences (e.g., competition, consumer law or child protection) is a common feature of polycentric administrations, the fragmentation of supervision of compliance with media regulation rules in Brazil has been criticized. The OECD Telecommunication and Broadcasting Review 2020 pointed out the need for a coherent regulatory framework, especially considering that '[a]s convergence gains momentum, both different licensing regimes for communication services and broadcasting, as well as separate agencies for communication and broadcasting, become anachronistic'. The report suggests that the fragmentation of supervision competences 'further hinders the effective monitoring of developments in communication services and markets'.[337] In this sense, it includes among its recommendations '[t]he creation of a converged regulator, established at arm's length from policy-making', that comprises both ANATEL's and ANCINE's competences, as well some of the function currently placed in the Ministry of Communications (so that a single entity conducts both broadcasting and communication spectrum assignments).[338]

537. Lastly, even though this section focuses on supervision performed by specialized public administration bodies, it is important to highlight that there are also institutions outside of the executive branch that perform law enforcement over the sector. This is the case, for instance, for the judicial system (as courts have competences to rule on conflicts of rights and law abidance) as well as the national and regional public prosecution offices (referred to in Portuguese as 'Ministério Público'). Overall, the institutional functions of public prosecution offices are focused on the initiation of criminal indictments and on a set of attributions aimed at the defence of the legal order, especially with regard to the promotion and defence of diffuse and collective rights. This includes, for instance, to promote civil enquiries, collective judicial actions or unconstitutionality lawsuits aiming at the protection of the public and social heritage, the environment, and other diffuse and collective interests (Federal Constitution, Article 129).

---

337. OECD Telecommunication and Broadcasting Review of Brazil 2020.
338. *Ibid.*

Chapter 1. The Ministry of Communications

§1. Organization

538. The number and types of ministries that become integrated into the national public administration can vary considerably. Ministries must be created by law, and it is typical that federal administrations promote the extinction and creation of several bodies according to their political interests, either by initiating bills of law in this sense or by implementing them through executive orders that are later turned into law (a legal manoeuvre whose constitutionality is questionable). The latter scenario reflects the actual situation of the current Ministry of Communications, recently recreated by Law 14.074/2020 (which turned into law Executive Order 980/2020), after being extinguished by President Jair Bolsonaro and integrated into the Ministry of Science, Technology and Innovation (then names 'Ministry of Science, Technology, Innovation and Communications'). Even though this type of transition always disrupts ongoing policies to some extent, they will not necessarily affect the core media regulatory structure, as long as most of competent organs are transferred to other ministries and not completely erased.

539. Currently, the Ministry of Communications is organized into several advisory units (e.g., press relations, parliamentary advisory, international affairs), administrative organs (responsible for budget, purchases, etc.) and secretariats, which comprise the departments responsible for implementing the communications policies under the Ministry's competence. They are the Broadcasting Secretariat (including two departments: 'Grants and Post-Grants' and 'Innovation, Regulation and Enforcement'); the Telecommunications Secretariat (which includes three departments: 'Public Policies for Telecommunications and Regulatory Monitoring'; 'Telecommunications Infrastructure and Broadband'; and 'Investment Improvement'). The third main secretariat is the Social Communications one, which is focused on functions that support the Presidency and encompasses three other secretariats: Promotion and Publicity, Institutional Communications, and the Press Secretariat. All these internal divisions are under the Minister's Office, and for the purposes of this chapter, we will focus on the first two secretariats, which are in charge of implementing media regulation frameworks.

§2. Tasks

540. The Ministry of Communications designs public policies to regulate and foster the use and adoption of information and communication technologies. Its overall activities encompass different media sectors, such as telecommunications, postal services, the Federal Government's communication and advertising policies, and broadcasting. Regarding the latter, it is possible to say that the Ministry acts as 'a quasi-regulator for FTA television (FTA), theoretically monitoring and controlling the broadcasting sector, directly and indirectly.'[339]These competences are detailed in Decree 10.462/2020, and in this section we highlight the main functions performed by each of the specialized secretariats.

541. The Broadcasting Secretariat is responsible for execution of public policies aimed at broadcasting services and the services that are ancillary to it (i.e., radio and television services, including retransmitters and repeaters, as per Part III, Chapter 1). These responsibilities include proposing and supervising initiatives aimed at promoting innovation in these services; proposing new and improving existing regulatory instruments, and a series of other activities that are peculiar to each of its departments. As one can presume from its name, the Department of Grants and Post-grants implements and monitors policies regarding the granting of concessions, licences and permission to exploit broadcasting services (including all analysis necessary for granting processes, post-granting and renewal of broadcasting grants). It also plans and coordinates the elaboration of calls for bids and other selection procedures for the execution of broadcasting services, and it decides on refusals or ineligibility to provide them. This is also the department that interacts with ANATEL in order to formulate and alter the National Grant Plan (*see* Part III, Chapter 2). The Innovation, Regulation and Enforcement department is mostly in charge of monitoring and enforcing the regulation of broadcasting, which it does by leading inspection processes, filing administrative processes in order to investigate and sanction infractions and deciding on the application of sanctions (which can include financial fees and cancellation of licences). This department also coordinates the implantation and updating of systems related to radio broadcasting services and the standardization and updating of the document models used within the scope of the Department of Radio Broadcasting.

542. Overall, the Telecommunications Secretariat handles the matters related to the production chain of telecommunications services including policy implementation, monitoring and proposals for new regulation. Specifically, the Public Policies for Telecommunications and Regulatory Monitoring handles, among others, technical standards, goals and criteria for the expansion of investment on telecommunications services and its infrastructure, as well as on the technological development of the telecommunications sector. In turn, the Infrastructure and Broadband department is mostly in charge of allocating funding aimed at the universalization or the expansion of telecommunications services, as well as carrying out and updating a national survey on the coverage of telecommunication networks and services that provide access to broadband Internet. It is worth bearing in mind that in the realm of telecommunications, the Ministry mostly focuses on general policy design, as the ANATEL is the main enforcement organization. Also, for both ANATEL and the Ministry, telecommunications attributions relate to a series of sectors that are beyond the scope of this monograph. The telecommunications services that are of concern in this monograph – Pay-TV services – are mostly regulated by ANATEL and ANCINE.

339. *Ibid.*, 130.

543. Lastly, the Secretariat for Social Communications is in charge of public opinion surveys, and a series of functions that support the Presidency's communication strategy.

§3. Sanctioning Powers

544. As shown above, inspection powers are distributed in different departments, according to their competences. It is worth highlighting that all processes of infraction investigation and sanctioning must abide by Law 9.784/1999 ('The Administrative Process Act'), which regulates all administrative processes led by the federal administration, including adjudicatory ones. This is the legal statute that sets out all guarantees for all that needs to be observed (such as due process, transparency, impartiality and legal counsel, as established in Article 3), as well as deadlines for replies, appeals and the different phases that these processes must comprise. This law applies not only to the Ministry of Communications, ANATEL and ANCINE but also to all public administration bodies, which in their turn, can still have specific provisions internally enacted, as long as they are not in conflict with this law.

545. It is important to highlight that there are relevant constitutional and legal provisions regarding grant limits and requirements for broadcasters under the Ministry of Communications competences, which have long been ineffective (and still are). This is the case, for instance, for the constitutional prohibition of monopolies or oligopolies in the media sector, and the ownership limits regarding the numbers of grants. Agent-centred requirements are also in force, albeit unenforced – notably, the 'impossibility' of politicians holding elected mandates and owning broadcast grants – a constitutional demand that is not only ineffective but also widely adopted practice that tarnishes an already concentrated sector. As highlighted by the OECD, compliance with these provisions was supposed to be guaranteed by the Ministry of Communications, and the sector remains in need of an integrated analysis to accurately assess the state of audiovisual markets in Brazil, and to capture emerging trends.[340]

340. *Ibid.*

Chapter 2. National Telecommunications Agency

§1. Organization

546. The ANATEL was created by Law 9.472/1997 (The Telecommunications Act, or in Portuguese, Lei de Geral de Telecomunicações – LGT), following the processes of privatization of the telecommunications sector. Until then, telecommunications services were fully provided by state companies, and the transfer of these service's exploitation by the private sector called for a regulatory body that would steer the sector towards governmental policies without directly intervening. This was the case for several economic sectors that went through the same transformation, and since then, regulatory agencies became key governmental actors for different policy fields.

547. Arts 18 and 19 of LGT provide a division of attributions between central federal government (i.e., the Presidency and the Ministry of Communications) and the regulatory agency. The former is responsible for ruling on which services are to be provided in the public or private regime; approving the general planning of grants for services rendered under the public regime and the planning for the progressive universalization of the same services; and for authorizing the participation of a Brazilian company in intergovernmental organizations or consortia destined to provide means or render telecommunications services (Article 18). In its turn, ANATEL holds a series of legal attributions that comprise different aspects of policy monitoring and enforcement, as well as the enactment of secondary norms that regulate legal obligations. To that effect, Article 19 stipulates a series of attributions, including: managing electromagnetic spectrum and regulating its use, issuing norms concerning grant-giving; provision and fruition of telecommunication services; issuing and terminating grants to exploit telecommunications services; monitoring and reviewing telecommunications tariffs and issuing and enforcing norms aimed at telecommunications equipment (these tasks will be further discussed in the next section).

548. As it is the case for every regulatory agency, ANATEL is linked to its supervisor ministry, in this case, the Ministry of Communications, in a relationship that was meant to be non-hierarchical, but which in fact is far from being shielded from interference and political pressure. Since its creation by Law 9.472/97, the agency rests on some foundational characteristics of this type of institutional model: it is an autonomous autarchy, which holds financial and administrative independency, and whose directors have a fixed tenure of five years (no reappointments allowed). This structure was originally prescribed in the law that created each regulatory agency, so that these institutions held a few organizational distinctions between themselves for several years. Since the enactment of Law 13.848/2018 (known as the 'Regulatory Agencies Act'), many procedural matters such as the length of directors' mandates, coordination inter-agencies and with the competition authority, and legal requirements for decision-making processes are now standardized across all agencies.

549. Nevertheless, some key aspects of operations are still ruled by LGT. According to Article 23, the directors shall be Brazilian nationals with a university degree, with a strong reputation in their field of expertise, and should be nominated by the President and approved by the Senate. Also, Article 49 provides that ANATEL's budget shall be elaborated by the agency every year, and included in federal Annual Budget Law after revision by the Ministry of Economy (Law 9.472/1997, Article 49).

550. ANATEL's internal organization is overseen by the Board of Directors, which is composed of five members: four commissioners and one President. This Board is directly advised by the Ombudsman Office, an advisory board provided by legislation. This Board is a consultative body formed by representatives of various stakeholders; it is composed of representatives appointed by the Senate, the House of Representatives, the Federal Government and entities representing telecommunication operators, consumers and society. The functions of this Board include: giving their opinions about the National Grant Plan (prior to sending to the Ministry of Communications); offering advisory support to decision-making on public and private service provision; analysing the Board of Directors annual reports; requesting information and proposing actions regarding the Board of Director's attributions. The Advisory Board's recommendations are non-binding and final decisions remain with the Board of Directors.

551. In turn, the Board of Director has attributions to deliberate collectively, by absolute majority, in a series of the agency's competences, and its decision takes the shape of resolutions, summaries, administrative acts and ordinances. The Presidency is in charge of performing high-level administrative powers and ensuring compliance with the functions granted to the Board of Directors. It is advised by a series of administrative units (such as technical advisory, press relations, institutional and international affairs, among others).

552. The performance of ANATEL's technical attributions lies with specialized units called 'Superintendencies'. There are eight superintendencies in total, responsible for the following sectors: competition, consumer protection, enforcement and inspection, internal information and data management, grants and service provision resources, management and finances, as well as planning and regulation.

§2. Tasks

553. In short, ANATEL's tasks can be traced to four main attributions: implementing the national telecommunications policy; enacting secondary norms that further regulate telecommunications activities; making grants for telecommunications services; and managing the electromagnetic spectrum.

554. Concerning broadcasting services, most of the policy enforcement and monitoring is led by the Ministry of Communications. ANATEL is only in charge of managing electromagnetic spectrum issues, which include auctions, licensing procedures, technical certifications and overarching planning (even though the actual grant process also includes the Ministry of Communications and Parliament).

555. Regarding Pay-TV, ANATEL is in charge of regulating and enforcing all aspects related to distribution – i.e., the use of the different types of infrastructure to provide these services. Content packaging and programming requirements are under ANCINE's oversight, as it will be further discussed in the next chapter. For all other telecommunications services, ANATEL is the main oversight authority. This includes mobile and landline services, broadband Internet, satellite and other telecommunications technologies.

556. As mentioned previously, ANATEL acts jointly with CADE to enforce anti-trust regulation in telecommunications. In a similar sense, it also has relevant consumer protection attributions, which can also overlap with other governmental bodies such as the National Consumers Secretariat (Secretaria Nacional do Consumidor, Senacon) and 'local departments for consumer protection'.[341]

§3. Sanctioning Powers

557. ANATEL has legal powers to investigate non-compliance with the regulatory framework under its oversight and to sanction infractions in accordance with the law – relevant legal statutes here are Law 13.105/2015 ('Civil Procedure Code'), Law 9.784/1999 ('The Administrative Process Act'), LGT and ANATEL's Resolution 589/2012 (which regulates sanctioning procedures). The first two are overarching laws that apply to ANATEL's activities subsidiarily – i.e., when specialized rules (LGT and Resolution 589/2012) are silent about a specific issue.

558. In Article 173, LGT provides that the applicable sanctions are: warnings, financial penalties, temporary suspension of services provision (applicable to broadcasting licences), termination of grants and declaration of ineligibility (applicable in the realm of grant auctions, when a candidate practices illicit acts aiming to frustrate the bidding objectives).

559. Due process and other procedural guarantees apply, as per LGT Article 175 and the aforementioned Law 9.784/1999 ('The Administrative Process Act'). In the realm of safeguards, Resolution 589/2012 further regulates these provisions to assure that: urgent precautionary measures are the only case in which decisions can be taken before the accused party is heard; all sanctions shall be applied by reasoned decisions of the agency, and defence rights are to be observed at all times. While sanctioning can be applied by different superintendencies according to their attributions, appeals are also guaranteed by law and will be adjudicated by the Board of Directors.

341. *Ibid.*

560. Sanctioning processes must abide by a series of criteria, such as the nature and severity of infractions, the resulting damage (to the service and to users), the advantage to the infractor that accrues from their illegal conduct, aggravating circumstances, the infractor's record and the specific recurrence will be considered. Financial penalty can only be arbitrated maximum at BRL 50,000,000 per infraction.

Chapter 3. National Film Agency

§1. Organization

561. The ANCINE is the regulatory agency in charge of the audiovisual sector. It is marked by a peculiar institutional arrangement, notably due to the fact that it fulfils regulation, funding and development functions. ANCINE was originally created in 2001 by MP 2.228-1/2001, under the supervision of the Ministry of Industry and Foreign Trade, with a focus on the development of the country's film industry. Around 2004, the government of President Luís Inácio Lula da Silva transferred it to the Ministry of Culture, and opened a debate about expanding its scope as a regulatory body with competences over the whole audiovisual sector.[342] After an intense political dispute that involved civil society and media conglomerates, this version of a media regulator did not thrive, but the agency remained within the Ministry of Culture.

562. Until 2011, ANCINE's attributions were in line with the original scope designed in MP 2.228-1/2001: regulating audiovisual production; developing audiovisual production; implementing national incentive policies for the film industry and monitoring the audiovisual market.[343] Besides the implementation of funding and development policies, regulating audiovisual production mostly meant keeping track of audiovisual works and audiovisual companies' mandatory registration before the organization (as provided by Articles 22 and 28 of MP 2.228-1/2001). Such registrations apply to audiovisual content in any media, and there is a series of obligations directed at the film cinema sector (including screen quotas for national films).

563. ANCINE's regulatory functions gained considerable scope with the enactment of Law 12.485/2011, which established a single regulatory framework for Pay-TV services (also referred to as 'Conditioned Access Services', or in Portuguese, 'Serviços de Acesso Condicionado'). This law assigned a series of content requirements enforcement to ANCINE, notably referring to the compliance with national and independent content quotas and with the insertion of Brazilian channels in bundles.

564. Also in ANCINE's case, its whole structure was originally provided by MP 2.228-1/2001, and later Law 13.848/2018 ('Regulatory Agencies Act') implemented changes in the sense of standardizing institutions across different regulatory agencies. ANCINE's internal organization is overseen by a Board of Directors, formed by four members, one of them being the Director-President (as appointed by the President of the Republic). The Board decides collectively on key matters under ANCINE's competences, administrative issues and as an appeal's body. When necessary, the Director-President holds the casting vote, and final decisions are

342. Jonas Valente, *Regulação Democrática dos meios de comunicação*, 38 (Coleção O Que Saber 2013).

343. *Ibid.*

mostly expressed in the form of deliberations (even though they can also be resolutions, ordinances or normative instructions).

565. Besides institutional support (like press relations and international advisory) and administrative units, the performance of ANCINE's technical attributions is divided into two main Secretariats: Funding Policies (which includes the superintendencies that handle direct and indirect funding, rendering of accounts and several types of coordinations focused on market development) and the Secretary for Regulatory Policies (which includes the superintendencies for registration and enforcement and inspection). There is a third secretary, responsible for internal management, who is in charge of administrative and budgetary functions.

§2. Tasks

566. ANCINE's tasks with regard to the enforcement of audiovisual legislation can be described according to its two Secretaries. The units that sum up to the Secretary of Funding Policies perform the attributions of funding and development for the audiovisual sector. This includes both the operation of tax incentive mechanisms established by different laws ('indirect funding') and of the Audio-Visual Sector Fund (FSA), which is a part of the National Culture Fund, aimed at investing on the development of the entire audiovisual production chain of audiovisual activity in Brazil (Law 11.437/2006). FSA is funded by the Federal Government's budget and, in its greater part, by collection of CONDECINE – Contribution for the Development of the National Film Industry (a federal tax applicable to the sector that will be further approached in Part III, Chapter 9, §2).

567. Besides these units that operate both tax incentives and the FSA's structure and selection processes, the Superintendency for Rendering of Accounts is responsible for analysing compliance of the agents that get access to funding with a series of legal requirements. This includes analysis and instruction of documentation, fiscal documents analysis and analysis of compliance regarding the object of funding (i.e., if the audiovisual project funded was indeed accomplished within the originally proposed terms).

568. It is worth noticing that the Brazilian audiovisual sector is highly dependent on public incentives to thrive. In fact, national audiovisual production in Brazil is massively consisting of branded works produced by broadcasters or Pay-TV channels or independent national production, funded by public federal and local resources. That is to say that this segment of ANCINE's operation holds a relevant role to the whole industry.

569. Under the Secretary of Regulatory Policies, one can find implementation, monitoring and inspection of compliance with regulatory obligations regarding the whole audiovisual sector. This includes audiovisual production and distribution, broadcasting services (to a minimum degree, regarding eventual obligations of audiovisual works registration), movie theatres and Pay-TV services. Regarding the latter, main tasks include enforcing programming and audiovisual content packaging; national, local and independent content quotas; programming standards for Pay-TV (such as limits for advertisement); and foreign ownership restrictions.

570. Also under the Secretary of Regulatory Policies is the Monitoring and Inspection Superintendency, which is responsible for investigating and sanctioning infractions, as we will further approach in the next section.

571. Last, ANCINE also has competition promotion tasks, in the shape of a general mandate provided in the Pay-TV Law ('defence of competition through free, fair and wide competition and the prohibition of monopoly and oligopoly in the activities of audio-visual communication of conditioned access'). There are no specific provisions on what specifically should be ANCINE's role,[344] an omission that is softened by the cooperation agreement signed with CADE, which gives the exercise of these competences a better shape.

§3. Sanctioning Powers

572. ANCINE has legal powers to investigate non-compliance with the regulatory framework under its oversight and to sanction infractions in accordance with the law – relevant legal diplomas here are Law 13.105/2015 ('Civil Procedure Code'), Law 9.784/1999 ('The Administrative Process Act'), MP 2.228-1/2001, Decree 6.590/2008 (that regulates administrative procedures for the application of penalties for infractions committed audiovisual sector) and Normative Instruction ANCINE 109/2012 (which regulates ANCINE's investigation and sanctioning procedures). The first two are overarching laws that apply to ANCINE's activities subsidiarily – i.e., when the specialized rules are silent about a specific issue.

573. In Article 12, Decree 6.590/2008 provides that the applicable sanctions are warnings and financial penalties. In the realm of Pay-TV services, sanctions of credentials temporary suspension or cancellation may also apply, according to the infraction.

574. Due process and other procedural guarantees apply, as per Decree 6.590/2008 and the aforementioned Law 9.784/1999 ('The Administrative Process Act'). In the realm of safeguards, Resolution 109/2012 further regulates these provisions to assure that parties under accusation: are treated with respect by the authorities and public servants, who shall facilitate the exercise of their rights and the performance of their duties; are informed of the progress of administrative proceedings in which they are an interested party and have access to the case records; are able to present allegations and documents, which shall be considered by the competent authority before its decision; can opt for being assisted by a lawyer (except when such representation is mandatory by law) (Article 4).

344. OECD Telecommunication and Broadcasting Review of Brazil, 225 (2020).

575. As it is the case for ANATEL, also for ANCINE's sanctioning processes must abide by a series of criteria, such as the consequences of the infraction for the audiovisual industry, the economic situation of the agent that committed the infraction and recidivism, as established by Normative Instruction ANCINE 109/2012, Article 19. The same provision also stipulates extenuating circumstances, including confession and voluntary adoption of effective measures to repair, avoid or mitigate the consequences of the violation; as well as aggravating circumstances (like the refusal to adopt measures to repair the effects of the infraction; withholding or providing incorrect information; and failing to comply with the requests made in the investigation procedure).

576. The Head of the Inspection Superintendence decides on the application of sanctions. Parties are entitled to appeal to the Board of Directors, which shall deliberate collective on the final instance.

Selected Bibliography

Alexsandros Cavgias, Lucas Novaes, Luís Meloni & Raphael Corbi. 'Edited Democracy: Media Manipulation and the News Coverage of Presidential Debates' (14 May 2019). https://www.insper.edu.br/wp-content/uploads/2019/05/Edited_Democracy_v2.pdf.

Andrea Monteiro A. Esmanhoto. *La Transparencia y el Acceso a la Información en Brasil.* Revista Internacional de Derecho de la Comunicación y de las Nuevas Tecnologías, 1, 3 (2010).

Antonio Moreira Maués. 'Constituição e Pluralismo Vinte Anos Depois'. In: Cláudio Pereira de Souza Neto, Daniel Sarmento e Gustavo Binenbojm (org.). *Vinte Anos da Constituição Federal de 1988.* Lumen Iures, 2009.

Bel Mercês, Cristina Charão, Daniele Ricieri, Diogo Moyses & Michelle Prazeres. 'A Sociedade ocupa a TV: o caso de Direitos de Resposta e o controle público da mídia'. *Intervozes,* 2007. Available at: https://www.intervozes.org.br/arquivos/interliv005asotvdr.pdf. Accessed 17 December 2020.

Carlos Eduardo Lins da Silva. *Censura judicial à imprensa no Brasil: autorregulação e maturidade democrática.* Revista de Direito Administrativo 253, (2010).

Cláudia Regina Fonseca Lemos, Cristiane Brum Bernardes & Antonio Teixeira de Barros. *TV Câmara, TV pública: As TVs legislativas brasileiras na transição para a plataforma digital.* Observatorio (OBS*), 5, 2, 1–22 (2011).

Cristiana Belon Fernandes, Renato Maluf & Gabriella Tuna Garamvolgyi e Silva Mamede. *Constitutional Law in Brazil.* Wolters Kluwer Law and Business, 2012.

Cristiano Aguiar Lopes. *Regulação das Outorgas de Radiodifusão no Brasil – uma breve análise.* Consultoria Legislativa, Câmara dos Deputados (2009).

Daniel Sarmento. *A Liberdade de Expressão e o Problema do Hate Speech in Livres e Iguais: Estudos de Direito Constitucional.* Lumen Jures, 2010.

Diego Werneck Arguelhes. *Ellwanger e as transformações do Supremo Tribunal Federal: um novo começo?.* Direito e Praxis, 2022.

Diolinda Madrilena Feitosa Silva & Maria Cristina Gobbi, 'Cenários e desafios da digitalização para as TVs públicas'. In: Maria Cristina Gobbi & Maria Teresa Miceli Kerbauy, '*Televisão digital: informação e conhecimento*'. Scielo Books, 2010.

Eneida Bastos Paes. *A construção da Lei de Acesso à Informação Pública no Brasil: desafios na implementação de seus princípios.* Revista do Serviço Público, 62, 4 (2011).

Enrique Saraiva. 'O novo papel regulatório do Estado e suas conseqüências na mídia'. In: Saravia, Enrique; Martins, Paulo Emílio de Matos e Pieranti, Octavio Penna (org.). *Democracia e regulação dos meios de comunicação de massa.* FGV, 2008.

Ericsom Meister Scorsim. *O controle dos serviços públicos de radiodifusão (Rádio e Televisão) no Brasil.* Revista da Faculdade de Direito da UFPR, 34, 161–175 (2000).

Eugênio Bucci. *O Estado de Narciso: a comunicação pública a serviço da vaidade particular.* Companhia das Letras, 2015.

Fábio Carvalho Leite. *Por uma posição preferencial do direito de resposta nos conflitos entre liberdade de imprensa e direito à honra.* civilistica.com, 7, 1 (2018).

Fabio Sapaio de Almeida, Maria Cristina Giorgi & Maria Vitória Silva Paiva. The Non-Representation of Black People in Brazilian Soap Operas: The Gabriela's Case, Educare et Educare UNIOESTE (July 2015). http://e-revista.unioeste.br/index.php/educereeteducare/article/download/12598/9012 10 20 573–583 (accessed 26 March 2021).

Fernando Oliveira Paulino. *As TVs Legislativas como instrumento de promoção do pluralismo e da diversidade.* E-Legis – Revista Eletrônica do Programa de Pós-Graduação da Câmara dos Deputados, 12, 21–28 (2019).

Guilherme da França Couto Fernandes de Almeida & Fábio Carvalho Leite e Ivar Allan Rodriguez Hannikainen. *Liberdade de expressão e direito à honra: medindo atitudes e prevendo decisões.* Espaço Juridico Journal of Law 21, n. 1 (2020).

Gustavo Schneider Fossati. *Public Broadcast Contribution: An Analysis in the Light of the Recent Decision of the German STF.* Revista do Direito 1, 57, 22–42 (2019).

Guy Thurston Hoskins. 'Beyond "Zero Sum": The Case for Context in Regulating Zero Rating in the Global South'. *Internet Policy Review* 8, 1 (2019).

Humberto Dalla & Renata Berlinski. *Civil Procedure in Brazil.* Wolters Kluwer Law and Business, 2020.

IAB Brasil. *Digital representa R$ 14,8 bilhões de investimento publicitário no Brasil em 2017* (21 May 2018). https://iabbrasil.com.br/digital-representa-r-148-bilhoes-de-investimento-publicitario-no-brasil-em-2017/ (accessed 17 February 2021).

Ivar A. Hartmann. *Crise dos precedentes no Supremo: o caso dos precedentes sobre liberdade de expressão.* Journal of Institutional Studies 6, n. 1, 109–128 (2020).

Ivonete da Silva Lopes. 'Political Culture and the Democratization of Communications in Brazil'. Latin American Perspectives 198, n. 5, 129–140 (2014).

J Aguilera & M. Baños. *Branded entertainment: cuando el branded content se convierte en entretenimento* (ESIC 2016). in K. Avelar & N. Prata, *O branded content como modelo de negócio*, 10, 71–88. Revista Geminis, 2019.

Jane Reis Pereira. *Classificação indicativa e vinculação de horários na programação da TV: a força das imagens e o poder das palavras.* Revista da SJRJ, 38, 169–197 (2013).

João José Leal. *Crimes hediondos: A Lei 8.072/90 como expressão do direito penal da severidade.* Juruá, 2007.

Jonas Valente. *Regulação Democrática dos meios de comunicação.* Coleção O Que Saber, 2013.

Jose Afonso da Silva. *Curso de Direito Constitucional Positivo*, 37 243. Malheiros, 2014.

Lucas Borges de Carvalho. *The Broadcasting Policy in Brazil and Its Legal Framework: From Authoritarianism to Ultraliberalism.* Revista de Direito Administrativo 264, 245–277 (2013).

Lucas Borges de Carvalho. *Os meios de comunicação, a censura e a regulação de conteúdo no Brasil: aspectos juridicos e distinções conceituais.* Revista de Direito, Estado e Telecomunicacoes 4, n. 1, 51–82 (2012).

Luciene Pazinato da Silva & Vera Michalany Chaia, *A descaracterização da Empresa Brasileira de Comunicação – EBC com o fim do Conselho Curador*. In: Edwaldo Costa, *Tecnologia e Estéticas da Comunicação no Brasil.* Atena, 2020.

Luís Gustavo Grandinetti Castanho de Carvalho. *Liberdade de Informação e o Direito Difuso à Informação Verdadeira.* Renovar: Rio de Janeiro, 2003.

Luís Roberto Barroso. *Temas de direito constitucional.* Renovar, 2003.

Luís Roberto Barroso. *Vinte anos da Constituição Brasileira de 1988: o Estado a que chegamos.* Revista de Direito do Estado 3, n.º 10 (2008).

Luis Roberto Barroso. *Constituicao, Liberdade de Expressao e Classificacao Indicativa. Invalidade da imposicao de horarios para exibicao de programas televisivos.* Revista de Direito do Estado, n. 11, 342 (2008).

Marcelo Gruman, *Lei de Acesso à Informação: notas e um breve exemplo.* Revista Debates 6, n. 3, 97–108 (2012).

Marcelo Ikeda. *Cinema Brasileiro a partir da retomada: aspectos econômicos e políticos.* Ch. 1, Summus Editorial (2015).

Marcia Maria Cabreira. *Cultura e identidade em São Paulo: a imigração síria e libanesa.* EccoS Revista 3, n. 1 (2001).

Marilena Chaui. *Simulacro e Poder: uma análise da mídia.* Editora Fundação Perseu Abramo, 2006.

Max Schoenthal. *Major Events and Reporting Rights.* IRIS Plus: IRIS Legal Observations of the European Audiovisual Observatory (2016). https://rm.coe.int/16807833ca (accessed 24 March 2021).

Media Ownership Monitor – Brazil, Empresa Brasil de Comunicação – EBC | Media Ownership Monitor (mom-rsf.org).

Michele Polo. *Regulation for Pluralism in the Media Markets.* 3 Universidade de Bocconi and IGIER, 2005.

Miriam Wimmer. *Direitos, Democracia e Acesso aos Meios de Comunicação de Massa*, 188 .2012.

Murilo César Ramos *A Contribuição para o Fomento da Radiodifusão Pública e o paradoxo de financiar o NBR* (17 April 2019). https://teletime.com.br/17/04/2019/a-contribuicao-para-o-fomento-da-radiodifusao-publica-e-o-paradoxo-de-financiar-o-nbr/.

Neide Lopes & Durval Campos. *Brasil: um país de imigração?*. Revista Internacional em Língua Portuguesa III, 24 (2011).

Organisation for Economic Co-operation and Development – OECD. *Telecommunication and Broadcasting Review of Brazil*, 228–229 (2020).

Selected Bibliography

Ronaldo Porto Macedo Junior. *Freedom of Expression: What Lessons Can We Learn from U.S. Experience?*. Revista Direito GV 13, 1, 274–302 (2017).
Teliti Suzuki. *A imigração japonesa para o Brasil*. Revista Institucional de Estudos Brasileiros 39, 57–65 (1995).
Venício A. de Lima Machado & Cristiano Aguiar Lopes. *Coronelismo eletrônico de novo tipo (1999–2004): as autorizacoes de emissoras como moeda de barganha política*. Observatório da Imprensa, Instituto para Desenvolvimento do Jornalismo, 2007.
Victor Nunes Leal. *Coronelismo, enxada e voto: o município e o regime representativo no Brasil*. 4ªed, Companhia das Letras, 2012.
Vital Moreira. *O direito de resposta na comunicação social*. 101–102 Coimbra: Coimbra Editora, 1994.
Wagner Machado da Silva. *A telenovela e os negros: A representatividade étnica na Rede Globo entre 2011 e 2017*. Intercom – Sociedade Brasileira de Estudos Interdisciplinares da Comunicação, 41° Congresso Brasileiro de Ciências da Comunicação (September 2018). https://portalintercom.org.br/anais/nacional2018/resumos/R13-0054-1.pdf (accessed 25 March 2021).

Table of Laws, Landmark Lawsuits, Decrees and Precedents

Table of Laws, Landmark Lawsuits, Decrees and Precedents

Lawsuits

Precedents

Other Laws

Table of Laws, Landmark Lawsuits, Decrees and Precedents

Index

The numbers here refer to paragraph numbers.

Index

www.ingramcontent.com/pod-product-compliance
Ingram Content Group UK Ltd.
Pitfield, Milton Keynes, MK11 3LW, UK
UKHW020142290926
15471UKWH00004B/659